REA

320.0
ROMNE
MOMEN

ALLEN COUNTY PUBLIC LIBRARY

ACPL ITEM
DISCARDED

D0572659

DO NOT REMOVE
CARDS FROM POCKET

ALLEN COUNTY PUBLIC LIBRARY

FORT WAYNE, INDIANA 46802

You may return this book to any agency, branch,
or bookmobile of the Allen County Public Library.

MOMENTUM

Women in American Politics Now

ALSO BY RONNA ROMNEY AND BEPPIE HARRISON

Giving Time a Chance:
The Secret of a Lasting Marriage

BY. BEPPIE HARRISON

The Shock of Motherhood

MOMENTUM

WOMEN IN AMERICAN POLITICS NOW

Ronna Romney and Beppie Harrison

CROWN PUBLISHERS, INC., NEW YORK

Allen County Public Library
Ft. Wayne, Indiana

Interview quote on page 38 copyright © 1987 by The New York Times Company. Reprinted by permission.

Copyright © 1988 by Ronna Romney and Beppie Harrison All rights reserved. No part of this book may be reproduced or transmitted in any form or by any means, electronic or mechanical, including photocopying, recording, or by any information storage and retrieval system, without permission in writing from the publisher.

Published by Crown Publishers, Inc., 255 Park Avenue South, New York, New York 10003 and represented in Canada by the Canadian MANDA Group.
CROWN is a trademark of Crown Publishers, Inc.
Manufactured in the United States of America

Library of Congress Cataloging-in-Publication Data

Romney, Ronna.
    Momentum: Women in American Politics Now.

    Includes index.
    1. Women in politics—United States.   2. Electioneering—United States.   3. United States—Politics and government—1981–   .   I. Harrison, Beppie.   II. Title.
HQ1236.5.U6R65   1988   320'.088042   87-27270
ISBN 0-517-56890-X

Book design by Dana Sloan
10 9 8 7 6 5 4 3 2 1
First Edition

For our daughters:
Ronna, Christina,
Martha, Mali, and Marianna

Contents

Acknowledgments

Anyone who doesn't realize after reading this book that politicians are busy isn't paying attention. It is for that reason that we are particularly grateful to all the women and men who took slices out of their time to talk to us. We appreciate their patience with our sometimes naive questions in the beginning, and their candor with us as we became more knowledgeable about the business of being a woman in what is still a man's political world. Most of their names are in the pages of this book; there were others, however, whose contributions were just as important in helping us understand the background and flavor of political life. Whether they are specifically named or not, we want to express our appreciation. For both of us, the interviewing process turned out to mean more than developing material for this book: we gained new friends and, above all, a deepened respect for the astonishingly high caliber of women committed to participatory democracy. People are too easily cynical about politics and politicians; it may be less fashionable to believe in idealism and dedication to public service, but we found them both, among politicians across the entire ideological spectrum.

There were also those who went out of their way to make our work easier, putting us in touch with yet others who could help. We want Nancy Kirshner of the Democratic National Committee, Jill Schuker, Stephanie Solein, Mitch Daniels, and Joan Sweetland to know how much we appreciate the time they took out of their busy days to set up interviews and contacts for us. The women at the Center for the American Woman and Politics, part of the Eagleton Institute of Politics at Rutgers University, were a wonderfully reliable source of statistical information: in particular, Martha Casisa was there whenever we needed a hand in locating elusive facts.

Both of us have families and children; while we were off discussing the ins and outs of professional political life, others were keeping the ins and outs of domestic life functioning. Ronna particularly wants to thank her mother, Eileen, her sisters Toby and Terry, her brothers Michael and Mark, her husband, Scott, and her children Kevin, George, Ronna, Mark, and Christina. Beppie wants to thank her family for their moral and practical support, especially Geoff, whose enthusiasm got her into the project in the first place and whose unfailing confidence got her through it.

1. Banners, Bunting, and All That

A woman politician may encounter some unexpected potholes.

It wasn't long after Pat Schroeder came to Washington as the new congresswoman from Colorado's first district that she was firmly ejected from a black-tie dinner at one of Washington's big hotels, simply because she was female. She hadn't been trying to make any big political point: she was new in town and didn't know how the system worked. The Touchdown Club was having a big dinner—Bob Hope was going to be there with star football players and lots of hoopla—and when the congressman in the office next door told her he'd bought some tickets he found he couldn't use, she said she'd take them. "I'm not really into sports, but my husband is," she said.

So they got a babysitter for their young children (two and five at the time), dressed up in black-tie finery, and went to the dinner. It took her under twenty seconds to notice that she was the only woman there, although there were lots of her male colleagues present. It was about then that a group approached her purposefully.

"I'll never forget the embarrassment," said Schroeder. "Here comes this group and they said, 'Are you going to walk out or are we going to carry you out?' And I said, 'Excuse me?' And they said, 'We've never had a woman at the Touchdown Club and we're not going to have one now.'"

Schroeder and her husband stared at them, totally taken aback. Meanwhile, there stood her congressional colleagues as well, looking on. "Now had I been a black, a Jew, a Hispanic, they'd have all walked out too," Schroeder pointed out. "Instead, they came over and said, 'Pat, what are you trying to do? For God's sake, grow up.'

1

So I said, 'I don't get dressed up and get a babysitter and come downtown because I don't have anything to do.' "

Patricia Schroeder, newly elected member of the United States House of Representatives, graduate of the Harvard School of Law, adult, mother of two—knowing perfectly well that apart from anything else this kind of stupid discrimination at a function held in a public place, with tickets sold publicly, was absolutely illegal—stood there uncertainly while the phalanx of men glared hostilely. Then her husband murmured, "Oh, forget it. Let's get out of here. I can't believe it."

So they left.

Now admittedly, that was in 1973, and fifteen years is a long time in politics. (Quick—who was president in 1973?) Fifteen years is long enough for a lot of things to change and for a lot of things to stay the same. In 1973, there were 16 women in the House and 419 men. In 1986, 23 women were elected to Congress, and 412 men. If this rate of change continues, women will reach representation fully proportional to their numbers in the population in a mere 406 years.

Will they? Should they? Given the dismal reputation politicians in general seem to have among nonpoliticians, why would they want to? Why take on all the aggravation of persuading a basically disinterested electorate to disrupt their routine and actually get out and vote for you, so that you can take on a sixty-, seventy-, eighty-hour workweek sorting out their problems and hammering out painful compromises (many of which will please nobody), traveling incessantly back and forth from your office to your constituency, and in the course of it all become a public figure whose most private life and finances might at any time be spelled out on the front page of any paper? Why expose yourself to debacles like the Touchdown Club's masculine revelries? Why bother?

·   ■   ■

Because politics is the business of deciding who gets to say what goes, and that's a compelling challenge. Pat Schroeder, when she came to Congress, had power easily defined by her vote as one of the 435 members of the House of Representatives. People spend hundreds of thousands, even millions of dollars to get elected and have one of those 435 votes.

2

But a lot—probably the majority—of women who stumble onto the fascination of political life and wind up as political animals don't originally have any intention of running for office. They get caught up accidentally. Many women start out with a specific issue—perhaps dismay over a toxic waste dump in town or the discovery that there is no program in the local schools for a disabled daughter or son. It's easy to start out grumbling that somebody ought to do something and, when no one else does, wind up organizing a campaign. Or, on the other hand, maybe the impetus is discovering a candidate who suddenly seems to be out there saying all the things that you've always wanted to hear somebody say. However it happens, a woman sticks up a hand to volunteer, or picks up the phone to call her party headquarters to see if there's anything she can do, or maybe, on an impulse, drops into that candidate's storefront headquarters to tell somebody she thinks they're right on the money. If she's the kind of person who enjoys chaos and crisis, the chronic working conditions of political life, she might well find herself sticking around to lend a hand, dropping in the next day to finish up, and the first thing she knows she's enlisted. If she keeps coming back often enough, she can wind up years later describing herself ruefully as one of the old warhorses, and mesmerize a new generation of casual drop-ins with the backstage stories of the good old days and good old candidates, victorious and defeated.

The most addicting quality of political life, according to everyone involved from the most basic grassroots level up to the White House (under any administration), is the fact that it's permanently challenging. Everything is always in flux. The book is always being rewritten. You can walk into headquarters and absolutely be guaranteed a different set of problems from the ones you had yesterday, whether yesterday's were solved or not. Even if there isn't a genuine crisis (and more often than not there is), there is always a pending crisis, or a perceived one. Politicians thrive on disaster. As Jennifer Dunn, chairman of the Washington State Republican Party put it, "You get in that little world, and you really have to stay with it to continue to be in the loop. It's fun to come to work because everybody is on the same wavelength. I have a full-time position, and it's like getting paid for an avocation. It's a lot of fun, and the only time it's not fun is when there's nothing scary happening, or

3

no crisis, and it gets boring. For people like us, that's just a real tough time to deal with."

The electoral calendar, serving up primaries and general elections with predictable regularity, and the unpredictable twists of national and international events guarantee that the adrenaline level is high enough to make life interesting most of the time. Who would have foreseen the Iran–contra arms scandal, for example, enlivening what might reasonably have been expected to be postelection doldrums in November 1986? Besides, even if there isn't a genuine crisis that anyone uninvolved might recognize, politics is an arena in which continual jockeying for position in future contests inevitably creates a burbling continuity of minicrises. For the citizen on the street, 1990 sounds a long way off politically speaking, past the watershed of the 1988 presidential elections. But back in 1986 both parties were already scrambling to identify promising candidates for winnable state legislative districts in 1990, since those are the legislators who will vote on the inevitable reapportionment of voting districts after the 1990 census. Who knows what the electorate will be looking for in those elections or what the major issues will be?

One other element that automatically jacks up the intensity level of political life is that there are always *us* and *them*. At least superficially, allies and enemies are well defined and obvious even when the arena is theoretically nonpartisan, as is typically the case at the local level. The good guys are the people who support your issue or back your candidate; the bad guys are the ones who oppose you. With battle lines thus drawn, you surge into combat. One of the enduring eccentricities of politics, of course, is that tomorrow's battle lines may lie in an entirely different direction, with a number of yesterday's enemies enrolled honorably as today's allies, aiding in the relentless assault on those who were yesterday's friends. Moreover, since the issues over which the wars are fought are more often than not genuinely important issues—choosing who gets to decide tax issues or, at the national level, planning military readiness, for example—there is unspoken license for emotional excess. Political opponents can, and do, wade into each other with undisguised public enmity that would be totally unacceptable in the more polite conflicts of ordinary society.

In the same way, political conventions—state or national—offer the opportunity for hilarious jubilation. Perfectly respectable people who look like anyone else at the grocery store wear silly hats, flourish banners, shriek themselves into laryngitis with passionate enthusiasm, and fall weeping into each other's arms whether they are celebrating victory or defeat. From the outside, the whole process looks incredibly juvenile. From the inside, it's a chance to abandon everyday inhibitions gloriously in the middle of a surging crowd of other people who feel as strongly as you do—and many of whom have been slaving away alongside of you for the past weeks and months. You don't have to be restrained. You don't have to be polite. You don't have to worry about looking like a fool. You can jump up and down and yell and shout and wallow in the communal emotion. Once the passion's in your bloodstream, there's no substitute for being there.

By and large, the people who get caught up in the political game, amateur or professional, are sociable extroverts, who genuinely enjoy the continual gatherings, the crowds and the hubbub, and the endless meetings. And after spending hours and hours together in the line of duty, they still relish trooping off together to the equally endless postmortems, over drinks or coffee, to analyze and evaluate all of the above. If there is one thing universally characteristic of all politicians, it is talk.

For a woman, particularly a woman who has had little working experience besides raising children and keeping house, politics can be an unexpected road to taking on more immediate responsibility than she's likely to be offered anywhere else except home. When a woman volunteers to work on a campaign, nobody checks out her resume. Many a woman novice has been assigned genuinely vital jobs simply because she happened to be physically present when somebody in charge decided that something needed doing and she was the one he, or she, happened to look at. If she turns out to be a skilled organizer—and if there is anything that being a housewife is specific training for, it is organizing chaos—as soon as she finishes that job, she'll move on to another, and when the original campaign draws to a close, win or lose, she'll get called for the next one. If the election ends in a particularly traumatic loss with her party demoralized and floundering, she may even find herself, greatly to her own surprise, sitting at the table in the meetings to decide what on earth to do next. As one party activist, a veteran of over twenty years of her party's fortunes waning and waxing, remarked, "When they're down and out they'll try anything. When they get fat, the goddamn place gets like a bureaucracy."

Because political organization remains incurably spontaneous, being in the room makes an enormous difference, as anyone who gets involved beyond a desultory basis rapidly discovers. Getting seriously involved in a campaign is not something that happens if you have only a couple of hours a week to spare. Without exception, the women who get into the game reorganize their priorities so that they are available most of the time. During a hotly contested campaign—an important local race, for example, or most statewide or national elections—the key people are on the scene seven days a week, for large chunks of the day and deep into the night. If you want to be a player, you have to be there. Problems arise unpredictably, decisions on strategy are made and unmade on the spur of the moment, and unless you're the candidate or the campaign manager, if you're not there, the decisions are made without you.

What this means, of course, is that if you really get into a campaign, you have very little time to spend with anybody who isn't. There are only twenty-four hours in anybody's day, and if most of them are spent working out the details of scheduling, putting together mailers, or perpetually pursuing funds, with the irreducible minimum spent grudgingly on earning a living, checking on what's going on with the family, and sleeping, what's left over is hardly adequate to arrange for clean clothes, let alone chats over the back fence or leisurely lunches with the girls. The result is that the people you work with on the campaign become family, bosom companions, and intimate confidantes (or mortal enemies)—at least for the duration.

Wilma Goldstein, a long-time Republican party activist and veteran of many campaigns, chuckled when she remembered a journalist remarking that the one thing women in politics had in common was they all liked to eat. Goldstein said, "It's one step further. It's the only opportunity we have to socialize when we're on the road, because it's an eighteen-hour day, and the only time you ever come together and sit down and relax is late at night over dinner and it's the only kind of pleasure you get. Sometimes candidates join you or staff people do, and then you can sit there and over a meal catch up on the day and get ready for the next one. It's almost like grown-up camp, to tell the truth."

That sense of esprit de corps under fire doesn't end with the campaign. Years later, when campaign alumnae bump into each other, the dormant intimacy is still there, in a way that it can't be with anyone who wasn't along for the ride. Even with the people you couldn't abide during the campaign, the warmth of reunion increases as the memories of the scars you inflicted upon each other recede.

■   ■   ■

The unpredictability, the intensity, the comradery are all there for anyone who takes a ride, however amateur, on the merry-go-round. But for some, the whole blend becomes irresistible. Political activity becomes too compelling to restrict to spare time; gradually, or suddenly, the volunteer moves over to the professional side. Men have been doing that for a long time, and it is no longer news when a woman does the same thing.

What triggers her varies from one woman to another, but there are patterns in common. For many women, it is an issue that becomes too important to leave to other people. Pat Schroeder, for instance, came to Congress not because of a single issue, but a confluence of them. It was 1972, and thousands of young men were dying and thousands more being wounded in a war that had already brought one president down. There were domestic social problems—the environmental issues, the plight of migrant workers, and the impoverished old, for example. Pat Schroeder and her husband James, both of them lawyers, were part of a group of young Democrats unhappy about the track record of the Nixon administration and determined to unseat their local Republican congressman. At one of the meetings to discuss choosing a candidate to take on the unenviable task of challenging a popular incumbent, Jim Schroeder remembers somebody turning to him and suggesting, "What about your wife?" Schroeder laughed and shot back, "What about *your* wife?"[1]

It was at home, talking it over afterward, that the Schroeders decided maybe it wasn't a joking matter after all. As unlikely a candidate as Pat Schroeder saw herself, considering she was a political unknown with two small children, she did have a flexible enough schedule to make a campaign possible and impressive credentials. And as her husband told her, "You say you're concerned about all these things; here's your chance to do something about them."[2] In any case they were initially talking about only the campaign: it seemed wildly improbable that she could possibly win. As she herself said afterward, "When I started running, nobody knew me but my mother."[3]

That may have been the state of affairs at the beginning, but it didn't last long. Pat Schroeder's congressional campaign was a textbook example of how it is possible to run a campaign on a shoestring. Her average campaign contribution was $7.50; much of her fund raising was done at wine and cheese parties. The national Democratic party kicked in a magnificent total contribution of $50. Her campaign relied heavily on the candidate's mastery of the issues and her hard-hitting miniposters, one of which showed a military cemetery and quoted President Nixon's assertion, "Yes, many of our troops have been withdrawn."

Schroeder was young (only thirty-two), attractive, and had an irreverent sense of humor. The voters of Denver were clearly impressed: she won in a stunning upset. The *New York Times*, reporting on the unexpected turn of events in Colorado, described her as "a little-known woman lawyer."[4] She isn't any longer. Pat Schroeder has since become the senior woman in Congress, one of the best-known women politicians in the nation—even, since Geraldine Ferraro's ground-breaking vice-presidential nomination, a potential presidential candidate. Her Denver district has become about as safe as they get: by 1982 the Republicans seemed to have given up making a serious challenge for the seat.

Antiwar and proenvironmentalist issues were the catalysts that moved Pat Schroeder from the ranks of involved spectators to those of professional politicians, but it was more a series of coincidences that put Colleen Engler on the ballot in Michigan. Schroeder was young to be undertaking her first campaign, but Colleen Engler was younger. She started only two years later, in 1974, at twenty-two, freshly graduated from college. She had been hired as a stewardess for Pan Am, but at that time the impact of the oil embargo was being felt sharply by the airlines, and her training class was postponed. So while she waited, she came home to Bay City, Michigan, where her parents lived, to find a temporary job until the training class could be rescheduled. Her parents used the opportunity to take a winter break down to the Bahamas, leaving Engler babysitting her younger sister, which was how she happened to be at home when a friend of her father's called. The friend was running in a special congressional election in their district and wanted her father to come to a finance committee meeting.

"My father's not here," Engler told him "but I'll come to your meeting." She did; she was the only woman there and she didn't know much about finance, but when it was obvious they needed volunteers on the campaign, she said that she was looking for something to do and became the campaign office manager. Her father's friend lost in the Republican primary, but Engler moved over to work for the candidate who won. He later lost to the Democratic candidate, who had been the representative to the state legislature for the district. With his election to Congress, there had to be another special election to fill his former seat in the state legislature.

Unfortunately, it wasn't a seat that seemed to offer a promising opportunity for any Republican. Bay City was a solidly Democratic area, and the local Republican party leaders, recuperating from the congressional election, thought they'd just put a name on the ballot and pretty much leave it at that. This struck Colleen Engler as absurd. "What would you think of me running?" she suggested. "I'd go out and try to really win the race." She says they told her she would be the closest thing they had to a winning candidate, but even so, the Democrats would take the race. Engler ran anyhow.

She used as her basis the work that had been done for the recent congressional races, when all the Republicans had been contacted. As she figured it, this was the Watergate year, and "if there was any Republican in a Watergate year that was going to vote for a Republican for Congress, they were going to vote for a Republican for state representative, even if she was twenty-two, and it was a she." So she went back to them for her support. She deliberately ran a very low-profile race so that the Democrats would not suspect anything was going on. They were unaware of her mail and phone efforts. "All the Democrats could see was just this twenty-two-year-old young girl going from door to door, and they thought it was cute."

She won, by a two-to-one margin, and went to the capitol in Lansing as Bay City's representative. Later she married, moved out of her district, and was elected as state representative again from her new district. In 1986 she left the state legislature to run for governor

9

in the Republican primary, and although she was defeated, was selected to be the candidate for lieutenant governor on the unsuccessful Republican ticket. Her launching into politics may have been less than carefully planned, but she has turned into a thoroughly professional politician.

Melody Miller, currently deputy press secretary for Senator Edward Kennedy, has worked for all three of the Kennedy brothers since she was first attracted to public service in 1960 by the Kennedy blend of charisma and dedication. There are few staffers with her longevity on Capitol Hill—she is certainly the staffer with the most seniority in Edward Kennedy's office and functions in many ways, as she puts it, "as an institutional memory—an alumni secretary for the three [Kennedy] generations. They check in through me when they're trying to find out something, because they don't know anyone else on the staff." The seeds of her career were planted when she was sixteen years old, living in Arlington, Virginia. John F. Kennedy was running for president, and although Miller was still years too young to vote, she was fascinated by him. "Then I discovered that to be able to defend him in class I had to start reading up on all the issues and I had to learn his positions and why they were right." She got active in Young Democrats and, being right in the Washington metropolitan area, found it was easy to follow political issues and news. For the 1962 congressional elections—Kennedy then being president—she went down to her local Democratic headquarters to volunteer. She still couldn't vote, but she could do everything else: "licking the stamps, stuffing the envelopes, pouring at teas, marching in parades for the candidates, canvassing neighborhoods, the works!" After the election she got a chance to work part-time in the congressional office of Joseph Montoya of New Mexico, who later became a senator. "So I was a girl Friday on Saturday, and while my colleagues in high school went off to picnics and everything else, I trundled down to work on Saturday, nine to five, the last half of my senior year."

It was while she was in high school that she was asked to the White House to meet President Kennedy. The invitation came about because of a minor disaster: she did a sculpture of the president in her art class, and when it was fired in the kiln, the thermostat failed, and the sculpture blew up. Being nothing if not determined, Miller painstakingly glued it back together, and it was exhibited in the school art show, cracks and all. One of the other student artists was the daughter of a *Washington Post* reporter who came to the show, and the story of the reconstructed Kennedy bust wound up as a human interest story in the newspaper. Quite unknown to Miller, someone in Congressman Montoya's office, having seen the clipping, sent along a letter to Evelyn Lincoln, the president's secretary at the White House, telling her about the sculpture and Miller's work on Capitol Hill and asking if she could be sent an autographed picture or something, since she was such an admirer of the president.

The result was electrifying. On a perfectly ordinary school day, in the middle of an otherwise routine journalism class, a runner from the office appeared and gave Miller the message that her mother had phoned to tell her that President Kennedy would like to meet her. At that point the bell rang, and Miller had to go straight to her English class—only four minutes between classes, no time to phone home—and lo and behold, another runner appeared with another message from the office. Only this time the English teacher looked at it, looked at Miller, and put the pink slip down on her desk. Miller sat for forty-five minutes, staring in agony at the pink slip. Time passed like molasses, but the class did eventually come to an end, and the teacher did give her the message, which was that Miller was to come to the White House at 12:30 on the day after next.

Two days later Melody Miller, the Virginia high school girl in her brand-new suit, clutching her brand-new purse and the bust, was duly ushered in to the Cabinet Room to meet John F. Kennedy and get her copy of *Profiles in Courage* autographed. The president had been well briefed on her activities, and for twenty minutes they chatted about the unfortunate accident to her sculpture and her political work, and they agreed she would work on his 1964 campaign.

It never happened. Instead, in the summer of 1964, during her summer vacation from college, Miller worked as a volunteer in the Executive Office Building next door to the White House, splitting her time between Evelyn Lincoln's office and that of Jacqueline Kennedy, helping sort out the sixteen million pieces of mail that had come flooding in after the assassination. That summer, she went to the Democratic convention with Mrs. Kennedy, and there she met Robert Kennedy. The next summer, Mrs. Kennedy having moved to New York, Miller came back to work in Robert Kennedy's office. She stayed there, working during school vacations until she graduated and then full-time until his assassination in 1968. "I helped pack up the Senate office, and we watched as the chair and the desk were rolled out the door, which was really gut-wrenching. It just so happened that I was the last person to leave on that last day. I turned out the light and closed the door and took a month off to let my nerve endings heal. Then I went to work for Edward Kennedy."

Twenty years later she is still there as the deputy press secretary and spokesperson. She is in her forties, looks as if she's in her midtwenties, and cheerfully suggests that when she is one hundred and three (by which time she might look fifty) she will still be standing on the street corner handing out pamphlets for whichever Kennedy is running then.

Melody Miller, Colleen Engler, and Pat Schroeder were all young women when they decided to make a career out of politics. Nancy Landon Kassebaum is more typical of the average woman politician in entering political life later on. In a sense, of course, it could be said that she entered political life the earliest of all: her birth in 1932 was news in Kansas because her father Alf Landon was a candidate for governor that year. He won, and four years later was selected by the Republican party to challenge Franklin D. Roosevelt's bid for a second term as president. The Republican ticket was soundly defeated (it carried only two states, neither of which was Landon's home state of Kansas). Alf Landon never again ran for an elective office, although he remained active as an adviser to other candidates and to his party. Kassebaum grew up surrounded by endless political discussions between her father and his politician friends, but otherwise her life was comfortably ordinary. In 1950, she went to the University of Kansas to major in political science, and there she met John Philip Kassebaum. In 1955 they were married, while he was in law school and she was getting her master's degree in diplomatic history. After they both graduated, they set up their first home in Wichita. For twenty years Nancy Kassebaum raised their four children, looked after their home, and busied herself with volunteer work in her community. In 1972 she was elected to the school board in the small town of Maize and served there for three years.

In 1975, her life abruptly took a new direction: she and her husband separated. Kassebaum picked up the three younger children—by this time her oldest son was in college—and took them with her to Washington, D.C., where she became a legislative aide to Kansas senator James Pearson, whom she had known back at home. She worked for him almost a year and found it interesting but exasperating in many ways. "It was a good experience working as a staff member," she said in retrospect, "just to see the day-to-day operation and how slow and ponderous it can be, and the frustrations of it." When she left Washington to return to Kansas, she intended to stay there.

However, not everything works out the way we expect. In 1977, Senator Pearson announced he was going to retire. Nancy Kassebaum found herself urged by friends to run for his seat. With no incumbent in place, the vacancy would offer a good opportunity for a woman to make a credible run for the Senate, and as the daughter of Alf Landon, she was uniquely placed to have a chance to win. In some ways it was a tempting proposition. She had always been fascinated by politics. She had majored in political science at college, and she had the Capitol Hill experience of of working in Pearson's office; this was in some ways an extremely logical next step.

For a woman who had been politically uninvolved until then, she made a shrewd analysis of her situation. In the first place, she was an extremely capable woman and she knew she was. The fact that she had devoted her energies to unpaid community activities and to raising a family made that no less true. Then, too, she knew people all over Kansas, partly through her family association, partly through her volunteer work, and in a large part because of her time at the University of Kansas. Kansas is a more homogeneous state than most, and people from all parts of the state know each other. Kassebaum says that there wasn't a community she campaigned in where she didn't know somebody. For another thing, she had money of her own she could put into a campaign. She also found it encouraging that there were eight other people in the primary already. With such a crowded field, Nancy Landon Kassebaum would have immediate name identification. "I think if there had been just two men and myself, I might not have [tried]," she says now.

She also took personal considerations into account. Her children were nearly grown—by the autumn of 1978, her youngest would be going into his senior year of high school. "I have always said I could not undertake this job with little children," she said. "I marvel at young women. I suppose in many ways I'm much more a traditionalist. I would not have wanted to miss going to the boys' football games or taking part in the children's activities." But that stage of her life had finished, and her marriage was over. Basically, she had only herself to consider—so she filed.

As she had foreseen, her father's name was a great help in distinguishing her from all the other Republican candidates, but she was continuously accused of riding on his coattails. As she amiably countered, what better coattails? "You couldn't disavow it," she points out. In any case, she thoroughly enjoyed debating the issues with the voters. She was initially apprehensive about public speaking, but she found she could do it. She loved getting out and meeting the people. She is a small woman who speaks gently and projects an immediate, almost tangible warmth. "I love visiting with constituents in Kansas," she said suddenly, in the middle of listing disadvantages of political life. "I love to work the county fairs and visit with people. That I enjoy. I detest fund-raising and the whole party apparatus in that respect."

Nevertheless, she did the fund-raising she had to do and took the primary in a clear victory. In the general election she faced a Democrat, former congressman William Roy, who had nearly defeated Kansas senator Robert Dole in 1974, when Dole was seeking reelection for a second term. Dole offered his help in Kassebaum's campaign, and when he came out to Kansas he stumped the state tirelessly on her behalf. She worked as hard, but in her own way. Her oldest son and daughter took a semester off from college to help: her son drove her back and forth all across Kansas, while her daughter worked at the campaign headquarters. "That was really nice," she says in retrospect. "It's great to be able to have some of your family there, and particularly driving you around, because then you can say, 'That was a real dog,' if it was. You don't have to put up a pretense."

She had no political record for her opponent to criticize: when Roy attacked her savagely for making only a partial disclosure of her financial records, she refused flatly to amplify, stating firmly that her husband, from whom she was legally separated at this time, had a right to privacy. She wouldn't respond with personal attacks on Roy, either; she stuck stubbornly to what she saw as the issues at hand. The voters apparently responded to her gentler style, and they gave her a 54 percent majority. Nancy Landon Kassebaum, who had spent the first twenty years of her adult life as a nearly apolitical wife and mother, went to Washington at the age of forty-four as the fourth woman to be elected to a full term in the United States Senate. She was reelected easily in 1984 and has become recognized as a thoughtful legislator who functions with a woman's grace but is nobody's patsy.

Schroeder, Engler, Miller, and Kassebaum: four very different women who entered politics by entirely different routes. What they share is a conspicuous zest for what they are doing.

■　　　■　　　■

A zest for politics inevitably includes a zest for power. As one of the most successful political women of our century, Margaret Thatcher of Great Britain, put it, "There is a magnetism about being absolutely at the center of the thing, something which draws you."[5] That draw works on this side of the Atlantic as well. Nor is the power entirely intangible. One of the attractive perks of political life is the magnificence of the official setting. The buildings that the tourists flock to admire are the places where the politicians go to work. The atmosphere breathes a sense of occasion. You can feel it in the corridors in Washington and in the state capitols spotted around the country. Almost always, the corridors are wide and high, asserting unmistakably that these are important places. There is the continual echoing sound of footsteps—everyone's footsteps, but of course high heels make the loudest noise.

The press is always there, too: whatever happens in those corridors is likely to be news. The reporters blend into the background, distinguishable mainly by their PRESS identification tags, but there is no missing the television cameramen, lounging against the wall or scrambling to set up their equipment in a committee room. An idle remark that might pass unnoticed almost anywhere else can turn up on the evening news or the front page of the paper: as Norma Paulus, former Oregon secretary of state, said, fresh from an unsuccessful gubernatorial campaign, "For sixteen years I have assumed everything I ever said would someday be on the front page of the *Oregonian*. Usually it was." In defense, politicians develop the arcane game of backing away from what they are about to say, by going off the record, or by making remarks not for direct attribution. Even so, political women, like their male counterparts, succeed and fail in the full view of anybody within reach of the daily newspaper, radio, or television. We expect a lot from our politicians. Cherishing our constitutional right to know, we expect to have their records available to us at all times, whether or not we have the interest to pay attention.

One result of all this public scrutiny is that the places in which politicians work, especially on the federal level, become subliminally familiar to all of us. They acquire a luster of celebrity all their own. A visitor to the west wing of the White House, where the president and his closest advisors have their offices, passes the permanent camera positions on the grounds between the guardhouse by the gate and the entrance to the office wing itself and suddenly recognizes the background to countless reports by White House correspondents on the network news. Walking into that building is not like walking into any other building, no matter how routine your actual business may be. A lot of people may walk into the west wing, but the business of clearances and the identifying visitor's tag around your neck makes it clear that a lot more don't—and at least temporarily, by virtue of being there, you are brushing up against power.

Having the White House be the place you work does not wholly obliterate that sense of importance. Even being a gofer at the White House is different, and grander, than being a gofer anywhere else. Similarly, working on Capitol Hill, or in one of the state capitols, or even being the mayor or a representative on the local council has its own cachet. There are considerably easier jobs, with shorter hours and usually much better pay, than working in politics. But being there is being part of the inner circle, being one of those who know, who get to have a voice in what's decided, and when that's weighed into the scales, the hours and the pay lose importance.

Sensing that power is a considerable high. Melody Miller, after twenty-five years on Capitol Hill, still feels the surge of excitement. "Driving to work," she said, "when you turn the corner and all of a sudden you're coming down Pennsylvania Avenue and you're going to the Capitol—and that is the Capitol of the United States, the symbol of freedom all over the world, and *you* are fortunate enough to work there. You get to walk down corridors with your tag that takes you into private areas where tourists can't go. You get to walk through that dome, where historic events have taken place, and you are making your own little contribution. And that is an extra privilege, and thrill, that you get from being in public service— and in politics—that nothing else can equal."

Miller is not alone in being gripped by that thrill. Wilma Goldstein wandered into Republican politics when she was looking for a job and heard that the Genesee County Republican Party had a clerical position open. During the initial interview she told them she wasn't sure if she was a Republican or Democrat, which apparently scored her enough points for blunt honesty that they hired her in the hope (fortunately justified) that she would turn out to be one of them. The headquarters were seedy offices in a dumpy old building, and the whole operation was managed on a shoestring, but Goldstein got right into it. "I started out doing everything. I mean the typing, the precinct delegate selection process, reapportionment, planning conventions, all of it, and I started to coordinate it and organize it. I think that's how I got hooked. It was probably the first time in my life I ever realized that a single human being—me, in particular— can really sit down and make stuff happen."

For most politicians, the central excitement is exactly that. Getting involved in politics brings with it the ability to "make stuff happen." It's quite possible to live comfortably in the United States and have little to do with the political system. The excitement in getting involved in political life is discovering the hands-on nature of democracy. For all the obvious truth that few politicians live in the rarified regions of Fourth of July oratory, the fact remains that on a daily basis, in legislatures across the land, somebody's ideas take priority and do prevail, and getting involved in the system means that you have a shot at having those ideas be yours.

For generations, women have been left out of that process. What the female politicians of the 1980s have decided is that those ideas are too important to be left solely to men.

17

2. Hitting the Hurdles

Political life is not and has never been an equal opportunity game. Most politicians are men, the power structure of both parties is overwhelmingly masculine, and there is still often a decidedly locker-room atmosphere in the offices and back rooms of elected or appointed officials. There are many men who think it ought to stay that way. Ruth Mandel, director of the Center for the American Woman and Politics at Rutgers University, tells the story of the New Hampshire man who was running against a woman for a seat in the state senate in 1976. During a newspaper interview, he claimed that he would make the better senator. When the reporter asked him why, he answered with jolly chauvinist humor, "Well, I'm a male and she's a female, for one."[1]

He is not the only politician convinced that politics is a man's business, although in his case his confidence was misplaced: the woman won. But Wilma Goldstein, now a political veteran who has worked for the Republican party on and off for most of her professional life, remembers that early in her political career, when she was working for a county Republican party in rural Michigan, her boss was fired. The county chairman told her regretfully, "Gosh, it's too bad you're a woman. You ought to have his job." At the time that seemed reasonable enough to her. "It was 1963 or '64, and I never thought to challenge it either. I just sort of thought, yeah, I guess it is too bad but you know, that's kind of how life goes." It was, after all, the period in which John Lindsay, mayor of New York City and sometime presidential hopeful, could tell a woman reporter on television, when asked why there weren't more women commissioners in his administration, "Honey, whatever women do, they do best after dark."[2]

But all that was nothing new. It was the way things had been long before women got the vote in 1920 and continued to be for fifty years and more afterward. The suffragists' idea had been that once women were voting citizens, government would be irrevocably changed. Corruption and bossism would come to an end, there would be no more war, and sweeping new social legislation would change the face of society. It was partly because the politicians believed them that it took so long for congressional enactment of women's right to vote. The suffrage campaign was well established with considerable nationwide support when Alice Paul opened the headquarters of the Congressional Committee of the National American Woman Suffrage Association (NAWSA) in Washington, D.C., in 1913, but it wasn't until 1918, after five years of vigorous suffragist campaigning, that the House of Representatives finally passed the nineteenth amendment giving women the vote nationwide. The Senate passed it a year and a half later, and on August 26, 1920, the thirty-sixth state ratified it and it became part of the Constitution.

What happened next was a giant anticlimax. Not only did women fail to surge into office to make their mark on the nation's legislation, most of them didn't even get as far as the polling place. The early quantitative analyses of female voting behavior are necessarily based on slim data, but it appears that in the 1920 elections—the first in which women were entitled to vote across the nation—only about one-third of the eligible women voted, as compared to two-thirds of the eligible men.[3] Women might have gained their rights, but the pattern of socialization was still more powerful, and when it came right down to it apparently voting and politics were considered slightly shady masculine endeavors in which well–brought-up ladies did not participate.

Nor did the figures improve significantly in subsequent elections. When it became clear that there was no dependable bloc of women's votes to count on, both the men who had worried about women's power and the men who had hoped for it went back to business as usual. The single issue of suffrage, which had united the women's movement, was no longer an issue. In its all-or-nothing simplicity, it had drawn in millions of ordinary American women who thought it was reasonable that they too should be entitled to vote (whether or not they actually did), along with the activists who were more concerned with developing social legislation for the underprivileged and the feminists whose first priority was total legal equality for women. But with the suffrage battle won, the movement lost its binding force. The factions went their separate ways. NAWSA itself became the League of Women Voters, a deliberately nonpartisan organization devoted to educating the voting public, male as well as female, and lobbying at all levels of government for legislation considered broadly beneficial.

There were *some* women in elected office. In 1931, there were seven women in Congress, six representatives (three of them widows who had been appointed to fill out their husbands' terms or elected to succeed them) and one senator (also a widow). Twenty-three states had women in their state houses. Forty years later there were thirteen women representatives in Washington, two senators, and 344 women in the state legislatures.

By the 1970s, however, there were thousands of other women involved in politics—the only trouble being that they were sitting at typewriters, passing out campaign literature, and fetching coffee. They did not make the decisions about what was to happen in the political organizations they served, but they were on hand to serve as willing troops once the decisions were made. "Women are on the outside when the door to the smoke-filled room is closed," said Millicent Fenwick, a four-term congresswoman from New Jersey who finished her political career as the first U.S. ambassador to the United Nations Food and Agriculture Organization. "We think it's possible to have a brave new world. The result is that the political operators have a sense that we will not understand the political realities—and they are often right. Maybe it's not a female characteristic as much as an amateur characteristic. Maybe some day we'll lose our amateur standing."[4]

One collision between feminists and the established political system that suggests that Millicent Fenwick was right was at the 1972 Democratic National Convention in Miami Beach, which nominated George McGovern. In 1971 four active members of the resurgent feminist movement, Bella Abzug, Shirley Chisholm, Betty Friedan, and Gloria Steinem, organized the multipartisan National Women's Political Caucus (NWPC) specifically to encourage women

20

to participate in mainstream politics. The 1972 Democratic convention was their most public introduction to the national scene.

In the aftermath of the shambles at their 1968 convention in Chicago, the Democratic party had set up a commission to define the ways in which future convention delegates would be selected. The commission, chaired by then-senator George McGovern of South Dakota, insisted that the state delegations reflect the population of the states, which in practical terms came down to something very close to a quota system in which women, blacks, and young people (defined as between eighteen and thirty years old) were to be represented more or less proportionately to their numbers in the population. This meant that since women were the largest "minority" (in fact, then as now they were the statistical majority) there were more of them than of any other individual pressure group: 38 percent of the delegates overall.[5]

At Miami, the NWPC discovered to its surprise—its internal communications not being particularly efficient at that point in its history—that it had over five hundred delegates, even more than the union had.[6] McGovern, unquestionably the front-runner for the presidential nomination, was the candidate most open to women's issues by far, and his commitment was more than theoretical. He had a good many women on his staff in top positions. Five of his ten regional directors were women; at the convention he had the first two women floor managers in the history of presidential campaigns, and one of them, Jean Westwood, he chose as Democratic National Chairwoman after his nomination. But the priorities of McGovern's woman staffers, most of whom had considerable political experience in less visible arenas, were clear: first get McGovern nominated and elected and then take up the agenda of women's issues. For many of the women on the floor, particularly NWPC leaders who saw themselves within sight of becoming players at the big table for the first time, the priorities were the other way around.

The resulting disarray and internecine warfare was no help to the McGovern campaign or the women's sense of participation. After noisy battles over the composition of South Carolina's delegation (there were only eight women out of thirty-two delegates) and an abortion plank in the party platform, an almost spontaneous last-minute NWPC push for Frances (Sissy) Farenthold of Texas as a

21

rival to Thomas Eagleton, McGovern's choice for vice-president, contributed to a delay in McGovern's acceptance speech, traditionally the climax of the convention and the rallying cry for the campaign itself. He didn't begin to speak until 2:48 in the morning. By then even in California most people had long since gone to bed. Live television coverage of the convention was reaching 17,400,000 homes at prime time, but by the time McGovern finally made his speech, the numbers had dropped to 3,600,000. (Three weeks later, when Richard Nixon made his acceptance speech at the Republican convention in prime time, the audience was 20,100,000.)[7]

The McGovern strategists were pulling their hair out by the roots; the Farenthold supporters saw the maneuver as an immensely important symbolic gesture. Both the NWPC group and the McGovern staffers went home disgruntled, each convinced the other was demonstrably guilty of ingratitude and betrayal. What the politicians had understood as bargains in the traditional political sense, meaning considerations to be delivered in return, the women had taken as promises, unconditionally guaranteed.

Looking at the whole episode in retrospect, the gains and losses for women in politics were probably fairly evenly balanced. In the first place, whatever the women did or might have done, McGovern's campaign was uphill from the beginning. McGovern may have had the hearts of the liberals, but the vast majority of American voters were suspicious of the drastic change in political direction he proposed, as they had been eight years earlier when Barry Goldwater advocated a similar swerve, but to the right. In November, Nixon was reelected by a margin of 17,998,810 votes. McGovern carried only Massachusetts and the District of Columbia. The party regulars who had been shoved aside by McGovern's forces moved back into power—party chairwoman Jean Westwood was promptly replaced. The suggestion that she should be succeeded by another woman was ignored: after Miami, the Democratic hierarchy had had enough of women idealists and their intransigence. Prejudice about the competence of women operating in the real political world was undoubtedly reinforced in several quarters.

On the other hand, 88 percent of the women at that 1972 Democratic convention had never been to a convention previously,[8] and for many of them being there was an eye-opener, which convinced them that participation in the political process was not strictly pie in the sky. The number of women at the Democratic convention inevitably had its influence on the makeup of the state delegations at the Republican convention: 30 percent of the delegates there were women, up from 17 percent at the 1968 convention.[9] Whether men intended it to do so or not, the system was creaking open, and the women who had been the lickers and stickers were getting a chance to see how things worked. They weren't players at the table yet, but at least they knew that there was a table, and they were even beginning to figure out where the table was.

After they went home, more women of both parties began to consider the idea of running for office. In 1971, there were 344 women in the state legislatures; in 1975, there were 604. In 1974, 41 women ran for Congress, 27 percent more than in 1972 and 43 percent more than in 1970. Three women ran for governor, 4 for lieutenant governor, 29 for other statewide offices, and a total of 1,125 for seats in the state legislatures.

They didn't all win, but by 1974 they were out there.

■   ■   ■

Lynn Martin was one of those women.

In 1974, Lynn Martin was serving her first term on the Winnebago County Board in Illinois. She was thirty-five years old, married, with two daughters, and had never held a political office before. In 1976, she was picked by the local Republicans to take on a Democratic incumbent for their district's seat in the state house of representatives. She won, concentrating her campaign on revitalizing the traditionally Republican precincts where the voters, dismayed by the Watergate revelations, had simply chosen not to vote in the previous election. In 1978, she moved on to the state senate: she was the third woman to hold that particular seat. In 1980, John Anderson, her district's Republican congressman, gave up his seat to run for president, and after considerable urging by her party, Lynn Martin decided the time had come for her to try to succeed him. She won a five-way primary with 45 percent of the vote and went on to win the general election.

Now in her fourth term in Washington, Lynn Martin is reasonably typical of the professional woman politician of the 1980s who has worked her way up through the legislative system. She said, "I didn't come with a mission. I want to know how [government] works and how *I* can make it work. I gravitated to money committees because I felt where and how you spent money defines government. What I really want to be is an expert on the rules, and when I say rules, I mean the whole structure of how to stop or to accomplish something."[10] She's been successful enough so that in her third term she was elected vice-chairman of the House Republican Conference, becoming the first and only woman to be part of the House Republican party leadership.

As Lynn Martin's career shows, a woman is definitely electable. As the careers of the thousands of women who ran for elective office in 1986 and *didn't* make it show, it still isn't easy. There are approximately eighteen thousand women holding elective offices in the United States in 1988, but they remain a small minority among an army of male officeholders. Sixty-seven years after women got the vote, the overwhelming majority of public officeholders, from the local level through the state and right up to the federal, are still men. Women hold 15.5 percent of all seats in state legislatures, which is impressive progress from 1974 when they held only 7 percent, but that still means that for every two women there are over thirteen men. There are at present 23 congresswomen, the most there have ever been, but there are 412 congressmen. There are 2 women senators and 98 men. Most of the names on any ballot are male, as the voters expect them to be. When John Q. Public summons up a mental picture of a politician, the politician doesn't wear a skirt.

This simple fact has a dampening effect on women's political careers for a couple of reasons. The most obvious is that when a woman throws her hat into the ring for an office—any office—the first thing that anybody notices is that she is a woman. Whether she is liberal, conservative, hard-line, conciliatory, middle-aged, young, senior citizen, strong on issues, strong on personality—or whatever else might be relevant—is seen only on the second look. "Women are basically outsiders to the voters in terms of the political process," says Harrison Hickman, the Washington pollster who has worked for Democratic women candidates across the country, among them the former governor of Kentucky, Martha Layne Collins, and Senator Barbara Mikulski of Maryland. "They get treated as outsiders, and it's tough for all types of outsiders to run."

What this means in terms of actual votes for a woman depends on whose polls you've been reading. For years, there have been polls showing that the electorate is prepared to vote for a woman, in theory at least. Even back in 1975, a Gallup poll found that over 80 percent of both men and women surveyed were prepared to support a woman candidate nominated by their party: nearly 75 percent were prepared to support such a woman candidate as a presidential nominee.[11] Those numbers look good, but as Norma Paulus points out, there's strength and then there's strength. Paulus was first elected to the Oregon state legislature in 1970, served three terms, and then was elected to the statewide office of secretary of state, where she served the maximum two terms. She ran for governor unsuccessfully in 1986. "When we started out," she said, "18 percent of the people indicated that they would not vote for a woman. Well, the longer I was in office the higher the percentage [of people who would] went up. When people were asked 'Would you vote for a woman for governor?' they kept saying 'Yes yes yes yes.' At the end of it, it was 87 percent that were saying they would vote for a woman, and I felt so smug about that until my pollsters said, 'Well, the flip part of that, of course, is that 100 percent will vote for a man.' "

On the other hand, according to Eleanor Smeal, former president of the National Organization for Women (NOW), there is data to indicate that, if anything, some women prefer to vote for a woman. "If there are two candidates on the ballot that have equal qualifications—nothing is ever exactly the same, of course, but if you could hold a constant—studies show that there is a little more of a boost for a woman: a 15 percent gender gap, actually, among women voters." In the rural parts of her Illinois constituency, Lynn Martin found voter discrimination in both directions, neatly cancelling each other out. When she was contemplating her first run for Congress in 1980, her survey showed that 11 percent were less likely to vote for a woman, and 11 percent were more likely to do so.[12]

Women candidates report, however, that there does seem to be a bedrock layer of stubborn resistance to a woman on the ballot. There is a minority of voters whose view of a woman's appropriate social roles simply does not include holding public office. One concern of many women politicians is the increasing political activity of the religious far right, with its emphasis on traditional values in all aspects of society, including roles for women. We've encountered it in our own experience: when Ronna Romney was running for the office of Republican national committeewoman for Michigan, she encountered a very determined fundamentalist woman who stood up in one meeting after Romney had just made what she personally considered a rousing speech soliciting support. This woman fixed Romney with a firm gaze and told her that she thought she had wonderful credentials and was splendidly qualified and a fine person and for all of those reasons she was going to work against her election. "You ought to be home with your children," she said, and sat down.

It seems reasonable that anyone so committed to maintaining the traditional roles of wife and mother would be equally disapproving of any woman who goes out to work without dire financial necessity. Anyone who chooses to run for office is clearly into it for more than the paycheck, which in many cases is a token payment anyway. Both women and men go through the tremendous effort of being elected to office for the satisfaction of being in a position to have some influence on decisions being made that affect their communities and the wider world surrounding them—but there is no overlooking the elements of personal gratification. People who hold fairly rigid definitions of appropriate sex roles are unlikely to approve of any woman who clearly relishes the spotlight. Some people aren't enthusiastic about a woman climbing the corporate ladder, or about a woman devoting her energies to becoming a doctor or other professional either. The difference is that a woman executive or a woman doctor doesn't have to go to the public to be voted into her job: the woman politician does.

While the political road is uphill for women, it is even steeper for black women. As Celinda Lake, political director of the Women's Campaign Fund, one of the stalwart sources of finance for women candidates, put it, "It's a double whammy. You have all the biases of gender, all the biases of race, and frankly, in the black community, there are biases against black women. So it's very difficult to come up through the ranks. But you have a lot of women who came out of the civil rights movement who are still in leadership at the municipal level, if you look at the city councils. What's depressing is that we're down in Congress. Cardiss Collins [of Illinois] is the only black woman there now. There *are* black women coming up from the state legislatures—if you look at the percentage of black legislators who are female it's about the same percentage as the percentage overall. And there has been steady growth in the number of black women state legislators. But it's tough. It's very tough."

Shirley Chisholm knew it was tough, but she was one of the few who made it. She retired in 1982 from Congress, where she had represented Brooklyn for seven terms—and she had been in the New York state assembly for four years before that. In 1972, twelve years before Jesse Jackson entered the presidential primaries and Geraldine Ferraro ran for vice-president, Chisholm ran for the Democratic nomination for president. The political pros didn't take her very seriously at the time—she had only three full-time staffers and no press secretary—but she saw herself as a candidate who spoke for the poor and disenfranchised in a way that none of the "credible" candidates did. In 1984 she was honest about admitting that she would have liked to have been selected for the vice-presidential slot, but realistic about her chances. "People won't look at my ability," she said. "They'll look at the amount of melanin in my skin."[13] Nevertheless, she perseveres, most recently organizing the National Political Congress of Black Women, a group whose purpose is to encourage black women to enter politics and to teach them how to do it.

What most other black women politicians do is much the same thing: get on with the job at hand, recognizing their circumstances but refusing to be daunted by them. "I don't wake up every morning thinking I'm a woman and a black," one state legislator said. "There are some things you take for granted." Her business is being a politician, and she reserves most of her energy for the same battles other politicians face.

If one stumbling block to women of any race getting into politics is the voter's notion that the "right image" of a politician is male— whether that is an unconscious assumption or a conscious decision by those so ideologically inclined—a curiously similar hurdle is the fact that all too many women who might otherwise consider a political career for themselves seem to share this assumption. It simply never crosses their minds to put themselves forward, to try. According to Ellie Smeal, much of the reason is a well-developed mythology about the handicaps a woman faces. "It's a form of job discrimination," she said with exasperation. "Where being a woman becomes a handicap is that they are discouraged from running. Women are talked out of running. They are told that they have to be better, or they are told that they can't raise the money. They are told a lot of negatives which discourage them. Well, if you don't run, you surely lose."

■   ■   ■

If would-be women politicians themselves are dubious about the possibility of being elected to public office, it is only reasonable that the local political parties, which gain their strength from recruiting candidates who do get elected, would be afflicted with similar doubts.

Traditionally, political party leaders played a more crucial role in the selection of candidates than they do now in most states. Changes in party procedure have greatly increased the number of direct primaries that any qualified person can enter. These primaries, in which the voters make the choice, are obviously much less susceptible to party control than the caucuses and conventions that used to decide which names went on the ballot. However, even if state and local political parties are weaker than they used to be, their support and encouragement do count. In Lynn Martin's career, for example, local Republican leaders originally asked her for advice on selecting a "good man" to run for the Winnebago County Board— and then Martin, encouraged by friends, decided to make a run for it herself. Knowing the local party was largely made up of long-time party stalwarts, she persuaded her whole neighborhood to come to the Republican caucus, which selected the nominee, and thereby got the party's nomination. From then on, each time she moved up to another office—first the state house, then the state senate, then Congress—it was because the party leadership came to her and urged her to do so. That Lynn Martin had had an unbroken series of successes at the polls is certainly in largest part due to her own competence and her popularity with the voters, but strong backing from her party has been a significant element in the development of her career.

A supportive local party can make a tremendous difference, as Barbara Trafton points out. She is now the Democratic national committeewoman for Maine and was in the state legislature there for six years. Depending on its resources and activity, a local party organization can provide a candidate with voter lists, furnish advice on strategies, pave the way to contacting funding sources for candidates, introduce the candidate to precinct officials such as election clerks and members of voter registration boards, and even come up with workers to help make lists of phone numbers for the get-out-the-vote part of the campaign. Every party needs to conserve resources for the general election and would prefer to avoid overcrowded primaries in which any failings of the ultimately successful party nominee are publicized by party rivals. Therefore, some of the most useful help a local party can supply is to discourage other candidates who have what is seen as a less viable chance for election.

The problem arises when any woman, by definition, is considered by her local party leadership to have the less viable chance. Until the last four or five years, that was a fair description of the attitude of the majority of local political parties across the country. According to Trafton, "Until recently, I would have hesitated to list political parties as a resource for women candidates. Political parties have been among the strongest of the old-boys' clubs, where men wheeled and dealed for power and women stuffed envelopes and cooked chicken suppers."[14] The situation, however, is changing, little by little and in spite of pockets of resistance. Gradually it is becoming obvious that women taking part in political life is not a passing phenomenon.

The main reason for the change is that women in our society are no longer content to remain in the niches to which they have been traditionally relegated. Women who are on the job shoulder to shoulder with men see no particular reason why the men should be offered opportunities to run for political office as a reward for their work, while the women who've worked every bit as long and hard are rewarded by being allowed to work longer and harder. The general raising of women's consciousness that was such a feature of the 1960s and 1970s took place in political arenas as well, and whether they were supported or not, women decided to run for office on their own. A lot of them still do, according to Celinda Lake. "Most women run outside the party, realistically," she said. "They're not now, and they haven't been, in that many smoke-filled rooms, and they run outside the party. I think Carolyn Warner [who ran for governor in Arizona on the Democratic ticket in 1986] is an excellent example of that. Of all the people who ought to have been an inside player, she was, and yet she was running outside the party. The party is what took her on. In the primary [outgoing Democratic Governor Bruce] Babbitt endorsed her opponent, and Bill Schulz [a Democratic businessman who entered the race late as an independent] and the business interests out of Phoenix took her on in the general election."

Carolyn Warner lost, but other women have taken on their party and won. Margaret Heckler, a Republican from Massachusetts, and Martha Griffiths, a Democrat from Michigan, both had given years of service to their parties, were refused party support for candidacies, went on to run regardless, and won seats as congresswomen. Such insurgent campaigns do little to strengthen the already-weakening control of the party organizations, and as Martha Griffiths points out with considerable enjoyment, one splendid dividend of the way she went to Washington was that once there, she owed nobody anything. Since political IOUs are a significant element of the grease that makes the system's wheels go round, local leaders would obviously prefer to have successful candidates feel a bit more beholden to the party back home. In one way or another, they are gradually becoming more prepared to consider women candidates seriously.

Another influence on behavior at the local and state levels is the indirect pressure from the national parties. While the long campaign for the ratification of the Equal Rights Amendment failed in its primary goal, it succeeded in producing a climate of opinion in which it is clearly unacceptable to discriminate overtly against women. Since 1972, both parties have explicitly claimed the goal of involving women more equitably in party decision making and encouraging them to become candidates for office. Both parties have formed task forces to identify and recruit women candidates; both parties have a variety of training programs to assist candidates and campaign managers in running successful campaigns. Ever since 1980, when women voters are shown to have supported candidates in different proportions and the "gender gap" was born on the front pages of the nation's newspapers, both the Republicans and the Democrats have kept an uneasy eye on what women seem to want, and this concern has clearly been felt in the local and state parties. It is a matter of opinion to what extent this concern is based on a universal genuine eagerness of the parties' male hierarchy to open political opportunity to women.

Women who have been around for a few years tend to observe much of this concern with a certain cynicism. Jeane Kirkpatrick, who for most of the years of her distinguished career in and around politics has been a Democrat, but who reregistered as a Republican after her service as ambassador to the United Nations under the Reagan administration, is unconvinced that either party's current attention to women is an expression of their generosity of heart. "I don't think there's token recognition of women today," she said. "I think as a matter of fact that there's obligatory recognition of women in both political parties. And, by the way, with better grounds than most people have for commenting on both parties, I would say that I do not think there is any significant difference between them in either their attitudes toward the role of women or men's attitudes toward women. For better or worse, I think that is the case."

While there are pressures on the political parties to encourage women, there are balancing pressures to maintain the status quo. Susan Carroll, a political scientist who has studied women in American politics, points out that the parties also have to consider the competing claims of men who are equally qualified by years of service for party endorsement. If a political office is seen as desirable, there are usually a number of interested aspirants. "To overlook these males in favor of women may, in fact, be a greater threat to party leaders' control over the candidate selection process than to overlook women in favor of men," she writes.[15] For one thing, men are typically in a far stronger position to run campaigns outside the party structure because they are usually more closely hooked in to the traditional business and professional networks that supply the money and the experience needed to run a campaign. If a man feels he has been unjustifiably bypassed by a woman, he may see her campaign as sufficiently vulnerable to take her on regardless of his own lack of party backing. One of the sharp lessons for women during the 1986 campaign season was that women candidates do seem to attract more competition in primaries and often third-party candidates in general elections. It happened to Barbara Mikulski in Maryland, to Carolyn Warner in Arizona, to Madeleine Kunin in Vermont, and to Arliss Sturgulewski in Alaska. As pollster Harrison Hickman put it, "I think that's another sign not so much of political weakness, I wouldn't say, as of their opponents just not perceiving

31

their strength." Whatever it is, it's likely to make the political leadership nervous.

In the same way, whatever the polls may say, the notion that the public just isn't ready to vote for women is still alive and well. If the race is important and winnable (an open seat, for example, in a statewide, congressional, or senatorial race), the chances are excellent that the party leadership's efforts will go to encouraging a male aspirant rather than a female, given equal or nearly equal qualifications. Unfortunately, the parties are a lot quicker to demonstrate their support of women candidates when the race is for a less prestigious office, or against a strong incumbent. When a "sacrificial lamb" is needed, all too frequently it's a woman who is placed on the ticket.

The pattern is beginning to change. For one thing, there's a lot of advice now from knowledgeable political women urging novices not to get into those hopeless races unless there is something else in it. If you're running now to collect IOUs from the party that you intend to use later (and they know that that's what you're doing), that's fair enough. Otherwise, forget it. Celinda Lake of the Women's Campaign Fund said that in her experience women were more likely than men to try the hopeless races. "Maybe in some ways we're more self-sacrificing, or we want to protect ourselves against loss," she suggests. "I've heard a lot more women then men saying, 'I'm gong to run this race to establish credibility for a future race.' Running a bad race is a lousy way to establish credibility."

Women are also less likely to be encouraged to seek the well-paid political jobs. It is no accident that the state with the highest percentage of women state legislators (New Hampshire, with 32.5 percent in 1987) is also the state with the lowest pay: $200 a year. Women unquestionably have a better shot at gaining an office when there is less male competition. Generally, most local political offices, like most state legislatures, are supposed to be part-time occupations. Increasingly, women are discovering that these offices are particularly adaptable to existing family or work obligations (as the men who have held those jobs for years already had figured out), and generally the campaigns are neither hotly competitive nor terribly expensive. It is not surprising that the number of women holding local or state legislative jobs is burgeoning: the number of women state legislators, for example, has almost quadrupled since

1969. Where the dramatic increases suddenly tail off is at the statewide or federal level, where the jobs are full time and perceived as desirable and the cost of campaigning is in the hundreds of thousands or even millions of dollars.

One result of all this is that among the electorate there now appears to be the general perception that women have crossed the threshold in legislative positions, particularly state legislative offices. There are more than a thousand of them out there doing the job right now, and according to the polls, most of the electorate has come to think they're doing it well enough, and even in some areas such as constituency service, doing better than the men. Women incumbents are as difficult to defeat as their male equivalents, if not more so.

But the number of women functioning in what might be called executive level positions—governor, lieutenant governor, secretary of state, or attorney general at the state level; president or vice-president at the federal—still varies from very few to none. Partly causing that, partly resulting from it is the public perception that women are more likely to be weak in dealing with crime, labor unrest, or other confrontations that may involve violence; that women are thought to have a problem saying no to special-interest groups or dealing with military issues. There have not been suffi-cient numbers of women elected to establish much of a track record. Those who have made the grade have seldom gained na-tional prominence. Even Geraldine Ferraro, who certainly made the headlines, never became vice-president and thus most people, unfamiliar with her legislative record, remember her only as a failed candidate. So the electorate is cast back on its own prejudices and preconceptions to speculate on what a woman would be likely to do at the highest levels. "I think that's what we have to overcome," said Celinda Lake. "What women in politics are experiencing is just a reflection of the general sex roles people experience out there in the broader society."

In the meantime, ambitious women seeking to move out beyond the state legislative level find they are banging up against a hurdle, the political equivalent of the glass ceiling women experience in the corporate world. The state legislatures have been the traditional launching pads for men's political careers in Washington. Women are beginning to progress as far as the state legislatures, but so far the numbers of women in Congress are creeping up only very slowly. In the Eighty-seventh Congress, which ran from 1961 to 1962, there were eighteen women, and then the number dropped off to ten in the Ninety-first (1969–70); in the Ninety-fourth (1975–1976) there were nineteen, and then again the number dropped off. Since 1980, there has been a steady rise, but the best we can say for 1986 was that in spite of four women retiring or leaving to run for other offices, the total number of women in the House of Representatives did not fall below what it was in 1984: twenty-three. There are at present two women in the Senate. Working within a system in which seniority still makes a big difference, the women are, relatively speaking, latecomers. Pat Schroeder, who was first elected in 1972, has the longest tenure for a woman in the House. Nancy Kassebaum was elected to the Senate in 1978; Barbara Mikulski, elected in 1986, is in her freshman Senate term. There are indeed women elected to help govern the nation in Washington, but there aren't very many of them, and by and large they aren't considered significant players.

Not yet.

■   ■   ■

Not all women end up in political life by running for office. Some women, like some men, find circumstances working out so that they gravitate toward working with another politician who is already in position and even, perhaps, moving toward prominence. Perhaps a political career begins by working on a campaign; perhaps it just comes about because the staffer-to-be and the officeholder seem to be traveling in a parallel direction, concerned about the same issues, and discover they enjoy working together. Wendy Sherman, for example, who was Barbara Mikulski's campaign manager for her successful run for the Senate in 1986, had known the then-congresswoman long before she came to work in Mikulski's Capitol Hill office as chief of staff. "I was active in both politics and women's issues in Baltimore, so we sort of knew of each other," Sherman explained. "Then I was working for the Washington Public Affairs Center of the University of Southern California on neighborhood revitalization issues and had come up with a policy idea of how to finance centers for dealing with domestic violence. She was working on a bill at the time, and my boss was very good friends with her out of the neighborhood movement, so I came up here to the Hill to say here's a way I think you might be able to do this. We became friends. We just became very good friends. We talked back and forth about issues: we're both social workers, both out of the University of Maryland School of Social Work. She was at a point where she needed a new administrative assistant, and we went to the movies one night and were joking around, and at first we laughed at the idea that I would come and do it, and then we got pretty serious. I knew that at some point I wanted to be on the Hill and have that experience, and I would not do it just for anybody. So I came and did it, and we stayed friends, which is really an achievement."

There have been women staffers for years, but the obstacles to a woman moving out of the semisecretarial functions of organizing an office and into the inner circle making decisions on strategy are curiously similar to the difficulties of a woman candidate for higher office. The woman candidate has to convince the party (usually) and the electorate that she can do the job, but the staffer has to convince her constituency of one: the officeholder or candidate she works for.

Sometimes convincing one person is significantly more difficult than convincing a whole raft of people. To start with, the sociology of politics being what it is, that person is probably a man. How close a woman can be to that man in a working relationship depends largely on the attitudes and assumptions he has developed over his career. There are a lot of men, particularly men of an older generation who have not grown up exposed to the idea of working with women as peers, for whom a woman will forever be another color of cat altogether. He may treat her with solicitude or with gallantry, may patronize her, or may not even notice that she's there, but for him her femaleness will always come before her qualities as a person.

Fortunately, there are others for whom a matter-of-fact working relationship with a woman is perfectly possible. A man does not always have to learn that at his mother's knee: sometimes it just takes being around a competent woman to figure it out. Newt Gingrich, Republican congressman from Georgia, credits Wilma Goldstein, who worked in his state for a while, with making a difference in his attitude: "Wilma Goldstein, I think, has played a role in changing the perception of women, because, being a person who could offer you qualitative advice about what you should be doing based on polling data and having a very aggressive personality in her own right, Wilma taught a whole generation of younger Republican candidates that women could be argumentative and important and that you had to listen to their opinion. She had an important impact on [former Georgia senator] Mattingly, for example; she was one of the people who really trained me. I think once you've dealt with a Wilma Goldstein it gets a lot harder to not have a sense of 'let's measure this next person on what they know, and not what their sex is.' "

On the other hand, other men can work with capable women and emerge apparently unaffected by the experience. Rozanne L. Ridgway, who has been in the foreign service for thirty years, is now Assistant Secretary of State for European Affairs, which meant she headed the presummit negotiating team for the Reagan-Gorbachev meeting in Geneva in 1985. "I sat next to [then White House chief of staff] Don Regan at lunch every day with the President during the course of the summit," Ridgway said—which meant she was as surprised and indignant as anyone when Regan hit the headlines by remarking patronizingly that women "were not going to understand throw-weights." As she said later, "I just shook my head and thought: what am I? The invisible woman?"[16]

But beyond knowledge and capability is the deeper abyss of mistrust. First of all is the issue of being trusted to do your job, which as Anne Stanley points out, is more difficult when you get out of the areas such as polling and fund-raising, where there are firm numbers to support you. Stanley, a Republican consultant who has been working on campaigns since 1968, says she almost wishes she had gone into a more specific aspect of the business, "But it's just that I don't have any of the skills. Because I'm a generalist, I do strategy advertising. Fewer women go into advertising. I guess because of all the problems women have in life in general, it is easier if you walk in with a product than it is if you are trying to get people to follow your strategy—after all, it's obscure, it's not something they can touch, feel, taste, measure. So that means they have to trust your judgment, which is a lot harder. Although it is getting better for women in politics now. As politics gets a little more scientific, and there are certain recognized skills, it gets easier. In the old days in the smoke-filled rooms, I think it would have been virtually impossible for a woman."

One of the politicians most widely recognized as relying on women in his innermost circle of advisors is Gary Hart, the former Democratic senator from Colorado. When he was the campaign manager for McGovern's presidential campaign in 1972, he persuaded Dotty Lynch, then an NBC News researcher, to join the campaign. After the campaign she served as vice-president of Patrick Caddell's polling firm, and then in 1984 in Hart's own presidential campaign she became his chief poll taker and close advisor. Kathy Bushkin, Hart's campaign press secretary in 1984, worked as a codirector of legislation in his Senate office for eight years and was a major contributor to his book, *A New Democracy*. She spent five hundred days on the campaign trail, going through the ups and downs of twenty-nine primaries, and was widely recognized as one of the most influential people surrounding the senator. When Hart was the front-runner for the Democratic nomination, before the spectacular demise of his campaign in the spring of 1987, many women had hoped that if he became president, qualified women might finally become part of the inner White House circles. Since a new president usually draws his White House advisors from the people he has worked with most closely over the course of his pre–White House career, it seems likely that women will only move into the inner circle of White House power after they have been accepted into the inner circle of presidential campaigns. After all, as Harrison Hickman pointed out, the fact that Ronald Reagan has not had close women advisors in the White House (apart from his wife) is not something that just happened in the rarified air of the White House. "Reagan's never had women advisors—it's not just because he's president. Same for Jimmy Carter—never had women. Same for [Vice President] Mondale. My guess is that may be the next big step: a woman would emerge as a key player in the presidential campaign."

Political life is inevitably life on the tightrope, watched by an audience eager for excitement, hoping for a fall. The more prominent a politician becomes, the more people there are to point out any misstep. It seems only natural that behind the need to be surrounded by staffers who can be trusted to do a competent job, any politician who aims to become a player also needs to have advisors and friends with whom he or she feels totally comfortable.

It is not surprising, therefore, that woman politicians tend to have other women as close associates, or that men feel it's most natural for them to employ other men.

Partly, it's a social problem, particularly with all the heightened interest in a politician's personal life. "I think that it is frankly easier for a male to be friends with males for a couple of reasons, and one is sexual," Newt Gingrich said. "If I'm going to go out in the evening and totally relax I'm more likely to do it with men, particularly since my wife is in school in Georgia. I'm not sure I want to go out with an attractive woman very many evenings and totally relax." On the other hand, becoming a social companion is not necessarily what many politicians expect from a staffer: for example, both Bob Haldeman and John Erlichman insisted after their departure from the Nixon White House that they had never had a social relationship with the president even when they were working most closely with him. But there is still a kind of compatibility a politician looks for in the people who become closest to him.

It is not only women who feel shut out. Former national security adviser Robert McFarlane, who attempted suicide in early 1987 as the Iran-contra revelations were spilling out, described his own sense of being excluded in a newspaper interview while he was recovering. "It finally came down to a feeling that, even though I knew and understood the substance of policies better than others in the Cabinet, I wasn't being listened to because I didn't qualify to be in the inner circle. The President is a man who admires men who have accumulated means and become wealthy and demonstrated considerable accomplishments in a chosen endeavor. [Secretary of State] Shultz and [Secretary of Defense] Cap Weinberger and [White House Chief of staff] Don Regan and the vice-president had built up businesses and made great successes of themselves. I haven't done that. I had a career in the bureaucracy. I didn't really quite qualify. It didn't do any good to know a lot about arms control if nobody listened."[17]

More than one woman must be able to identify poignantly with McFarlane's forlorn analysis. Sometimes, in the end, qualifications are only part of the equation. Before women are truly accepted in the innermost circles, the men who are already there have to become completely comfortable in their presence. No one who is in any way an outsider is going to be a player when the going gets rough. As Celinda Lake put it, "When the shit hits the fan, and the door is closed, how many woman are in the room?"

Sixty-six years after American women were made full voting members of their society, the answer still has to be damn few, if any.

■   ■   ■

Not all the hurdles in the career path arise from the attitudes of others. The time demands of political life are based on a man's life-style, and the life-style of an extraordinarily energetic man at that. To accommodate those demands to the different patterns of a woman's life is not easily managed.

Pat Schroeder, who came to Washington when her youngest child was only two, remembers the stir it made among her friends and constituents when against all expectations she won the election. "Everybody was saying 'How are you going to do it?' " she remembers, laughing ruefully at herself. "Right after I was elected I got a phone call from Bella Abzug, and I was thinking, here's *one* phone call when I won't have to go through that. And she said, 'I hear you have two little kids.' And I said yes, and she said, 'How are you going to do it?' And at that point, I thought oh my goodness, maybe I'm not!"

Every woman running for office has to cope with questions during her campaign about how she is going to handle her personal life, but the problem is more complicated than that. Working out an acceptable answer is a strategic problem; working out a solution that she and her family, if she has one, can comfortably get along with is a master-class jigsaw puzzle of flexibility, shifting priorities, and all hands to the pump when necessary.

There are a lot of responsibilities to be taken care of, one way or another. The most recent (1983) comprehensive research project on women in public office by the Center for the American Woman and Politics found that the majority of women in both appointive and elective office were married and had children. However, less than one-third of the women appointed to office and less than one-fifth of the women elected had children under twelve—statistical evidence that the Pat Schroeders of the world who undertake the rigors of political life with young children are still few and far between. Even for women with older children, the logistics are formidable.

Political life almost invariably requires considerable travel. Holding a local office may only involve a bit of driving back and forth, but a state legislator has to get back and forth from the capital, which in all but the smallest states probably involves overnights away from home, especially toward the end of a session when the legislature is sitting late to get the business done. Depending on the size of her constituency, a legislator may have additional miles to cover just to keep in touch with the people who elected her in the first place.

Going to Washington magnifies the whole problem. Connie Morella, a former Maryland state legislator elected to Congress in 1986, points out that she is the only congresswoman (or congressperson, come to that) who, because she and her family live in the Maryland suburbs of Washington, is closer to her job now on Capitol Hill than she was when she had to travel to the state capitol in Annapolis. For most members of congress, election means a continual process of traveling back and forth from Washington to the constituency. Congressmen or congresswomen from the Far West must quickly feel that they see more of the interiors of airplanes than either Capitol Hill or their home turf. Unless a congresswoman's family travels with her—an impractical option for most and a grueling prospect for all—she and her family must inevitably spend a substantial amount of time apart. This unavoidable separation is the first thing many women state legislators mention when they talk about the possibility of running for federal office. It's hard on a marriage; it's hard on children, even those who aren't young and don't need around-the-clock attention.

Parallel to the distance problem is the time dimension. Politics of any flavor—appointive or elective, campaigning or serving in office—is not a nine-to-five job. There are committee meetings, groups to visit, speeches to make, Jefferson Day dinners for Democrats, Lincoln Day dinners for Republicans, and similar fund-raising festivities the rest of the year, parades and ice cream socials during the summer—all in addition to the normal business of doing whatever job the politician was elected or appointed to do. Some of it is obviously important to getting the job done; all of it is important for somebody or other as visible evidence that the job is being done. No matter how committed a woman public official may be to her job and the opportunity it gives her to have a hand in the decisions being made, the fact is that no one can use the same hour more than once. An evening spent speaking to the Future Farmers of America or working out what can usefully be done for a distraught constituent caught up in the coils of bureaucracy is an evening not spent with husband or children—which gets more stressful for all concerned when it happens to be the sixth (or sixteenth) consecutive evening on which something unavoidable has come up. Time spent politicking all too often has the same effect as distance to be traveled in separating the politician and her family.

Clearly, there are ways in which women politicians manage to cope with it. Pat Schroeder is everybody's shining example because she managed to maintain a congressional career and become a national political figure while her children were growing up, but as she points out, she had advantages a lot of women don't have: "In a way what I'm doing is what almost every American woman is having to do in this generation. They don't even have the options I had because shoes now cost what a coat used to cost and cars now cost what a house used to cost, and nobody's salary has maintained that level, so everybody who's got children is having to work and there is this incredible conflicted area. In a way I've been hesitant to talk about it too much because my feeling was always that with the kind of salary I make, I've found it fairly easy to hire people, but what about these other people who can't afford to hire anyone?"

Her philosophy of holding public office while remaining a wife and mother is straightforward. "What I have done with the job that's really quite different from what most politicians do is I have viewed it as my job and not as their job. My husband doesn't do thank-you notes, and he doesn't go to Ladies' Teas, and he does not go back and campaign and set up housekeeping and smile and do all that, nor do the children. I post the schedule and anything they don't want to do, fine. It's my job and not theirs. And we've spent a bloody fortune doing it, but I've treated the job as a seminar. Anywhere I go, they can go. And we pay for the tickets. That doesn't mean they have to go and sit through boring meetings. They can sit through what they want. Therefore, they think the job is a million laughs. They've been all over the world—they've been everywhere. I couldn't pay for that kind of an education. But we spend our money on airlines. As a consequence, we live in very small houses and we do not drive fancy cars."

Even so, even given the money and the hired help and the advantages she admittedly feels her family gained from the whole experience, meshing family and a political career was not always a barrel of laughs. When she remembers back to when she was a new arrival in Washington and the children were very young she still sounds almost incredulous that she made it through. "They were only two and five when I got here. There were days when I would sit down and see flashing lights on the wall and it was just absolute exhaustion." That Pat Schroeder exists is proof that it can be done, but not everybody can be Pat Schroeder. It takes determination, a strong and flexible marriage, money, and a high level of energy, sustainable for years. Most women don't even try running for office until their children are older, not primarily because that plays better with the voters—although it does—but just because it simplifies an already grotesquely complicated life-style.

Children grow up and into independence. The relationship of a husband and wife is presumably intended to be a more permanent arrangement. Jeane Kirkpatrick, in her study of women state legislators, *Political Woman*, identified four different patterns of husbandly behavior found among her sample of forty-six women, all of whom had served more than one term and were judged by competent observers to be effective legislators. She categorized them as participant husbands, who took an active part in their wives' careers; helpful husbands, who might not have become directly involved themselves, but were willing to take on extra responsibilities at home so their wives could be freer; acquiescent husbands, who generally approved of their wives' activities but left the job up to them; and jealous husbands, who disapproved of their wives getting involved and wished they would stop.[18] Her study was made in 1972, but from what women politicians currently serving have to say, the patterns haven't changed much since then.

The classic example of the jealous husband remains the husband of congresswoman Coya Gjesdal Knutson, a Democrat from Minnesota who was elected in 1954 and served two terms. Just before she made her announcement to seek a third term, her husband sent a letter, which promptly became known nationally as the "Coya Come Home" letter, to his hometown newspaper. In it, he wrote that as a result of her wifely neglect, his "home life has deteriorated to the extent it is nonexistent." As a direct result of the letter, she was defeated in the 1958 election, the only Democratic incumbent in the House to be defeated by a Republican that year. Either the marriage or the political career seems to fall by the wayside when a politician's husband is fundamentally opposed to her activity. In Coya Knutson's case, it was the career that came to a full halt; more typically (as in the two cases among the study group reported by Kirkpatrick), it is the marriage that suffers and ends in separation or divorce. In both cases, the husband had initially been acquiescent to his wife's career. It is a rare wife who would attempt the obvious difficulties of combining marriage and a political career if her husband were flatly opposed to it in the first place.

Most husbands fall in the other three categories, and some of them are magnificently supportive. Pat Schroeder's husband Jim moved his legal practice from Colorado to Washington when she was elected to Congress; Charlie Smeal, whose wife Ellie has had two separate periods of holding the presidency of NOW, has not only moved the family from Pittsburgh, but has changed his career twice to make her work possible, because he and their children believed what she was doing was unique and important. "They made a decision to move and so they moved," Ellie Smeal says about it. "You don't know if you make the right decisions or the wrong decisions in life, but you decide just like anybody else would. Just like you would move for a man's job."

Not all husbands are willing or able to redirect their own careers in the service of their wives' political advancement. Almost by definition, most women who choose to enter politics are successful, high-achieving women, and it is not surprising that by and large such women, if they are married, are married to successful, high-achieving men. Few of those men can pick up and move the way the wife of a male politician traditionally has done. In practice if a married woman's political career requires that she be in one city and her home and husband somewhere else, what usually develops is some variation on a commuter marriage. When Bella Abzug went to Washington in 1971, her husband Martin stayed in New York and she traveled back and forth. Most of her time in Washington she lived in a hotel because she felt lonely in an apartment: "I'm a family person. Living apart from my husband was the only part I didn't like," she said.[19] In 1979, eight years later, when Geraldine Ferraro went to Washington she and her husband had a similar arrangement: he stayed at home with the children, and she spent part of each week with them and part at her job in the Capitol. Other women in Congress and the vast majority of women state legislators are living out their own variations on the same pattern. Since few women marry their husbands and have children expecting to live separately from them, working out these compromises is often a matter of choosing the least disagreeable alternative. More than one woman contemplating a political career—or a move upward from a local office—has decided the whole stressful game, with all its complicated logistics, simply isn't worth the candle. More than one husband of a defeated woman candidate, supportive though he may be of his wife's ambitions and committed to her political goals, has unquestionably been relieved that he gets to go on living with the woman in the ordinary daily way to which they're accustomed.

Even so, the other couples who are managing to accommodate the whole set of conflicting demands find their own kind of satisfaction in the exercise. Judith Miller is a Michigan state legislator who lives about ninety miles away from the state capitol and thus spends her fair share of time on the road and away from home. She and her husband have found their own accommodation to the difficulties. "My husband isn't particularly interested in politics at all," she said, "and yet he said to me the other day, 'you know, even when it's challenging and you're doing more than I would like you to do, even then I wouldn't have you doing anything else.' " Often the people who speak with the most feeling about the difficulties of combining a married or family life with political ambitions are those women politicians who are unmarried and childless, who know about the pressures and stress but don't have the experience of the pleasure in undertaking a project that demands the best from the whole family, and rewards them with unique satisfactions. The negatives are right out there in public for all to see; the pride a whole family can take in good old mom tends to be more private and personal.

Fitting together the priorities and rhythms of a woman's life with a political career remains one of the highest hurdles of all, but it's not insurmountable.

■　　■　　■

Looked at from the negative side, when you contemplate all the difficulties facing women in political life the wonder becomes not that there are so few, but that there are so many. However, women politicians are generally optimistic by nature and disinclined to brood over their personal problems. What many of them prefer to emphasize instead is that anything anybody chooses to do has disadvantages, and if being a woman involved in politics is at times frustrating and exhausting, so are a lot of other things.

"My mother lived a traditional life as a full-time homemaker," Ellie Smeal pointed out, "and she used to be overextended just from her family and all the other kinds of obligations. Everything in life is tiring. You can be tired walking a precinct and you can be tired washing the floor, too. I don't know if you can do whatever doing it all means, but if you want to have a profession in this area and have children I not only think it is possible and doable, I think it's as possible and doable as anything else in your life."

In focusing on the problems women face in political life, it is easy to forget that it's not necessarily a piece of cake for the man either, and they have centuries of role models to fall back on. In some ways, being a woman and thus visibly distinguishable from the majority around you isn't all bad. As Millicent Fenwick observed during her last term in Congress, "We have an advantage that too few of us are willing to admit. When we are one of 18 women in a House of 435 people, we stand out. When we go down to speak, people notice us. That makes a difference."[20]

Even in the 1980s, American political life has a long way to go before it approaches gender-blindness, but it sometimes helps to consider how far women have come, and how recently. In 1974, Jeane Kirkpatrick was able to write in *Political Woman*, "Half a century after the ratification of the nineteenth amendment, no woman has been nominated to be president or vice-president, no woman has served on the Supreme Court. Today, there is no woman in the cabinet, no woman in the Senate, no woman serving as governor of a major state, no woman mayor of a major city, no woman in the top leadership of either major party."[21] In 1988, there are Geraldine Ferraro, Sandra Day O'Connor, Elizabeth Dole, Nancy Kassebaum and Barbara Mikulski, Madeleine Kunin and Kay Orr (with Martha Layne Collins having left office only in December of 1987), Dianne Feinstein and Kathy Whitmire, and all the others. It may not be happening all at once, but slowly, gradually, it's happening.

3. The Campaign Trail

Months later Norma Paulus still remembered that day. In 1986 she was campaigning for governor in Oregon—one of those spacious western states where the population is more thinly scattered than clustered—and, during the day, "In one twelve-hour period I was in five vans, two helicopters, on a sternwheeler on the Columbia River for a good part of the day, and on a conventional aircraft. For all of those twelve hours I was either speaking or 'on stage.' " She added thoughtfully, "I think I have changed clothes in every public restroom in the state." She remembers that day not because it was unusually demanding (it was reasonably typical of her life on the campaign trail), but because the wind was roaring down the river gorge, and for once she was frightened during the helicopter ride up the river.

Altogether she campaigned every day, all day, for a year and a half: she started in 1985, a year before the Republican primary in May, which she won. In the course of the eighteen months the campaign raised over two million dollars, but her opponent in the general election, Neil Goldschmidt, a former mayor of Portland and President Carter's secretary of transportation, raised more than three million. In November, Paulus lost by about forty thousand votes. Maybe she lost because there wasn't enough money at the end; maybe she lost because she was too liberal for the right wing of her party; maybe she lost because she was a woman and enough of the electorate thought being the governor was a man's job. Whatever it was, she didn't lose because she didn't campaign hard enough.

Similarly, Arliss Sturgulewski crisscrossed the vast expanse of

Alaska, stumping the state in her own 1986 gubernatorial campaign. "Campaigning is tough," she said. "I flew, of course. Our road system is relatively limited." Even Juneau, the state capital, can't be reached by road: the road extends only a few miles north and south of town. When the legislators convene there, they arrive by plane or boat. "I campaigned on everything, all the way from going on our state ferry, which we call our marine highway system, to helicopters, to small planes, to executive jets, to regular commercial air—I certainly went by auto to hit the road system we do have, but you just do a lot of stumping in a lot of areas and the distances are vast. It's difficult because of cost, really, to hit the number of places that you would like. There were always great calls to get to the Eskimo and the Inuit and Indian communities and many of those would have a population of two hundred or three hundred and a tiny airstrip and simply no way could you have the time or the financial resources to get to them." Sturgulewski beat eight men in the Republican primary and was in a strong position to win the general election until one of her defeated Republican rivals, former governor Walter Hickel, launched a write-in campaign and siphoned off enough votes to put Democrat Steve Cowper into office.

For the politically uninvolved, a campaign is mainly literature stuffed under the door or hanging on the doorknob, repetitious commercials on the radio and TV, yard signs and bumper stickers blooming abruptly, and—if the race is an important one—saturation news coverage in the media. For the people caught up in it, a campaign is a mushrooming obsession that gradually overtakes every other element that used to be important in their lives. The phones never stop ringing, there is always someone at the door, someone waiting for an answer, always a crisis either full-blown or just about to explode. However much money there is, there is never enough, so there is always the drumming pressure of fund-raising to conjure up more. For the candidate, there are always more places to go and people to meet than there is time to do either, so there are always choices to make and cold sweats in the middle of short nights wondering if the right choices are being made. For the staff, there are thousands of details to be attended to against a background of constant veiled or unveiled struggle between would-be policymakers, and forever and always, more people available who think their job ought to be making policy than there are people willing to do the work to carry it out.

It's on the campaigns that the heroes are made and reputations established. Stars are made overnight. On a campaign, exaggeration comes easily, and events inevitably appear larger than life: nobody can really know what is going to be the crucial factor in the end, and so any detail can be decreed critical by somebody. The combination of the cachet of being an insider and the adrenaline-rich stress is sufficiently addictive so that there are always those people who surface to volunteer for campaigns alone, and then, even if their candidate won, drift away rather than get involved in the routine of actually doing the job they fought so tenaciously to help win. The campaign insiders—the ones who prove they can be counted on to do what they said they'd do—grow more and more tightly knit as the campaign progresses. Each day of the campaign the tension seems to heighten as there is one day less to do everything that has to be done, until in the last weeks being part of the campaign can feel like being aboard a freight train hurtling down a track toward the brick wall of election day—and then, suddenly, it's all over. The voters vote, they tally up the score, and that's it.

■   ■   ■

Campaigning, like so much else in politics, is different for a woman. Some of the differences are obvious to everybody; some are subtle. It is possible, of course, to overemphasize them—after all, as one longtime political observer pointed out, "It may be a woman, but the species is still politician." Getting 51 percent of the vote is a respectable challenge for anyone, male or female. Still, practical current experience shows that in some distinct ways the hurdles are still higher for women.

Take for example Barbara Mikulski's run for the Senate in Maryland. Looking back at it with the knowledge that she was elected with over 60 percent of the vote, it seems almost a foregone conclusion that she was unbeatable. Baltimore born, she still lives in her old neighborhood in the Polish east section of the city, down the street from the corner grocery her family ran. She started out as a social worker and first moved into political action by organizing local resistance to the extension of an interstate highway through the neighborhood. It worked, and the community was left intact.

Mikulski went on to win a place on the Baltimore City Council and in 1974 made her first bid for the Senate, challenging Republican senator Charles Mathias, then seeking reelection after his first term. She lost—but with 43 percent of the vote—and in 1976 she ran for the House of Representatives and won. She served five terms, winning by impressive majorities each time. When Mathias retired in 1986, it was an obvious opportunity.

It's tempting to believe that a male Democratic politician in her position with her record would have gone for the Senate seat without a moment's hesitation—and that his strength would have been apparent enough to would-be rivals so that more than token competition would be unlikely. Might-haves and would-haves being forever debatable, the fact is that it took Barbara Mikulski about a year to make the final decision to risk her rock-solid House seat in the gamble for the Senate. According to Wendy Sherman, her campaign manager, "She did a lot of political consultations. I did a fund-raising assessment to try to figure out where we could raise the money from. We had long meetings and discussions to try to sort through whether she would run. She had to decide whether she wanted to run, take the risks, and even if she wanted to, should she be a senator, and if she wanted to and she should be, could she be? Were the numbers there for it to happen? Once we sorted that out, we knew how we were going to approach it. We knew that we were going to build from the bottom a metropolitan base; we knew sort of how much money we thought we would have to spend. We budgeted *very* tightly and were very cautious in spending money. So when we began, we were pretty clear about what we were going to do."

It turned out that she needed every bit of that planning. In the primary, two popular Maryland Democrats took her on: the governor, Harry Hughes, and Michael Barnes, a four-term congressman from the Washington–Maryland suburbs. According to pollster Harrison Hickman, who had been heavily involved in Mikulski's decision-making process, "Both of them got into the race against her without ever doing a poll and just assuming that she was weak. But we had been polling her off and on for about nine months, and the fact is that she was one of the strongest politicians in Maryland. In retrospect, it all seems so simple as to why she won. But at the time these guys who were bright, both officeholders, each had a pretty good political base, just didn't have a clue. They just didn't understand how strong she was. If it had been a man, they would have understood. There wouldn't have been this problem of underestimating her strength." They figured it out when the primary returns came in: Barbara Mikulski rolled over both of them, capturing 50 percent of the vote.

As it happened, a woman won the Republican nomination as well. It was Linda Chavez, the former White House director of public liaison, and the national political media licked its collective chops at the prospect of this woman versus woman race. The contrast between the candidates could not have been more striking. Barbara Mikulski is short (four feet eleven inches), stocky, and her fashion style has been aptly described as being "like a nun whose order has just abandoned its blue wool habit for Toni home perms and polyester suits from K mart."[1] Linda Chavez is also petite, but slender, exquisitely groomed, and beautifully dressed for all occasions, with the modulated voice and gracious manner that plays beautifully on television. In political orientation she now describes herself as a neoconservative. Mikulski is a forthright feminist with a national reputation for supporting feminist causes, liberal, and uncompromising about pursuing her legislative goals. She is invariably described as "feisty," which appears to be mediaspeak for being a short, tough woman.

Chavez, however, turned out to be no shrinking violet. She kicked off her campaign emphasizing her own traditional status as the mother of three sons and describing Mikulski as "a San Francisco-style feminist," and then went on to make a major campaign issue out of an episode back in 1981 when Mikulski had hired Teresa Brennan, an Australian radical feminist, as an aide in her congressional office. For two months, while looking for a place of her own, Brennan stayed at Mikulski's house in Baltimore. Before long, Brennan's aggressive feminism had created enough friction in the office so that she was asked to leave. Altogether, her tenure lasted for about five months, and was reported by the Baltimore *Sun* at the time. The voters, having read about the whole thing, still returned Mikulski to Congress in 1982 and 1984, each time with about 70 percent of the vote. Mikulski was apparently exasperated by Chavez's exhuming of the incident five years later as an event of major importance. As she said, "We have spent more time talking about Teresa than she spent in my congressional office."[2] It appeared to some observers that what Chavez was questioning was not so much Mikulski's judgment as her sexuality, but when reporters asked Chavez, she said no such inference was intended.

Whatever was intended, it is generally agreed that Chavez, who never made any significant inroads into Mikulski's lead, conducted one of the nastiest campaigns fought in what turned out to be a fairly nasty season—negative campaigning flourished generally in 1986. Mikulski proponents had a few countercharges of their own: Chavez had credibility problems. Although her current political stance was firmly conservative, she had started out her career as a liberal Democrat and was a political appointee in the Carter administration, changing her party affiliation less than two years before the election, when she went to work for the Reagan White House. Further, the press brought up questions about whether she was Catholic as she claimed or had converted to Judaism when she married, as the rabbi who said he had instructed her reported.

The fact that the Maryland race was only periodically spread across headlines from coast to coast was in part a deliberate decision on the part of the Mikulski campaign. "I think that part of the reason that Barbara Mikulski is a senator is because Gerry Ferraro ran for vice-president," Wendy Sherman said. "I think that we learned an enormous amount from that. I think we learned some of the things that people were going to look at and for in a woman running for higher office. I think we learned about fund-raising. I think we learned that it's very important to distinguish between celebrity status and candidacy. When after the primary election everybody wanted to make the Mikulski-Chavez race into a national race, two women running against each other, we wanted to keep it to a Maryland race. We did not do the national television news shows after the primary. We did not believe that our opponent had the same credentials that Barbara Mikulski had, so we were gong to run it as a Maryland campaign, not as a national campaign."

To what extent the mudslinging in the general election came about because both candidates were women is of course open to conjecture. Ed Rollins, formerly Reagan's political director and now a political consultant who functioned as an unofficial advisor to the Chavez campaign, said he told her that, "If you don't raise the following five or six things, they are going to say you choked in the course of the campaign, so you better decide whether you want a future in Maryland or you want a future with the conservatives." This advice may have been the basis of her decision to seek national media coverage, but perhaps her need as a woman to prove she could play hardball like a man also came into it. Mikulski's countering toughness was no surprise to anyone.

Even back in Mikulski's primary campaign, the gender issue had surfaced in her opponents' campaign tactics. There was little in the way of issues separating the three Democratic candidates, and a lot of the campaign appeared to boil down to the peripheral issue of which candidate looked the most "senatorial." As Mikulski said with typical belligerence, "A lot of Americans, black or white or female, are always told that they don't look the part. It's one of the oldest code words."[3] Wendy Sherman said more matter-of-factly, "Some of the money people were skeptical that this hard-talking, working-class–roots woman could be a senator. That was gender, that was her height, and that was class." Looking at the astounding variation in physical appearance among the ninety-nine other individuals elected to the Senate, it's a little difficult to come to the conclusion that looking "senatorial" might refer to anything other than gender. Otherwise dissimilar they may be, but ninety-eight senators *are* male.

■　　■　　■

If Barbara Mikulski had not been female, then her campaigns, both primary and general, would probably have been different. In that way she shared the experience of other women candidates. But obviously she had a much higher profile than the average woman candidate, partly because she already had a national reputation as a committed feminist, partly because it was only the second time in United States history that women took both major party nominations in a Senate race. (A woman challenged Maine's Margaret Chase Smith in 1960.) Senatorial campaigns are big business and cost big bucks: the Mikulski campaign raised and spent $2,057,216, and Chavez spent $1,699,175. That's one of the big reasons that few women run for the Senate and fewer yet get there: Mikulski is only the seventh woman senator to serve there.

So far, most women are still getting their campaign experience in much less visible and much less expensive races. (As did Mikulski originally—she started out in 1971, after all, with a local campaign for the Baltimore City Council.) Generally speaking, campaigns can be divided into two main categories: the local campaigns where it is possible and practical for the candidate to meet a reasonable proportion of the voters personally, and the statewide or federal campaign where the distances and numbers of voters involved inevitably lead to a lot of the campaigning being done with as much media advertising as the candidate can afford and by a far-flung network of campaign staff, paid and volunteer. Most campaigns for state legislative seats can still be conducted locally, which keeps the cost and complication factor down—another reason why the numbers of women are burgeoning there.

Every campaign, on whatever level, is fueled by two main resources: people and money. Campaign consultant Matt Reese explained it neatly. "I know how to run a campaign with lots of people and little money. I know how to run a campaign with lots of money and few people. I love it when I've got lots of money and lots of people. I don't know what to do when I don't have any money and any people."[4] Generally, women's campaigns have had more volunteers and ingenuity than cold cash.

For many races, this is not as crippling a disadvantage as it might initially appear—which is not to say that money isn't important. Years ago, longtime California politician Jesse Unruh earned political immortality when he described money as the mother's milk of politics, and it is as true now as when he said it. However, the best that money can buy is generally more sophisticated methods of communication to substitute for the candidate discussing the issues personally with each voter, and in the local race it's possible for the candidate to get out and talk.

That kind of personal contact seems to be something that most women do well—there is even considerable political opinion that most women do it better than most men. Barbara Trafton, speaking from her experience of successful campaigns for the Maine state legislature, says that one of the main advantages women candidates have is their potential for successful door-to-door visits. "People tend to respond well from the start to the female office seeker, who they see as more direct, honest, and sympathetic than the average male politician," she writes. "Besides, they feel much safer inviting an unknown woman into their homes than an unknown man."[5] Moreover, she adds, since dusk comes early (around 6:00 P.M.) in Maine during a general election campaign in the fall, and since people are more likely to trust the intentions of a woman on their doorsteps than the intentions of a man, she figures she gets an extra hour of campaign time each day that her male opponents don't get.

If women in our society, by and large, absorb any specific training simply by being socialized as women, it's training for amicable interpersonal relations. The skills of listening and being responsive that women unwittingly develop (and as often as not don't give themselves credit for possessing) are admirably suited for the small group and one-to-one situations that are so much a part of a local campaign. Those skills are not acquired only by women as a result of working outside their homes. Women who have spent their adult lives going to showers and to coffees for their children's schools and doing volunteer work are just as able to make the transition to a political coffee or wine and cheese event, and generally do well at explaining themselves and their programs on an informal, personal basis. It is still unusual enough for a woman to decide to undertake a political campaign that almost every one who does makes it her business to be well-informed and articulate about the issues. Curiously, the same voters who take it as a matter of course that a male candidate knows what he's talking about are likely to be actively impressed by a woman who is obviously knowledgeable. It's still true that a woman is expected to be *more* qualified than a man to get the same opportunities, but the voters, having listened to the more qualified woman, often remember her better.

A local campaign is also usually an operation of manageable scale. A candidate can keep most of the control in her own hands, if she wishes. Fran Ulmer, now a state representative in Alaska, started out her elective career in 1983 with a successful campaign for mayor in Juneau. Although it is the state capital, Juneau is really a very small town where most people know each other. "I was really my own campaign manager in both my mayoral campaign and the legislative campaign," Ulmer said, describing her way of going about the job of organizing her two successful campaigns. "I had a lot of help, and had what I called the coordinator who was working at a full-time job doing something else. She helped keep the glue together. You have to have somebody keeping the glue together or you just burn yourself out—I certainly didn't do it all myself. I used a team approach in both campaigns. I had a cabinet so to speak, of campaign workers, each of whom were responsible for a piece of the action. There was a media coordinator and there was a door-to-door coordinator, there was a special events coordinator, and those people each had other networks of other people who would work on individual pieces of the campaign. Then we would get together once a week at a 'cabinet meeting' and discuss the schedule and what needed more money. You'd know what was coming up that somebody had to work on. We used that sort of system, which I think really works better than having a campaign manager go off and do it—but part of that is just a matter of personal style. I would never feel comfortable totally turning over my campaign to someone else. Of course my campaigns have been small enough geographically to be able to do that. If I were running in a statewide race, I'm sure I couldn't do it that way."

Ulmer also pointed out that one of her advantages as a woman was that she didn't have to do anything elaborate to differentiate herself from the other candidates. Particularly in the mayoral race, when there were four other candidates in the race, all male, she didn't have the job her rivals had of setting themselves apart from the pack. This is obviously an advantage that women have at any level of campaign, as long as they're running against men.

Susan Molinari, New York City Council member, commented on the same phenomenon from her own experience among her Staten Island constituency. Getting attention, she said, is not the problem. A woman is bound to be noticed. "There are still lots of areas where you are the token, where they need a woman on the dais, when they need a woman to fill out an advisory council," she explained. Being a token may be exasperating, but a determined woman candidate can turn it into an advantage. It gives her an opportunity to be visible while her male opponents tend to blend into the background. On the other hand, the same woman who gets attention easily may find that gaining credibility is considerably more difficult. "Sometimes you might have to stand up, you have to yell a little louder, you have to be a little more assertive," Molinari went on to say. "Politics is like journalism or anything else—you have to work. I believe you have to work five times as hard to establish the credibility a man has. It's easier to get the attention at first. It's harder to get credibility."

Should they be in one of the infrequent races where woman faces woman, of course, the advantage of being the visible woman evaporates. Nebraska had an all-woman gubernatorial race in 1986 when Republican Kay Orr defeated Democrat Helen Boosalis. Harrison Hickman, who had done the polling for Boosalis, remarked with some chagrin, "It was a little bit frustrating, and I said this all along, even before we were on the losing end of the score. The voters were going around patting themselves on the back for having the good judgment to have nominated two women, and it was very difficult to get them to focus on the differences between the two women."

Whether the campaign is big or small, one element that any political woman is bound to encounter is the electorate's concern over how she is going to organize her private life in order to hold public office. As Ruth Mandel put it, "Political women contend with curiosity and scrutiny in a society not yet comfortable with the idea that women might be able to arrange their life patterns so as to function as public leaders."[6] The immediate result is that a woman is asked personal questions that male candidates are never faced with. Barbara Trafton suggests that the standard two are "Who's taking care of your children?" and "Who's fixing your husband's supper?" This is sufficiently aggravating when everything at home is going well, but it can feel like the final straw when under the stress of adjusting to the difficulties of having wife and mother out on the campaign trail, the family is indeed having its problems, and everybody has to smile regardless, knowing that if they can all just hold out to election day, the worst will be over and life can return to something a little closer to normal.

If a woman doesn't happen to have either children or a husband, vocal members of the electorate want to know why. Learning to cope with this curiosity, usually brought up at the most inconvenient times, is part of the education of every woman politician. As Barbara Mikulski, who is single, said after her 1986 campaign against Linda Chavez, "Our marital status is criticized, whatever it is. If you're widowed, you killed him; if you're divorced, you couldn't hold on to him; if you're married, you're neglecting him; and if you're single, well, you're a little funny, aren't you?"[7]

Elizabeth Holtzman of New York sees definite sexism in the course of her campaigns. A former congresswoman, she won the

Democratic senatorial primary in 1980 and narrowly lost the general election, by less than seventy-two thousand votes—only 1 percent of the votes cast. She has been Brooklyn's District Attorney since 1981. "When I ran for the United States Senate in 1980," she said, "a major New York newspaper ran an article about the Democratic candidates. The writer's main concern about me seemed to be that no one could imagine me wearing a 'plunging neckline or a skirt slit to the thigh.' A year later, when I ran for district attorney, my opponent had radio commercials of a similar nature—a woman said, 'Liz Holtzman, she's a nice girl; I might even like her for a daughter, but not as D.A.' The message of the commercial was: a woman in a traditional role, yes; a woman in a nontraditional role, no. Neither of these incidents prompted any outcry; plainly, only six years ago, even in a presumably enlightened city like New York, these kinds of blatantly sexist attacks on women candidates were considered perfectly acceptable."

There may be some signs that this situation is improving. Congresswoman Connie Morella, who started out in politics with her race for the Maryland state legislature in 1974, said that her 1986 campaign for the House showed her that the electorate was willing to consider a woman as something other than a disturbing novelty. "Times have changed," she said. "Now, no matter what my sex, people know I can deliver, but when I started they worried whether I could take care of my kids and do the job."[8]

Monica McFadden, former political director of the Women's Campaign Fund, who has been active in organizing and assisting women's campaigns nationwide since 1978, says she can track the developing differences in attitudes toward women running for office in the Iowa races she has been associated with over the years. "I had an opportunity to watch three generations of women go through this," she said. "Nineteen seventy-eight was the first campaign I was involved with, and Minette Doderer, who was a wonderful state legislator, ran for lieutenant governor. Well, I mean women didn't run for lieutenant governor then, they just didn't do it, and Minette was asked all the nutsy questions. This is a woman who is in her fifties, she was highly qualified, she had served as a state legislator and as a state senator for over ten years. A dynamite woman. A feminist, definitely a feminist, no question about it. But they weren't ready for a woman. We watched the boys, the good old boys, literally go after her quite publicly. They arranged for another male candidate to run against her. She was asked all the nutty questions. 'What about your children?' Her children were in their twenties. 'What about your husband?' She and her husband had worked out an arrangement for ten years while she was a legislator in Des Moines. 'Was she a lesbian?' Never mind that she had a husband and children. All that kind of stuff. It was interesting to watch that.

"Well, four years later Roxanne Conlin runs for governor, and I worked on that campaign, and things had changed a little bit. Women had been sensitized by then to ask, 'What do you mean just because she's a woman she can't do this?' But we still ran into unbelievable attitude situations. My favorite was the time I was out on the road with Roxanne on one of the early trips and a man walked in, looked at the two of us standing side by side, and said, 'Which one of you dames is running for governor?' It was that attitude, and the constant theme 'Is Iowa ready for a woman governor?' A lot of talk about how a woman couldn't run this or that or the other. But there was a change in tone. Women got excited about this woman, and a lot of the blatant sexism had been driven underground. You couldn't just say you were voting against her because she was a woman because you were going to get beaten around by three or four women in a room and a lot of the men, too. It began to sound stupid to say you were against someone just because of her sex.

"Now in 1986, there were four women, two running for secretary of state, and two for lieutenant governor. The personal questions still get asked, but they seem silly. They're not even asked publicly, although they are asked privately. The difference, I think, is Ferraro. She gave this country a chance to get the sexist mentality out of its system. People had the chance all at once to ask the silly questions. People had a chance to look at it and say, 'Why not?' "

■　　　■　　　■

Stepping up from the local or state legislative race to a statewide or federal campaign is coming to bat in a whole new ball game. For one thing, there are almost always considerably vaster distances involved, which means that the candidate is constantly traveling. Wherever she is, there are more places where she isn't, and thus her message has to be carried by others, who have to be recruited, directed, and above all organized by somebody else. There is no way that the candidate herself can remain in complete control of the campaign. It is absolutely essential to trust other people to take crucial roles and further to trust that in carrying out their responsibilities they will work in her interests and will not make stupid mistakes. That can be a scary leap in the dark, particularly for the woman who has typically made her own way, relying on her own competence.

There are some things on a campaign that only a candidate can do. She has to be available to the voters. Although in a statewide or federal campaign she will never get to meet all of the voters—or even many of them—she still has to be out there meeting as many as she can, and she has to be available to the press and other media who report on her activities. She has to be actively involved in the fund-raising: there are many political donors who want to talk to the candidate personally before they make out the big checks. She has to have some time with her campaign staff to remain in touch with what is being done on her behalf. She has to find more time to keep up with what's going on in the world besides her campaign, so that a sudden question out of left field doesn't leave her standing there looking and feeling blank. She has to have some sleep and a few minutes here and there to maintain the minimum of a personal life. It is not possible for anyone else to do any of those things for her.

The campaign manager exists to do, or to delegate, everything else. A good campaign manager is a tactician who can keep the overall picture in mind while supervising ten thousand details, an expert in human relations who can soothe ruffled feelings while getting maximum productivity, a walking memory bank of what was tried and what worked and what didn't, and not least, a buffer for the candidate, absorbing and deflecting as much as possible of the run-of-the-mill gripes and intramural bickering that seem to be an integral part of any organization. Most of any candidate's staff members are people who were originally drawn to the candidate because they felt a personal commitment to her, but it is humanly impossible for the candidate to be as available to each of them as each of them would like her to be and still get out on the road to meet the electorate. The campaign manager is ordinarily the one who sets the limits of availability. This is not always a popular role.

Obviously, picking a campaign manager is one of the most

critical decisions of the campaign. Almost universally, political experts (and particularly women who have weathered less than ideal campaigns) emphasize that getting the right person is worth paying what it costs. Managing any campaign beyond the local level is a full-time job, and few capable politicians are in a position to volunteer their labor on that basis for very long. Unfortunately, all too often a woman who has been elected a couple of times to a local office continues to rely on the help of the devoted amateur friends who fought the early elections with her. Inexperienced and frequently loath to confront an old friend directly even when the job of the campaign manager should be to point out to the candidate where mistakes are being made, most of these amateurs (however willing and energetic they may be) find the job is more than they can handle.

"She was my best friend," one state legislator who had tried for Congress explained about her erstwhile campaign manager. "We'd always struggled through together. This time we just struggled. She was out of her depth and by the time I figured out why everything was going wrong, we were in too deep a hole to crawl out. I don't know if a win was ever there for me, but the campaign was in shambles by election day and we were just buried. I figure if it was her fault for letting everything go to pieces, it was even more my fault for handing her all that responsibility in the first place." Sadly, and very typically, not only the campaign but the friendship foundered irretrievably. More experienced politicians, male and female, flatly recommend that an aspiring candidate hire the best help available and find a place for the old friends on a board of advisors, where their useful suggestions can be utilized without swamping them with responsibility.

Women's campaigns tend to have more women in them, which can be simultaneously a strength and a weakness. As Ruth Mandel points out, women working for a female politician tend to identify personally with her, to take her as a mentor figure, and to realize from her example that women can be not only campaign workers but candidates themselves.[9] That close identification often leads to an intense loyalty, a special intimacy of pioneers caught up in a perilous adventure together, and virtually every woman politician has tales to tell of the extraordinary devotion of women working on her campaign: how they will go not only the second, but the third, sixth, and tenth mile if necessary. Many of these women are getting their first political experience, and so they may have a freshness and enthusiasm that more experienced hands lack. At the same time, their inexperience means the campaign organization may waste time reinventing the wheel and, at the worst, may make elementary mistakes in the allocation of energy and resources that someone more politically practiced would never make.

In theory, the quickest way to acquire political expertise is to hire a political consultant, and increasingly consultants are becoming an essential part of all major campaigns. A murmur in political Washington back in January of 1987 was that if Jeane Kirkpatrick were serious about taking a run at the presidency—a persistent rumor around then—she had better get moving because all the good consultants were already making their commitments to the hopefuls of 1988. The idea of proceeding without a seasoned staff of consultants was dismissed by several campaign professionals as impractical nonsense. When in the summer of 1987 Pat Schroeder started investigating the practicality of making a run for the Democratic nomination, she was mainly concerned with making sure that the finance was available. She did not feel she could use her sparse resources to take on consultants—and she ran into formidable problems in getting the political establishment to take her seriously as a potential contender. Did that have anything to do with the lack of recognized names aboard? She insisted it didn't, but interested political observers from both parties were not so sure.

The choice of consultant adds not only political technology to a campaign, but credibility—if you've signed up one of the first-rate consultants who watch their win-loss ratios closely you must have a reasonable chance of election, or so the reasoning seems to go. There are also those skeptics who claim that the proliferating political consultants are simply better educated, better groomed versions of the old political party pros who instructed novices on how the game was played while belching smoke from their cigars.

Political consultants are divided into all kinds of specialties: polling consultants, media specialists, direct-mail specialists, professional fund-raisers, organization specialists (who help in assembling the candidate's staff), and generalists who do a bit of everything, but often got started in one specialty or another. Political scientists trace the birth of political consulting back to California in the 1930s, and in the fifty years since, professional consultants have been playing an increasingly important role in political life. They are primarily involved only in statewide or congressional races, mainly because few state legislative or local campaigns have sufficient funds to afford their services. A good political consultant does not come cheap.

A presentation by a practiced consultant of services available for a fee can be an overwhelming experience. Particularly if a candidate is trying a major race for the first time, and thus is unsure of her own political judgment, it is very easy to place total trust in the serene assurance of the expert, who comes in with the mantle of authority, armed with sheaves of numbers, reports of past successes, campaign statistics, and an impressive win-loss record. Male chauvinism is not dead in the ranks of consultants, who are apt to see themselves as vastly more knowledgeable than any woman, even if she happens to be the candidate. Harrison Hickman, himself a consultant, remembers an early meeting he had with Martha Layne Collins when she was launching her ultimately successful gubernatorial campaign in Kentucky. "In the first meeting I went to," he said, "I was working with Bill Hamilton there, another pollster, and all these male consultants were in the room. Poor thing, she sat beside me at this meeting, and she never said a word during the entire meeting. These people were sitting there determining her fate politically. She and I got on famously eventually, and came to where we're fast friends today, in part because I was the only one who really took her opinion very seriously in terms of politics."

Dianne Feinstein, mayor of San Francisco, believes firmly that the candidate has to keep the upper hand and remember who's running. "I don't believe the consultant should control the campaign," she said. "I believe candidates run their own campaigns, and not to do so I think is a major sign of weakness. I think that the candidate should approve everything that goes out, the candidate should participate in the strategizing of the campaign, the candidate should review every single [television and radio] spot, every single piece of literature that's prepared, because that literature is *you*. Nobody accepts, I think, the excuse that, 'Well, my campaign manager did it, and I don't know anything about it.' I think that there is a weakness now because people come into the arena who are willing to give themselves over to a political consultant. I've just got to say I never have. I've won, and I've lost, and I've never blamed a consultant for my loss. I think when you have weak candidates, they give themselves over to a political consultant and say, 'Here, merchandise me, make me.' That's a big mistake. Because the chances are that that political candidate isn't going to know what to do when they get elected."

One major problem that afflicts the political consultants as much as it afflicts women candidates themselves is the fact that the book is still being written on how women should campaign. Should it be any different from the way men campaign, and if so, how? Electoral technology is still more an art than a science for anybody's campaign. Longtime Democratic political consultant Matt Reese, who has been in the business for twenty-five years, is engagingly honest about what he's doing: "All of us, including the new ones, sell magic; that's what the client wants to buy. . . . In those early days, I thought it *was* magic. I thought, Jesus Christ, this stuff works! Since I've matured, I've realized the hard steps that must be taken and the inevitable problems that arise. They're like arguments in a marriage—the same arguments come up time after time after time. As a consequence of knowing more and understanding more, and attempting to be an honorable person, I have greater trouble selling the magic. I have to tell clients what's real—and they don't want what's real."[10]

Reese's point applies just as much to women candidates, who are also looking for the magic and hoping to find a guaranteed successful formula. Celinda Lake, who as political director for the Women's Campaign Fund has been involved in dozens of campaigns for women candidates, points out that right now, in the late 1980s, women are at a crossroads in political life, moving from the point of being rare trailblazers to becoming an institution (however underdeveloped) of the American political scene. "But one of the disadvantages of being at a crossroads," she went on to say, "is that it's like every race is an experiment for us, because the environment for campaigns in general is changing so fast. The kinds of women who are running and the offices that they are running for are changing right now. So it's hard. We don't have a lot of past experience to learn from."

One of the areas of uncertainty for both women candidates and their consultants that was highlighted by the 1986 campaigns was the advisability of using negative campaign tactics. Broadly speaking, there are two methods available to candidates who are attempting to persuade the electorate to vote for them. They can either point out how qualified they are for the job (positive campaigning), or how unqualified their opposition is (negative campaigning), generally accomplished by pointing out the opposition's "negatives." The classic example of a negative would be Chappaquiddick for Ted Kennedy—but less tragic indiscretions do just fine. Former astronaut Jack Lousma was doing reasonably well on his campaign for the Senate in Michigan when his opponent, incumbent Democrat Carl Levin, came up with a film clip showing that Lousma had commented on the virtues of his Toyota car when he was speaking to an audience in Japan—not a popular move in the heartland of the American automobile industry. Levin subsequently took 52 percent of the vote. Negative tactics are generally considered to have turned dirty when a campaign not only emphasizes but exaggerates an opponent's liabilities. Even when playing straight, traditional political wisdom has been that negative tactics are somewhat like dynamite: a little goes a long way.

The year 1986 was one in which many campaigns emphasized the negative, but postelection analysis seems to indicate that particularly for women, the dangers of going negative might outweigh the possible advantages. Republican Linda Chavez's outstandingly negative Maryland campaign against Barbara Mikulski did Chavez considerably more damage than it did Mikulski. Chavez started out her general election campaign on what was widely interpreted as a negative tack: her accusation that Mikulski was a "San Francisco–style Democrat" was part of her primary election victory speech. Interestingly, Ed Rollins, whose consulting firm advised Chavez (although he himself was not directly involved in the campaign, giving his own advice only as a longtime friend) claims that Chavez did not deliberately go negative until two weeks into the campaign, after she had spent $250,000 on positives and failed to shift Mikulski's lead by one point. Whether she meant to go negative early or chose to later on, she lost the election. Democrat Harriett Woods, in her Missouri campaign for the Senate, followed her consultants' advice and purposely went negative before going positive in what is now described as a crucial campaign mistake. One of her earliest campaign commercials, which was produced by her Washington-based media consultant, used very emotional tactics to place much of the responsibility for a Missouri farm family losing its farm on her opponent Christopher Bond, a popular Republican former governor. Woods lost, too.

Celinda Lake, looking back at the Woods campaign in particular, came to the conclusion that there may be lessons there for women candidates in general. "There was a lot of negative campaigning in '86, and everybody broke all of the rules on negative campaigning. Harriett went negative before going positive, and that's something that a lot of candidates did. One of the things that we're certainly thinking about is that that may not be such a good idea for women, because women tend to get an advantage from the fact that they are not the usual politician. When you come straight out of your race and run a hard-hitting ad, then it makes it easier for your opponent to say, 'This is not something special here, this is a run-of-the-mill politician. Look at what she just did.' And that's in fact what Bond did, very very ably, and really kept hammering home with that. That tainted the whole campaign, that structured the whole rest of the debate in the voters' minds. That's a lesson that we learned, but we had no place else to learn that, except in the actual race." The point is not that the political consultants, the experts in the field, are singularly unqualified to advise women, but that everybody is learning new rules, if there are any.

The professionals are not the only ones putting forward their opinions. In any campaign, everybody from the candidate to the senior staffers, even the junior staffers who don't make policy, is surrounded with advice. Colleen Engler, running for governor of Michigan in 1986, said that she got advice from somebody or other on a daily basis every place she went and concerning everything she did. A candidate's loving family, well-intentioned but generally badly informed about what is going on in a campaign, is the bane of campaign managers and consultants coast to coast. Family members hear all the murmurs about things going wrong that are a part of every campaign and are quick to run to the candidate. Of course they have automatic access, which so few other staffers do, and the candidate is predisposed to accept their counsel, whether the would-be advisors know what they're talking about or not. Reminding the candidate why the disputed strategy was adopted in the first place—and why it should be continued—takes up a lot of staff time and energy when there isn't enough of either.

As Celinda Lake said, "The problem in any campaign is that there are probably five or six people who honestly see that something is being done stupidly, and another sixty who think they see that. So campaigns get told every hour that 'This is going absolutely crazy.' What I try to tell my campaigns is that unless they've gone irretrievably off the track, stay the course. You really will lose if you try to run three or four campaigns. And, in fact, I think Harriett [Woods] in some ways tried to run three different campaigns."

What experts are learning about conducting women's campaigns is still tentative. Even the campaign schools that specialize in training candidates are still feeling their way a lot of the time. It may indeed turn out that the women candidates who insist on keeping things clean, on confining their campaigns to the issues, are as naive as some of the more hard-nosed political pros say they are, and that women will have to learn to come out fighting. It may turn out that Woods and Chavez, for example, were anomalies whose problems were more in the particular circumstances of their campaigns than in their tactics. On the other hand, it may turn out that the increasing nastiness of negative campaigns will be shown to be counterproductive not only for women but for men too, and the pendulum of current political wisdom will swing back to less gritty tactics. In the late 1980s, not enough well-qualified, well-financed women, seasoned by the system, have run major races for firm conclusions to be drawn.

Ten years from now, perhaps the women—and the political consultants—will have figured it out.

■　　■　　■

In the meantime, conducting a political campaign is an exhausting and exhilarating experience for any woman. There is the excitement of getting to talk about the issues that have concerned you, of getting to offer what you've figured out may be solutions. There is the good old-fashioned high of being on stage with the bright lights and the crowd applauding. As Norma Paulus of Oregon pointed out, "This political business is very much like the theater. Some days you are on and some days you are off. Some days you can stand up and make these speeches in a row that will bring people to their feet, and the next day you are just a little off."

There is the sense of closeness with the other people on the campaign. You become more than friends: you're blood sisters, with a whole new vocabulary or allusions to mistakes and successes that convulse anybody who's been there on the campaign and is in on the joke and are meaningless to anyone else. You know more about each other than you know about any of your other friends in what you remember increasingly remotely as your civilian life; you eat cardboard chicken and take-out hamburgers day after day together, you fall asleep in the back seats of cars leaning heavily on each other and put on your makeup elbowing each other to peer into a gas station restroom's mirror.

If you're a staffer on a typical woman's campaign, you may find yourself briefing the press in the morning and ironing the creases out of the candidate's dress in the afternoon. If you're the candidate yourself you get the exasperated feeling that half of your time is spent struggling in and out of clothes: a male candidate can handle a heavy day of campaigning in a suit with an extra shirt, taking off the vest and jacket for the tour of the plant, putting them back on to make a speech at a Rotary luncheon or a cocktail party. Most women candidates feel uncomfortable about climbing open-tread stairs in a factory wearing a skirt or attending a dressy event in pants, and finding a place to change from one to the other (or back again) while on the road is a continual nightmare. Colleen Engler of Michigan, who ran not only for governor in the Republican primary but for lieutenant governor in the general, remembers, giggling, the time she threw herself on the mercy of a priest at his rectory, asking if she could use a bedroom there to change her clothes halfway through a campaign day that involved travel from one end of Michigan to the other. Nor is it simply a problem of clothes. A man can just fall into bed at night and get up in the morning, shaving on the way to his first event if worst comes to worst: a woman candidate usually has to spend considerably more time making sure her hair looks right and that her makeup is in place. With depressing regularity, precious time has to be spent at the hairdresser's. One of the cardinal rules for any woman politician is that the women in her audiences notice and remember.

Then of course there are the people. Norma Paulus remembers

the two women who stared at her when she darted into a store for five minutes between speaking engagements to pick up something she had seen advertised, and after muttering between themselves (still staring) one finally approached her to ask if she was really Norma Paulus. Paulus admitted that she was, and the woman retreated triumphantly to her friend, who promptly rushed back to Norma to tell her, "Well, you can't be because you're not tall enough."

After a while the faces blur into each other, with only the sudden isolated individuals (the old man at the back of the hall, the young mother balancing the heavy baby on her hip at the rally) standing out from the mass. In her autobiography Eleanor Roosevelt wrote of her bewilderment facing her first political campaign: "I never before had spent my days going on and off platforms, listening apparently with rapt attention to much the same speech, looking pleased at seeing people no matter how tired I was or greeting complete strangers with effusion."[11] And she was just the candidate's wife. For the candidate, it is not just a question of listening to the same speech attentively, but of delivering it with the same vigor and enthusiasm even if you've already given it three times that day. Plus, there is the terrible loneliness of looking around you at the good, trusting people on your staff who are working themselves into exhaustion on your behalf because they believe in you—and you know, because you know yourself, that you're not the heroine of your pamphlets, but a perfectly ordinary human being who blows her nose and makes mistakes. (And, if you're like one woman politician who says ruefully she is perfectly regular the rest of the time, you get your period on election day every time—proof positive of the effect of stress on the female hormonal system.)

Along with the lows come the highs. Colleen Engler remembers the low day when she hit total exhaustion during her wearing, underfinanced primary campaign for governor, but she also remembers the high of the state Republican party convention when she was selected as the nominee for lieutenant governor and stood triumphantly on the platform in front of the cheering party faithful. "I won't ever forget that. I was standing there, thinking about the fact that I was accepted back into the fold—because I had been a renegade Republican running in the primary, when I wasn't the chosen person. And then all of a sudden I *was* the chosen person, chosen by the party."

Win or lose, election day always comes. In a small campaign, the final two weeks are probably the most frenetic, trying to reach as many voters as possible, knowing that the majority of them are still undecided (and unless reminded again and again will probably not even vote). Local endorsements and media coverage are crucial, and arranging for those, as well as taking care of the last-minute leafleting and door-to-door effort and organizing the get-out-the-vote element of the campaign means that everybody has to pitch in. In a large campaign, by the final week most of the decisions have already been made, the machinery is in motion, and apart from the field workers who are out there supervising, much of the headquarters staff is likely to be wandering around without a great deal to do except to be anxious and to study the polling reports. The candidate, of course, is still on the treadmill, meeting people, people, always more people, making statements, and trying to look as fresh and enthusiastic as she looked months ago, when she was.

Those are the days when the press is circling, trying to pin the candidate down when she's off her guard, knowing that the off-the-cuff remarks are likely to be the most newsworthy. The campaign manager has to move in to protect the candidate from the mistakes born out of exhaustion. If the campaign is going well, the senior staffers are likely to be jockeying for position if they have their eye on postelection jobs. If the polls, and the scent in the wind, are sour, there is a great deal of stiff upper lips and talk about Truman—and a desperate hope that someone will think of a last-minute ploy that will turn it all around and that the dwindling stream of money can be spun out to election day. When the whole thing seems still to be a toss-up, there's not much to do but pray that your opponent will make a major blunder and that your campaign won't. That, and wait for election day.

When it's going well, election day can be euphoric. The Mikulski campaign sailed into election day triumphantly ahead—over twenty points in the polls—and the returns were a kind of coronation. Her staff was exhausted, wrung out, and gloriously, triumphantly proud. "We were very proud of the campaign," Wendy Sherman said. "We're proud of her having won, which she certainly should have done—as the senator says, she's a twenty-year overnight success. We were attacked tremendously, and it was a very disciplined campaign." Surrounded by all of her family and friends, standing on the little metal suitcase she had used all through the campaign so she'd be tall enough to be seen over the podium, the senator-elect was the local girl at home with her people at the victory party, loving the cheers, loving the jubilation of having done it. The only member of her family who wasn't there was her father, who has Alzheimer's disease and lives in a nursing home, and when the camera zoomed in on her, Barbara Mikulski looked right at it and said, "Dad, if you're watching—and I know you are—your daughter is a U.S. senator."[12]

Moments like that go a long way to explain why people give up a year or more of their lives for a campaign. Whoever wins, whoever loses, the drama is palpable. Election night has its own rituals. In a local campaign, there is usually more waiting for the votes to be counted, and the campaign faithful, the candidate, and her family gather at somebody's house—sometimes the candidate's own—to talk it all over and be nervous together, while scouts run back and forth from wherever the votes are being counted to report on how it's going. In the major elections, most campaigns rent a hotel ballroom for the victory party (it is always called a victory party even if everybody knows the campaign is going down in smoke), and the candidate usually stays upstairs in a suite, sequestered with her family and the innermost ring of her advisors, unavailable to any-one until she descends to make her appearance before her support-ers. Since anybody who knows anything is thus unreachable by the press, the media is forced to interview a succession of people who have no information but show lots of enthusiasm, real or forced. Given the new sophistication of exit polling, within minutes of the polls closing there is usually a fairly clear idea of what the outcome will be, but since nobody concedes on the strength of an exit poll, the ritual spins out in its traditional way.

Eventually, win or lose, the candidate appears before her support-ers to make her speech, flanked by her family. Unless she won, she must not cry, as Pat Schroeder discovered when the tears accompa-nying her announcement that she would not enter the presidential race were discussed as much as what she said. If a woman is victorious, a perceptible glistening of her eyes is humanizing. This

70

last rally is the time for everyone to come together, and the theme of the speech, whether delivered in victory or disappointment, is usually about unity and going forward from here. If she lost, she has already made her phone call conceding defeat. It's not an easy call to make, although graciousness is the order of the day: the winner is gracious about victory, the loser gracious in defeat. Some defeated candidates make a virtue of the extra mile and go to the opposition's headquarters to see the winner personally to concede.

In every major campaign the press is everywhere. Initially, they are probably most interested in the loser, since everybody wants her reaction at the very moment of loss, wants to measure just exactly how much it hurts. If it's a woman candidate, they not only want her to tell how she feels personally about being defeated, but how she thinks her failure reflects on the success of women in politics in general. It's this sort of question that makes all experienced candidates, male as well as female, treat the press with guarded wariness sometimes mixed with distaste. Once she's been gracious to them, too—and again, being emotional is not acceptable, if she has any further political ambitions—they're off to track the winner and the loser is old news.

■　　■　　■

Curiously, the emptiness at the campaign headquarters the next day is not that different, whether the candidate won or lost. "It's postpartum depression," Celinda Lake said. "I mean, I get postpartum depression after every campaign. I don't think there's anything else equivalent. A week out, you're running a $500,000 to $2,000,000 business, you've got staffs of twenty to forty people, you're running eighteen-hour days, and the day after the election, there's nothing. There's nothing else like it. If you win, then you have quite a bit, but there's still that feeling."

Campaign headquarters is usually terminally untidy, which didn't bother anybody very much when they were working full speed ahead, but everyone notices in the new silence. The phones that were ringing constantly are quiet, and most of them are swiftly disconnected. Staffers wander in and out, cleaning out their desks and surreptitiously collecting lists to use for the next campaign. There are piles of unused leaflets and bumper stickers around—the leaflets have only historical value, but a good handful of bumper stickers can be used for years to take lint off dark clothes. In the total tempo change, a new distance is beginning to creep up even in the closest of campaign friendships. Now that it's over, the old intimacy is perceptibly fading. Everyone will be going different directions, and even if you wind up together again working on somebody else's campaign, nothing will ever be quite the same. People stand talking to each other by the elevator, the open door bumping against a hand, lean on cars in the parking lots, making arrangements to get together. Sometimes you will (and many political operatives say their closest friendships were forged in the fire of a campaign), but most of the time you won't. Knowing that is like a chill autumn wind. It is, after all, very often early in November.

When you lose, it's worse. "It's an incredible mourning period for everyone involved," Celinda Lake says, who in her work for the Women's Campaign Fund has seen lot of women's campaigns, many of which do lose. "It's a mourning period for the staffs, who've become very dependent, a mourning period for the loss of the candidate and a lot of the people who were your best friends. It's almost like that shunning quality that you see in a mourning period. It's very hard all the way around. A lot of women will come back, will try to run again. And in fact, 60 percent of the people who are in Congress today lost some major race along the way."

Arliss Sturgulewski, who came heartbreakingly close to winning the gubernatorial race in Alaska in 1986—she lost by only four percentage points—says the impact of defeat didn't sink in right away. "It was an incredible thing," she said, talking a couple of months after the election. "I sailed through the losing night being extraordinarily gracious and everything was just fine. About four or five days after the campaign it really hit me. Hey, you know, I've lost all of this. And that's it. I was in my midterm as state senator so obviously I still have that to look forward to. But I needed to reach out to people, and what I found across the state was that the people who had worked on the campaign were so incredibly into this that really they were suffering, and I looked to them for strength and they had none to give me.

"So I took a couple of weeks with my son's family in Hawaii. I went to a health spa, and I had to do a lot of thinking because you just commit your total self, your resources, your personal strength, and everything to the campaign. I came out of it with a lot of thinking and a lot of walking, just by myself working through it because it is a very personal experience. I worked through that, and decided, hey, you gave it a good crack. There were factors you learn from. There are things you could control, there are things you couldn't, but for Arliss Sturgulewski personally, I know I am a leader. I have something to give, and that is communication. I am doing a great deal of that, and that brings me satisfaction and an opportunity to be involved, to influence public opinion. I'm a little bit like a car that's idling. I haven't set major goals, but I have set those kind of short-term goals that I can accomplish that make me feel okay about myself, and the other will come in time."

Win or lose, a campaign is only the beginning of something else.

4. The Money Game

"When I first heard that this campaign was going to cost $650,000, I laughed and gulped," said Connie Morella, a Maryland Republican who ran a successful campaign for a seat in the House of Representatives in 1986. "I thought, 'No way! Are they off target!' But we raised it, almost all of it—it was more like $640,000. We have a little deficit, but basically we raised it. I am absolutely amazed that we were able to do that. But nothing happens easily. You have got to make it happen. I had to call people to ask for money directly when I knew they had it, and I needed money for radio or something. My adage was that it only hurts for a few minutes. I learned that I had to pick up the phone. Once I heard their voices then I could do it, but it took a lot of guts to go through lists of names. Some were almost cold calls, recommended by somebody else. Amazing the success you get. It really is."

■   ■   ■

Money and politics have always been wound, vinelike, around each other. In order to talk about the special relationship of political women and money, you have to look at what has been going on with campaign finance in general for the last twenty years or so. After all, female and male candidates have to cope with the same ground rules, whether or not the way they work out in practice is equivalent.

From time to time in the United States, particularly since the Progressive Era at the beginning of this century, reformers have tried to untangle the relationship here or there, but few have been so starry-eyed as to believe money would cease to be important in political life. At most the reformers have aimed to assert some control over where the money comes from, and how much of it is spent by whom, in the hope of producing something a little closer to a level playing field for all contestants. Nevertheless, in spite of sheaves of legislation, "level" remains a pious hope. In politics, all men are equal, but some are more equal than others—and women are usually the least equal of all.

Running for office in the late 1980s isn't cheap for anybody. In 1986, about $425 million was spent on House and Senate elections, up from $259 million in 1980—and less than half that in 1976.[1] Connie Morella's House campaign was a particularly expensive one: the location of her district, primarily composed of the Maryland suburbs of Washington, D.C., means that she has to buy her media in the pricey Washington market, which includes vast numbers of Virginia residents—and even though they are irrelevant to her campaign, those numbers are added into the equations that determine how much her campaign had to pay for airtime to reach the Maryland voters they were aiming at. The average spent by a winning House candidate in 1986 was $340,000: up from $177,000 ten years before. An average Senate campaign in 1986 cost $3 million, up from $600,000 in 1976—and more than one commentator was horrified by how much it cost back then.[2] Of course a senator, once elected, has a comfortably six-year term ahead of him (or her): Connie Morella and her colleagues in the House, having raised and spent hundreds of thousands of dollars in 1986, have less than two years before they have to raise it again.

Where on earth does all that money go?

The best nutshell explanation is the increasing sophistication of campaign technology. It is seen most full-blown in the quadrennial extravaganza of presidential politics, and the fact that both voters and the candidates for less rarefied offices can see it working means that there is an inevitable trickle-down effect. The most dramatic element (and the most costly) of sophisticated campaigning technology is clearly television. From 1912 to 1952 each national party committee spent about the same amount of money per vote cast in national elections. In 1952, television entered the presidential campaigns: both Stevenson and Eisenhower ran television ads. From that point on, campaign expenditures skyrocketed.[3]

Television can't be pinpointed as the whole reason, however. Just as television added a new level of sophistication, so did other techniques of communication and information gathering, simultaneously adding to the cost of getting elected to public office. While ordinary garden-variety polling is expensive enough, there are more costly, but informative, embellishments. One of them is focus-group polling, in which small groups of people, selected, say, for their age, sex, economic, or life-style characteristics, or whatever, are gathered together under the direction of a trained discussion leader to talk generally about the campaign and the candidates. Clearly, if enough of these are conducted, you learn a lot about voter attitudes and therefore can spot opportunities for a candidate to shape a campaign successfully. But the process isn't cheap. Neither are tracking polls, used most frequently in the late stages of a campaign, in which shifts in sentiments among voters are measured by phone interviews on consecutive nights, with the same questions asked of each set of individuals polled. These give the campaign strategists invaluable information on trends in voter perceptions of the candidate or the issues as new events or tactics by an opponent force changes during the campaign or in the vital final weeks or days. Clearly, politicians (and their campaign managers) made tactical decisions for years without focus groups or tracking polls, but once everybody knows that that kind of information can be purchased, it's an easy next step to decide that if the funds can possibly be found, it *must* be purchased. It becomes even more compelling if your opponent is already using similar information. And inevitably the overall cost of the campaign goes up.

The existence of the computer, and its applications, has also made campaigns more expensive. The computer has made it possible for a candidate to target the geographic areas where the greatest number of sympathetic voters may be expected to be found, using such bases of information as past voting and turnout patterns, census figures, survey research results, and even relevant commercial marketing data—all of which produce clear indications of where campaign resources should be concentrated. Similarly, the computer becomes an invaluable resource for scheduling, maintaining lists of voters for canvassing or phone banks, and of course keeping track of the endless financial records of contributors and their contributions, required not only for the purposes of the campaign itself but for compliance with the federal or state campaign financial disclosure laws. To a certain extent, the existence of the computer makes it cost less (if not less money, then at least less volunteer time) to provide information than it would cost to generate the same information manually, but the fact is that without the computer much of the information was never generated in the first place. Few campaigns would willingly go back to the days when it wasn't, but the new tools still have to be paid for.

They also require campaign technicians who know how to use them. Increasingly, particularly for major campaigns, this means using paid staff. Part of the reason is obviously that as the techniques used are more complicated, a candidate needs people who don't have to learn from the beginning. There isn't time in a campaign for that. Another reason the pros are necessary is that few people are in a position to volunteer their full time, unpaid, for the year or more that is now required for anyone working in a senior capacity on a major campaign—and even many lower-level campaigns. Furthermore, hiring professionals with a good reputation gives the campaign instant credibility, which can be used to raise funds, which you need to pay the professionals.

In any case, multitudes of unskilled volunteers are nowhere near as available as they used to be: most of the women who traditionally made up the peon army are no longer at home during the day with free time to donate. The fact is that the majority of American woman are now part of the work force, even the young mothers: 70 percent of women under the age of thirty-five are now employed.[4] When candidates attempt to use substitutes to do some of the basic tasks the local volunteers used to do, some odd incongruities can show up. Republican political consultant Eddie Mahe, Jr., said that in the 1986 election, the Republicans had Hispanics in a phone bank in San Antonio, Texas, calling people in Anchorage, Alaska, to get out the vote. "If I could have gotten a local Boy Scout troop in Anchorage, saying, 'As Boy Scouts we urge you to go vote,' it would have gone a great deal more good," Mahe admitted.[5]

But the serious money in political campaigns goes into getting the message across, whether by mail or media. The cost of first-class mail has steadily escalated; so has the bulk mail rate used by candidates for their thousands of pieces of campaign literature. Twenty-five years ago it cost 2.2 cents per item. It now costs 8.9

cents for a flier. Doing a single mailing—and most campaigns do many more than one—is a considerable investment.[6]

Media rates have gone up even faster: one knowledgeable estimate was that the price of a minute of air time has been going up about 40 percent every two years, assuming the same time slot and station.[7] The advertising industry figured that candidates spent about $200 million on television spots for the 1986 elections. Prime time costs can be astronomical: in 1986 a thirty-second spot in the Dallas–Fort Worth area, only the eighth-largest television market in the nation, went for $100,000,[8] a significant dent in any campaign budget, particularly when you consider that most media consultants figure a typical ad needs to be seen several times before it is likely to make much of an impression. Prime time costs go a long way to explain why most candidates wind up putting most of their ads in the more affordable off-peak hours—but cheaper than $100,000 is still far from free.

What all this means is that media soak up greater and greater proportions of available campaign finances: Connie Morella estimated that between the primary and general elections, her campaign spent 70 percent of its resources on media. In 1986 in Missouri, a much less expensive television market, both senatorial candidates, Republican Kit Bond and Democrat Harriett Woods, were spending $250,000 a week in the last month of the campaign. By election day, approximately 60 percent of both campaign budgets was going for television spot commercials alone.[9] Radio and television time has to be paid for before a spot goes on the air. When you see or hear a paid political advertisement, somebody has come up with the money already. The problem of financing media buys is a chronic one for almost all campaigns. Morella in Maryland was no exception. When she needed radio time and the money wasn't in the bank, she had to get on the phone to contributors and raise it. This means going back to the proven contributors who have come through before, and all campaigns do it. "I don't like raising money because I feel like a blood bank," Morella said in the quiet after the election. "I am going back for more infusions, time and time again." Or as Harriett Woods put it, "The price of running for the Senate today is spending more time than you'd like to spend asking people for more money than they'd like to give."[10]

Connie Morella was fortunate in that when she needed it, she always got the money. That doesn't always happen. In 1982 Woods, then a little-known Missouri state senator, won a surprise victory in the Democratic Senate primary and was coming astonishingly close to upsetting incumbent Republican John Danforth. Being a former television producer, she was communicating effectively using television ads and closing the gap with Danforth in mid-October, when she ran out of money. No money, no ads. She was off the air for a week, during which an October 15 poll, taken just before she had to pull her ads, showed she had drawn even with Danforth. Ironically, it was only then that the big money started to come in. During the final two weeks of the campaign $550,000 was contributed, half of the total raised by her campaign.[11] But by then it was too late. Danforth's campaign had taken advantage of her week-long silence and counterattacked, going negative to accuse her of distortion. By late October, when she was able to place her ads again, there was simply not enough time to answer his charges effectively. On election day, Danforth won, 51 to 49 percent.

It is thus not only a question of how much money a campaign can raise, but when it comes in. In politics, it's the early money that is hard to get and crucial to have. The early money is important partly because it enables the candidate to hire staff, arrange for a headquarters site and set up telephone service, get expensive initial benchmark polling to provide a reasonably reliable basis for strategy, and work out a coherent plan for the campaign, with money in the bank ahead of time for printing and air time, both of which have to be paid for up front. Practical as all those elements are, the early money is almost more vital because of its psychological effect. Prospective donors are always more likely to contribute if the candidate has the demonstrated ability to raise money, and the earlier the candidate demonstrates that, the better. Money follows money, and donors are most comfortable with bandwagons. Nothing stimulates givers to give more than the vision of bigger givers giving. It confirms their own political wisdom, it reassures them that their money is not being wasted, and it underlies their sense that they're getting in on the ground floor of something important. Big money is smart money, the theory goes, and thus political fund-raising offers the purest illustration of the old axiom that he who has, gets. And all too frequently it *is* he, not she.

Even within that narrower subdivision of the campaign, media advertising early can carry more weight. Months before the election, ads often are taken not so much to persuade voters (most of whom aren't paying attention yet) as to make the campaign itself appear more credible. Political scientist John Carey called the bid for credibility the "metacampaign,"[12] a campaign within the campaign, which is intended less for the voters than for the players—the big contributors, party workers, reporters, and the rest of the political elite who make the judgments about which campaigns have a chance and which ones don't. If the metacampaign works, the campaign as a whole can be seen to be succeeding (and be reported as doing so), even in the face of such relatively objective data as polls showing the opponent ahead—as long as the enhanced credibility enables the campaign to make up enough ground so that the disparity between appearance and reality does not become undisguisable. Waging the metacampaign involves signing up important consultants, putting together a campaign staff that even in the initial stages behaves in a coherent, professional manner, producing impressive media right from the start, and not least, having enough money so that all of this can be accomplished smoothly, without jerks and false starts.

This may require a great deal of start-up money. Speaking in 1987, White House chief of staff Howard Baker recalled his own abortive presidential campaign in 1980, when he raised $4 million, enough to compete in a couple of primaries, and then recognized that his campaign wasn't going anywhere, which meant the money wasn't there either. To pursue his presidential ambitions further inevitably meant he would have to lumber himself with colossal debt. Given the mushrooming numbers of primaries, all taking place within a matter of weeks of each other, he pointed out that now the luxury of trying a couple of primaries and seeing what happens no longer exists—and thus the cost of getting into the race at all is becoming prohibitive. You have to have $20 million to begin, he said.[13] Clearly, a lot of otherwise qualified individuals simply can't raise that kind of money to get started.

It is certainly true that the gargantuan challenges of presidential fund-raising directly affect only a very few individuals, but the trickle-down phenomenon of rising expectations and increasing—and expensive—campaign technology means that everybody feels some of the pressure. And that pressure is not limited to candidates.

Officeholders also need to keep raising money, either to pay off any debt accumulated in the last campaign or to begin amassing the war chest for the next one.

It is not only politicians elected from marginal districts who are stashing funds in the bank for future campaigns. Democratic Senator Lloyd Bentsen of Texas was elected in 1982 for a third term with a 59 percent majority and is in an excellent position for reelection in 1988. The Republican party in Texas was deeply divided by the 1986 gubernatorial primary and most of the likely GOP challengers for his seat in 1988 are still in debt from that primary. Nevertheless, Bentsen, using his powerful position as chairman of the Senate Finance Committee, was busy raising money years before his seat came up. One enterprising method caught the attention and the ridicule of Capitol Hill: Bentsen offered two hundred Washington lobbyists and political action committees (PACs) the opportunity to join his Chairman's Council and have breakfast with him once a month. The price was a neat $10,000 a meal. Capitol Hill humorists were promptly asking each other, "What is yellow and white and costs $10,000?" and answering, "Egg McBentsen."[14] Stung by the merriment, Bentsen withdrew his offer but continues more orthodox fund-raising, presumably aiming to acquire a big enough treasury to allow him to make contributions to other candidates' campaigns, as well as to intimidate would-be challengers in his own race.

In a different arena, June Roselle, primary fund-raiser for Detroit's mayor Coleman Young, is quite forthright about the purpose of her current money-raising efforts for the mayor, who has over $2 million in the bank, doesn't face reelection until 1989, and hasn't had in the past, nor is expected to have in the foreseeable future, any credible opposition. "It's a matter of power," she said. "It gives him power, and it makes the price of running against him so high that no one will try it."

Even without the obstacle of an incumbent sitting on a massive war chest, challengers have a harder time of it. Much of what an incumbent already has—name recognition, a corps of volunteers, and lists of proven contributors, among other advantages—costs a challenger money to acquire, and it is a fact of political life that money comes harder to a challenger than to an incumbent. Donors want to give their money where it will do some good: the idea behind making a political contribution, presumably, is to aid in the election of an official who intends to pursue actively the political agenda the contributor advocates. In addition, it is assumed that the official might listen to the contributor with special attention if he has legislative problems or at least would be broadly sympathetic to the contributor's point of view. Having the ear of a defeated candidate is not a lot of use. Incumbents usually win: in the House of Representatives, for example, approximately 90 percent of all incumbent members of the House who have sought reelection since 1950 have indeed won.[15] In 1986, it was 98.5 percent.[16] Therefore, whether a prospective contributor is an individual or one of the political action committees that have come to play such a major role in campaign finance, it does not take a genius to figure out that if they are trying to support someone who will probably be elected, they should support an incumbent. Mainly, they do.

There have been major campaign finance reforms since 1971, and much of the main thrust of reform activity has been to control the influence of the old-style fat-cat contributor. As the law now stands, the only source of unlimited funds is the candidate, if he or she is fortunate enough to possess them. Some do. In 1984, Jay Rockefeller spent $12,055,043 to win a Senate seat in West Virginia, of which $10,250,000 was his own money. Generally coupled with Rockefeller in tales of candidates spending their own megabucks is Lewis Lehrman of New York, who spent some $7 million of his own money in 1982 trying to defeat Mario Cuomo for governor. Lehrman took the Republican primary in a landslide, but Cuomo was elected, although he was far outspent both in the Democratic primary and the general election. The only restriction on a candidate's own spending that the Supreme Court has found does not infringe on the candidate's First Amendment rights of free speech is a spending limit imposed as a condition for accepting public financing. So if a candidate chooses to go for broke, he or she does it without matching funds.

Other campaign finance reform provisions have increased the pressure for more and smaller donations from individual donors. Although the limit for an individual's contribution to a federal candidate is $1,000 per election, matching funds only apply to part of that—for presidential elections, for example, only to the first $250, which makes four $250 donations worth $2,000 to a campaign, whereas one $1,000 donation only brings in $1,250. Many states have similar arrangements for state or local campaigns, limiting the matching funds to the first $100 or so. Campaign fund-raisers rapidly become expert in the vagaries of the laws that regulate their particular campaign, and spend considerable energy trying to work the pattern of their donations into the form that creates the most dollars according to whichever rulebook is applicable.

Although the political parties are permitted to make larger contributions to candidates' campaigns, the fact remains that you can't give what you don't have, and in recent years the Republican party has had a vastly greater treasury to draw upon than has the Democratic party. The Republican party turned to direct mail solicitation of funds in the shambles after Watergate, and since then the lists have grown steadily. Although the Democratic party began a similar effort after the 1980 election, it still lags far behind: for the 1986 election, for example, the Republican party raised $82,780,000 and the Democratic only $17,234,000.[17] The only thing that keeps the equation from getting totally out of whack is the fact that Republican contributors seem more inclined to give to the party, while Democratic contributors give more to the individual candidates, so that on a campaign-by-campaign basis the competition is more equitable than it would appear looking at the party treasuries alone. In 1986, for example, the Republicans outspent the Democrats in Senate races, and the Democrats outspent the Republicans on House campaigns.[18] On the other hand, the greater wealth of the Republican party does permit the national party and the national party congressional committees to offer sophisticated services and training to their candidates (as well as money), which the Democrats are not yet in a financial position to match.

The Republicans may raise more money from individuals, but the Democrats still hold the edge as far as PAC money goes, mainly because there are more Democratic incumbents. The flourishing PAC community is one other direct result of the election reform laws. PACs can give more to a campaign than any individual, and although the donation of any one PAC is limited by law, a PAC's impact can be greater because of its ability to bring along other PACs that contribute as well. Whether PACs are a good thing or a bad thing, like so much else, depends on your point of view. Political scientist Larry Sabato defines a PAC as either a separate, segregated campaign fund of a sponsoring organization, or the campaign fund of a group formed mainly to give money to candidates.[19] PACs come in many shapes and flavors. There are corporate PACs, labor PACs, trade PACs, ideological PACs, Washington-based PACs, and PACs with headquarters all over the country. There are PACs that spend most of their funds in donations to campaigns and PACs that specialize in independent expenditures, often by waging negative campaigns against the opponents of candidates they favor. Some PACs have a great deal of money; most have limited amounts and are trying to get the most bang for their bucks. This usually means that PACs prefer to give to incumbents, and, since PACs usually want to have some effect on legislation as well as on electoral results, the seniority and committee assignments of incumbents can be important, and often even decisive, in deciding who gets how much money. There are PACs, particularly ideological PACs, who choose to put their money into challengers taking on incumbents the PAC finds objectionable, but there is little doubt, looking at the overall picture, that PAC money most often goes to bolster incumbents.

This is not to say that PACs are not quite capable of working both sides of the street. The citizen watchdog group Common Cause identified 150 instances in seven 1986 Senate races where PACs first donated to the Republican candidates, and then to their Democratic opponents when the Democrats won the seat. In North Dakota, thirty-nine PACs gave to the Republican incumbent and postelection gave to Democrat Kent Conrad, who won; in Alabama, thirty-one PACs gave to another GOP incumbent and then switched to the winning Democrat.[20] And so it went in other races as well. There is a lot of money up for grabs: PACs contributed more than $125 million of the $425 million spent in the 1986 congressional election cycle. There are those who blame the PACs for the vast amounts of money being spent on elections these days, claiming that the system only intensifies the influence of special interests, increasing their control over elections, and subsequently legislation. There are others who identify the PACs as more a symptom of the high cost of campaigns than a cause, pointing out that the statistical evidence shows that few PACs donate in the ways you would expect them to donate for maximum legislative leverage: to uncommitted candidates who might be persuaded by their support. Instead, as political scientists Theodore J. Eismeier and Philip H. Pollock III point out, "political action committees tend to reward the past behavior of congressmen positively predisposed toward the interest group's legislation to begin with."[21] Clearly, there are more efficient methods of tilting the balance in your favor, but so far, most PACs have chosen to stick with the guys they know.

The only money harder to raise than early money is money to retire a campaign debt. With the soaring cost of campaigning, winners as well as losers may find they still have bills after the campaign is over, and raising money to pay them is not easy. The winner is obviously in far better shape to find help in clearing the debts: losers have an uphill job. It takes an unusually loyal contributor to put money into something that is not only over and done with, but was manifestly unsuccessful. "Debt money is the toughest political money in America to raise," Nathan Landow, a Democratic fund-raiser, has said.[22]

Some women, having been elected, feel even more reluctant to try to round up contributions after the campaign is over than they did before. "'It's interesting, my attitude about fund-raising," said Seattle city councilwoman Jane Noland, who won a hotly contested race for her seat, but was left with a debt of about $20,000. "I do want to erase this debt," she said, "but I am much less comfortable now that I am in office. It was fine while I was running, and I never made promises to people, and I never had the feeling that with the $350 limit anyone expected to buy my vote on anything. I'm glad the city made that rule. I feel it is much less comfortable once you are in office to raise the money, even though I will have to take some steps to reduce the amount. Obviously I am not selling my vote at this point either, but it's just less comfortable."

If it goes on long enough, of course, a debt can have a significant impact on a candidate's subsequent political career. Colorado's Gary Hart had a $4.7 million debt in January of 1985 left over from his 1984 race for the Democratic presidential nomination. Although the amount was gradually reduced over the years to $1.3 million, when he announced his candidacy for the 1988 presidential campaign, the debt immediately made news when creditors seized $30,000 at a fund-raising party in California in the first week after his announcement. It marred the bright start any candidate would want for a major campaign: in the end, of course, it was the celebrated adventure with Donna Rice that sealed Hart's doom, but the finance story was already creating bad publicity. As the campaign manager of one of his opponents remarked at the time, "Obviously, any time you get a negative story of that magnitude, it's a problem."[23]

At the start or after the finish, too often money problems just won't go away.

■   ■   ■

If finding a way through the world of political finance is a maze for the men who have been playing the game all along, what is it like for women who, relatively speaking, are newcomers in the field?

So far, the main money hurdle for women politicians is getting some to start out with. The primary obstacle is credibility. It is only very recently that women are being seen as candidates even marginally likely to be elected, and the men who have traditionally been the big donors or now control the PAC money tend to play it safe. They want to put their money behind the winners. The situation has not been helped by the fact that as long as 90 percent of all officeholders are men, most women candidates will necessarily be challengers, and statistically speaking, challengers, male or female, are seldom successful in replacing an incumbent.

Further, as the numbers of women in congress show (only twenty-five out of 535), women have not been very successful in high-visibility races. In 1984, for example, there were nine women challengers for the Senate, and they all lost. Only two out of forty-one challengers for the House won. In 1986, there were six women running for the Senate, and five of them lost. Seven women lost gubernatorial bids, and thirty-five out of fifty-eight contenders for the House were defeated. It is also true, of course, that over four hundred men lost in those same races as well, but women, because there are so few of them, stand out in the crowd. Whether it's fair or not, one woman's loss is too often seen as confirmation of the fact that women in general don't win—and that becomes a reason for the money men to wait and see before getting out their checkbooks. It's the famous catch-22 all over again: the money men say that there's no point in contributing to a woman's campaign because women can't raise enough money to win.

"It's always hard for a woman to raise early money," said Ann Lewis, formerly political director of the Democratic National Committee and now executive director of Americans for Democratic Action. "Our advice to women is to assume that the guys aren't going to do anything for you until you look like the winner, at which point you should be prepared to greet the prodigal son. Meanwhile, you've got to figure out what you can raise from other women and from relatively low donors." Or as Stephanie Solein, former executive director of the Women's Campaign Fund put it, "The early money, which is the toughest money to get—the primary money—does come from the women's community."

This is particularly true of Democratic women, who can't look to their party for the kind of support the better-financed Republican party can offer GOP women. Women's PACs are springing up to fill the gap, with the deliberate intention of learning to use the existing system in the hopes of bringing more women into political office. Some of them, like the Women's Campaign Fund and the National Women's Political Caucus, are bipartisan, but they do require their candidates to be "good on the issues"— which means supportive of the Equal Rights Amendment and prochoice on abortion. Conservative women candidates still need to look elsewhere for their money, particularly for primary money, since the party money is not normally available to primary candidates.

One obvious source of early money for men or women is to use their own, if they have it. Since the Founding Fathers gathered in Philadelphia, men of property have been prominent in the government—originally, of course, a man had to own property before he was even qualified to vote. It is not surprising that there are still many wealthy men in government or that they are quite prepared to invest substantial amounts in their own campaigns— usually with the idea that they will be repaid once the campaign is underway and other contributions are coming in. It has taken women much longer to feel comfortable about using their own resources, or for it to be fully acceptable in the electoral context for them to do so. Because our society is still framed in patriarchal terms, it is perfectly all right for a man to use his wife's money to further his political ambitions—that's considered to be family resources. But when a woman uses family money it's looked at differently: too often it's seen as a case of her husband trying to buy the election for her.

Perhaps the climate is changing. Nancy Kassebaum of Kansas, elected to the Senate in 1978, is a wealthy woman, one of the millionaire senators—roughly a quarter of the senators are. When she started out in a crowded primary field of nine candidates, it was on her own money. "I was going to put in $30,000 at first," she said, "then I went up to $60,000. I decided I could go up to sixty, but I ended up going almost to ninety. Not quite, but it was way beyond what reasonably I told myself I should. But at that point the polls showed me that I was really making some advances and that some last-minute TV could help. Now that's where Jan [Meyers, one of her primary opponents, now a congresswoman] would argue that she didn't have the same opportunity, which is true. But I didn't spend as much as two of my male colleagues who lost." Once she won the primary, of course, the money started to come in—the familiar story. Altogether, the campaign cost about $850,000.

In 1986, Arliss Sturgulewski, running in the Alaska gubernatorial race, dug even deeper into her own pocket to finance her campaign. Sturgulewski gets irritated by the press describing her as a rich widow—"Nobody said, damn it, that I had educated myself, that my husband was killed in an air crash in '68, and that I have made the money"—but considered that she needed to put up the money to compensate for a softer approach to fund-raising that she realized was a liability for a candidate. "I had targeted for a personal contribution of $250,000, and it went $150,000 over that. I knew that the money was going to be a hard thing, but I had never considered myself that good a fund-raiser. I think we did very well to do over one million dollars. Hindsight, I think, would have caused me to structure the finance committee differently. Unfortunately raising money, big money, is a hardball operation, and I am not a hardball politician, nor do I surround myself with those kinds of people. So we didn't have that kind of knocking-heads approach to raising money and that is the name of the game. That is something that would need to be really very carefully evaluated, how you do raise the money. Since I was in a position where I could raise the money myself, it was never a question of well, we couldn't do something because we didn't have the money. We can say that we might have targeted and used those dollars differently, but it wasn't a question that the campaign faltered because we couldn't get out that last media." In the end, she lost by less than 6,500 votes, mainly because one of her primary opponents launched a write-in campaign.

Still, all women candidates are not able to dig into their own deep pockets, and all of them need money to get started. One new PAC that calls itself "EMILY's List" exists for the sole aim of electing Democratic women to the Senate and addresses exactly this problem of the starting-up money. The name is an acronym for "Early money is like yeast"—it makes the dough rise. Founded in 1985, the PAC has already grown to a twelve hundred member network. In 1986 EMILY's List provided $350,000, split evenly between the two Democratic women senatorial candidates, Barbara Mikulski of Maryland and Harriett Woods of Missouri. Like all PACs, EMILY's List itself could contribute only five thousand dollars to a single campaign, but the rest of the money came from individual contributions that could legally be "bundled" and passed on to the Mikulski and Woods campaigns. Since EMILY's List is intended to be early money, seed money for the very first stages of the campaign, and is raised and dispersed right away, it gave Mikulski, for example, a flying start. "Because the money came early," Mikulski herself said "it gave me a good campaign infrastructure. I had the money to do polling."[24] Or as her campaign manager Wendy Sherman put it gratefully, "EMILY's List was just a *tremendous* help."

By itself EMILY's List money couldn't guarantee either Woods or Mikulski victory: Woods went on to lose her campaign, Mikulski to win. But both were truly competitive in their races, and the early money made an important difference in that. Given a sound start, both women were able to raise a lot more money from other sources—Woods raised $3.5 million, Mikulski over $2 million. "The big boys who give the most judge your chances by the money you can raise at start-up," Kathleen Currie, a spokesman for EMILY's List said. "For the first time, we're seeing financial godmothers. Women have finally got control of that piece of political machinery."[25]

Unfortunately, the problem of early money is not limited to Democratic women for the Senate, which is all that EMILY's List has funded. What the other women who need money are learning is that they simply have to take their courage in their hands and go out and ask for it. It's hard for men to go ask people to give them money for a campaign. Hubert Humphrey went through a lot of campaigns in his long and distinguished political career, and what he had to say about it was that "campaign financing is a curse. It's the most disgusting, demeaning, disenchanting, debilitating experience of a politician's life. It's stinky, it's lousy. I just can't tell you how much I hate it."[26] Women have generally been socialized to believe it's somehow more appropriate to provide your services on a volunteer basis, whether in a domestic or community context. Many of them thus find it even harder to ask for money for themselves. Those women know exactly what Humphrey meant.

The problem is sufficiently universal so that the Women's Campaign Fund has done a fair bit of research on it. "We did a videotaping where we watched men and women ask [for campaign contributions] and we use it now in our training," Celinda Lake explained. "Our communication people talk about it as throwing a ball in the other person's court. And men *will* throw it—they will ask, and they will leave it there, and then you have to throw it back. The idea is even if you're going to come back and say, 'No, I'm not going to give' you're probably going to say, 'No, I'm not going to give it all, but I'll give $250' or 'No, I'm not going to give now but come back to me in a month.' Women almost reach out and grab it back, as if to say, 'Oh my god, I can't believe I asked for one thousand dollars, I'm sorry, forget it.' Women are almost apologetic that they asked at all."

The odd thing is that many women who decide to run for office were quite used to asking people for money before—many of them have been doing fund-raisers for charity or even asking for money for another candidate, having first got into the political game on somebody else's campaign. What seems to make the words stick in their throats—often to their own surprise as much as anyone else's—is the fact that they are saying "please give money to me for me to use myself." Some women find it almost impossible to come out and ask: the women political pros have a repertoire of disgusted stories of putting would-be candidates together with potential donors only to have the hopeful candidate circle round and round the issue without ever "closing"—the simple business of asking for a given amount and making arrangements to collect it. "You'd think she was waiting for him to volunteer," said one pro with exasperation. The first political rule all women candidates have to learn is that nobody is going to volunteer money.

It is not only the shy, introverted women who have problems going out and persuading people to come up with contributions. Bella Abzug, nobody's definition of a shrinking violet, has said she found it hard to ask people for money for her senatorial campaign in 1976. "It's difficult to ask for money," she said. "I overcame it because I was so determined to win this race."[27] She raised $600,000—a lot of money for a woman politician back in 1976.

The new breed of women candidates are learning that if they are that determined to run, fund-raising has to be done whether they feel like it or not, and once they get started, it may not be as bad as they fear. After all, as Connie Morella told herself, it only hurts for a few minutes. Picking up the phone and asking a disembodied voice to write out a check so that you can run for office may not be the jolliest way to pass time, but men have been doing it for years, and women can learn to do it too.

The Women's Campaign Fund's candidate training school for women would-be congressional, statewide, and state legislative candidates is designed to teach precisely those skills. As Celinda Lake of the WCF explained it, "One of the things we tell our people is to sit down and write a list of fifty $1,000 people, because no PAC will look at you until you raise $50,000. You've got to put down the name of the person and attach the amount of money that you're willing to ask them for. In the training school, one of the things we do is to tell folks one of their assignments is to go out and raise $1,000 overnight. If you can't do that, you can't raise a million. That's the pace they're going to have to start raising it, at $1,000 a night. Even at $1,000 a night, if you work at it a whole year you raise only $365,000." That's just a shade more than the average it cost the winners to be elected to the House of Representatives in 1986, and it will almost certainly cost more in 1988.

It is only recently as more women have been moving into the business and professional worlds that they have known whom to ask to get those big donations. Even now, as Ann Lewis of Americans for Democratic Action pointed out, women don't have the same personal relationships that a man might have with the people who write $1,000 checks. A woman doesn't go out and play golf with the chairman of the Community Chest or other local powers who make contributions—if she plays with anybody, it's probably with their wives. And wives don't make out the same kind of checks. "Now you can have a very happy marriage," Lewis said, "and if the guy's law school roommate is running for Congress he will write him a $1,000 check and if the woman's college roommate is running for Congress she will write her a $100 one, and it is a joint checking account. Women don't feel they can spend that money in the same way. That's one problem, and some of that will get changed as women start earning more of that money. But it's a problem now."

A further irony is that when men do give to women candidates, they seem to think that women don't need the big bucks a man might need. Representative Claudine Schneider, a four-term Republican congresswoman from Rhode Island, has said, "There has been many a time when I stood before a contributor and he wrote a check to me for $500 and one to my male colleague for $1,000. Now, I certainly respect the fact that this gentleman thinks that as a woman I have the capability of stretching the dollar twice as far, but the fact remains that I have to pay as much for my advertising as a man does. So we have to train the men to recognize that, like betting on three horses, some of us are going to win, some are going to show, and we're all worth putting the money on."[28] Not only that, she went on to say, but women need some training too. Women feel free to spend $35 on a scarf, but they won't make out a contribution check for $35.

The women staffing the feminist PACs in Washington see that need for women's political education about fund-raising very clearly. As Stephanie Solein said, sitting in her Washington WCF office, "I think that the more money women can raise and the better they are at it, frankly, the more power we have. Because money is what makes this town tick, and we've learned that. We've learned it the hard way. It's been interesting to see the women's movement progress. I think you started out with a great many idealistic people who were very cause-oriented. The idealism is still there, but I think we've realized that we've got to be pragmatic and sophisticated and play the way the boys play or we're not going to ever be a part of it." She talked about the ways the WCF is trying to involve women who would probably otherwise be outside the political game altogether: "We did a breakfast in New York last year that was hosted by

Chemical Bank. It was not a fund-raising event—we invited a number of top women in the banking community in New York to come and meet Governor Madeleine Kunin of Vermont, and at the time lieutenant governor candidate Evelyn Murphy from Massachusetts, who won afterwards and is now lieutenant governor. We had forty women there, a number of bank vice-presidents, women from Wall Street who came at eight in the morning and had coffee and heard two really very strong speeches. It wasn't on why it's important to be a feminist as much as it was about what the governor and Evelyn Murphy had done on their jobs—Evelyn had run an economic commission under [Governor Michael] Dukakis. They were talking about business issues that were of interest to the women in the financial world, but at the same time, talking as women about the different approaches they'd taken. In the case of Madeleine Kunin, she was able to balance the budget and do away with the deficit they'd had in Vermont, but at the same time put more resources into education and into programs that women do have a lot of concerns about. After that, a couple of those women wrote large checks to our organization, and several others got involved later on with a fund-raising event we were doing. It made them see what women can accomplish once they make it and why it's important both for their own self-interest as well as for the country in general to get more women into public office. What we hope is after they have an initial opportunity to meet candidates like that, or to meet elected officials, they will get involved, get interested, will see the reason. It's the key to expanding the donor base, I think, particularly for women candidates' own organizations."

In 1986, women candidates finally began to be financially competitive in their races. Women running for office in that election cycle raised 25 percent more money than women candidates had in 1984, only two years previously.[29] More of the women running for high-visibility offices had held enough other offices to have developed the political skills—including fund-raising—to make themselves credible candidates. They came into the elections with a following of men and women who believed in them, and who were further prepared to back up their faith with money. In several outstanding cases—Barbara Mikulski, Harriett Woods, Paula Hawkins of Florida who raised $5.3 million in her bid for reelection to the Senate, Norma Paulus of Oregon, to name a few—they were able to raise enough money so that their campaigns could concentrate on other elements. They didn't all win, but then half of the candidates always lose. You still have to get 51 percent of the vote, and money isn't everything. Ed Zschau of California was the top fund-raiser of 1986, gathering up $9.2 million in his attempt to unseat incumbent Senator Alan Cranston. Cranston is still California's senior senator. In fact, six of the top twelve Senate fund-raisers lost their races. As Fred Wertheimer, president of Common Cause, put it, "Money never guarantees winning, but having money makes a big difference."[30]

In 1986, women candidates demonstrated they had grasped that point. The question is what happens from here on: a few women attaining financial credibility is only a beginning. If significant numbers of women candidates are going to be taken seriously in the big races, they will have to learn to tap into major fund-raising sources one way or another. At present, the women's PACs are a great help to liberal women candidates of either party (although a greater proportion of their help does go to Democratic women). Over the years, the PACs themselves are becoming more professional in their own fund-raising: for example, in 1974, the year that the Women's Campaign Fund was founded, it gave $20,000. In 1986, it was able to donate $450,000 in cash and services. That's a pretty penny compared to what it used to be, but with federal campaigns costing hundreds of thousands or millions of dollars, the contribution the women's PACs as a group can make to any single woman candidate is still only one dollop in the bucket. The women's PACs, all considered together, are small potatoes compared to many of the national PACs. AMPAC, for example, one of the monsters of the PAC community, contributed $4.2 million to its chosen candidates in 1986. The money was mainly disbursed to incumbents, and since only a sprinkling of women fall into that category, the money went mainly to men. Celinda Lake, who has seen a lot of campaigns from her WCF viewpoint, and participated in the discussions about how much money should go to which candidate, says bluntly, "If you sat down the whole feminist PAC community and everybody anted up at that point in time the maximum that they could give to a candidate, which would never happen, there's no more than fifty thousand dollars at that table.

That's why it's so critical that we expand the resources available for women candidates."

So far, most women candidates are still at the local and state legislative level, where the amounts of money needed to campaign are less daunting. But there, too, there are fund-raising lessons to be learned. Traditionally, women have been more comfortable arranging fund-raising events—fashion shows, potluck suppers, anything in which the would-be donors appear to be getting something in exchange for their donation besides the satisfaction of making a contribution to a candidate they (presumably) believe in. For a lot of women candidates, this somehow feels fairer than simply asking somebody to write out a check. Unfortunately, by the time the costs of putting on the event are subtracted from the total receipts, too often what's left is hardly worth the expenditure of time and effort invested in it—particularly if, as still does happen, the candidate sees herself not only as candidate but as hostess and is helping out in the kitchen and wiping up tables afterward, instead of leaving the mess to her staff and moving on promptly to the next event on her campaign agenda or perhaps even going home to collapse into the bed she has seen so little of during the rigors of the race. The hard facts of political fund-raising are that even at the local level, events for small donors can be only part of a campaign (and even then have to be planned carefully so that the cash return is maximized and the time of preparation and effort involved minimized). Serious candidates have to put much of their fund-raising time into the personal visits, letters, and telephone calls to major donors that are the ways in which most men raise their money. As former state senator Barbara Trafton of Maine pointed out, women can't continue to think in pennies when the cost of campaigns has to be paid in dollars.[31]

Given the fact that the cost of campaigning will continue to escalate, the small donations so typical of a woman's campaign may present a serious problem if women intend to move up into higher office. Celinda Lake is matter-of-fact about the problems women can face, if they continue to raise their money in dribs and drabs. "The major difference for women still is that they do not raise as much money in high donations, so they have to make it up in small donations," she said. "That is a real Achilles heel, particularly in two kinds of scenarios. The first is statewide races, where you usually don't have the same proportion of PAC money. The other is in races where you come into September and you thought you needed $500,000 and all of a sudden you find out it's a $750,000 race. Well, if you're raising your money in thousand dollar clips you can make that adjustment. If you're raising your money in twenty-five dollar donations, you can't make that adjustment. You just never catch up." Exactly how women candidates—or the women's PACs—are going to cope with that dilemma is anything but clear.

Perhaps there is no answer in the short term. In the long term, the best hope may be to expand the base of women who contribute to women's campaigns by educating women in general to recognize that it is in their own best interests not only to go out and vote (which women already do in larger numbers and larger percentages than men) but to back their chosen candidates with money. This is something that must be realized not only by the professional, high-salaried women who are presumably in a position to make major donations but by the other women who can only come up with small amounts. The Republican party, after all, came out of the shambles of Watergate by going into direct mail fund-raising looking mainly for small donations: in 1986, the Republican National Committee raised nearly $83 million, with the average donation being less than forty dollars.

Perhaps the important number will turn out to be not how big the average woman's donation might be, but how many donations there are. One of the glowing successes of Geraldine Ferraro's campaign for the vice-presidency was the astounding amount of money she raised from women. All together, she ended up raising a record $2.1 million from women-sponsored events, another record $2 million from direct-mail requests, and another $2 million from general events. For the first time in Democratic history, the vice-presidential candidate raised as much as the man at the head of the ticket.[32] "It was not me, it was the candidacy," Ferraro said in 1987, looking back at it with bemused amazement. "It was not 'Gee, we're going to see Geraldine Ferraro,' forget that. It was 'We're coming to see this first woman who's doing this national bit—let's see what she looks like.'" But they brought their checkbooks. Many of Ferraro's donors were new political contributors: the Democratic

National Committee was able to add twenty-six thousand new names to their lists, a lasting legacy to candidates who follow her. Women who had worked on her campaign recalled with grins that it was far from uncommon for a woman contributor to ask *not* to have her donation acknowledged. "We figured they had Republican husbands," one former campaign staffer said.

Ellie Smeal has been fund-raising among women for years, mainly for NOW, of course, and she gets fire in her eyes when she says, "You have to ask not once, not twice, but numerous times, and you have to realize that asking people to give is giving them an opportunity. Not to ask them is to exclude them." She remembers the older woman who came up to her after a rousing fund-raising speech and to Smeal's surprise, thanked her warmly, telling her that the check she'd just written out was the very first check of that amount she'd ever written without asking somebody. " 'I would always have asked for a check that size,' she told me, 'but I thought about it and I said this is so important to me and I really want this to happen. I want to be part of it. So I took it out and I wrote it for what I wanted.' And she said, 'You know what that makes me feel like? I feel like I have come of age.' "

■　　■　　■

It is not only women with ambitions to run for office who are learning how to work the money end of politics. The new girls in the back room are discovering that learning about money and where it is to be found can be the high road to being taken seriously by the campaign hierarchy. Political scientist Xandra Kayden explains it succinctly: "Because so many people do not like to ask others for money and because money is so crucial to politics, the woman who helps with the fund-raising can quickly become part of the campaign decision-making group."[33]

June Roselle, primary fund-raiser for Detroit's powerful mayor Coleman Young, believes a lot of it comes down to the plain old question of access. On any campaign, power is derived from a staffer's closeness to the candidate. June Roselle has raised money for the mayor for fourteen years now and serves as one of his major appointees. "Being his fund-raiser is a very key position to the mayor to this day," she said. "There's something emotional about fund-raising to a candidate. They always feel closest to their money.

I can call him, and I get immediate access. There's other appointees—they don't have that. The person that does the fund-raising is close, very close to the candidate. He has to trust that person."

The person who does the fund-raising rapidly becomes the master of the lists of contributors, and the lists are crucial—in the final winding-down phase of any campaign, one of the things that people are scrambling to hang on to are the precious lists. Those lists serve as the basis for the next campaign (whether the candidate of this campaign won or lost), and the fund-raiser spends hours merging and purging the lists, developing and protecting a special, private list of high donors and working to widen the base of donors at all levels. The lists become the fund-raiser's individual stock in trade, and a successful woman fund-raiser from one campaign finds that she is taken into the loop of the players planning the next important campaign, simply because she knows where the money is to be found.

Celinda Lake says that even women who *are* thinking of undertaking a candidacy of their own in the future ought to get into the fund-raising end of other campaigns. "Raise more money than you need, give it away, do it for the party, but get used to raising that greater volume of money," she said. "Most of the state legislature races in this country, a couple aside, are still ten- twenty- thirty- forty- to fifty-thousand-dollar races. It's a huge jump to a half million dollar race. Women just aren't used to raising that kind of money, but we say get on the committees, fund-raise for the party or whatever, so that you start to know where the money is buried and so you know those people as individuals."

The whole business of campaigning is fraught with uncertainty. Nobody knows—nobody *can* know—exactly what is going to make the numbers come out right on election day, so everybody can take credit for themselves for any apparent successes along the way, and they do, and everybody can point fingers at somebody else when things go wrong, and they do that too. In the middle of all this vagueness and ambiguity, the successes and failures of fund-raising are clearly quantifiable. Either you got the money, or you didn't. It's even better if you got more than anybody expected to get. Your rating as a fund-raiser is almost independent of whether or not your candidate won: if you brought the dollars in, you did a good job. Not only that, but it is very difficult for anyone else to take the credit for the job you did—a not unknown phenomenon elsewhere on the campaign trail. It may be possible for the titular finance director to sweep in, present the sums, and look good temporarily at the expense of the woman working for him who has actually been on the phone raising the dollars, but unless he has the personal contacts that will enable him to go back and get more, his glory is short-lived. The people who give the money know who asked them for it.

The woman fund-raiser who is honest with her donors and treats them fairly and with respect can go back to them over and over again. The respect is not only a ploy: "You know, in a way, I almost have the greatest admiration for the guys who give," one fund-raiser said musingly. "They give because they really believe in somebody, or his program—and they back it up with money they could spend other places, just like everybody else does. And they ask for so little back—I've raised money from thousands of people, and I've had maybe four, five people come back to me and ask for a favor, and it's never been anything big, anything I wouldn't have done even if they had never come up with the money. I try to give them something if I can, the major donors who always come through when you call up and say, 'We've got to do this media buy. I don't know if it's going to make the difference or not—I can't promise you it will, but we have to buy the time.' I figure I owe them something for just being there for me, for taking my call even if they groan to themselves when they're told it's me on the line. So if I can put them on the dais, maybe give them complimentary tickets to another fund-raising event, I do it. It's such a little way of saying thank you."

Most of the time, the quid pro quo is as simple as that. Only an innocent child would claim that all politicians and contributors deal only with clean hands—the potential for corruption is always there no matter how comprehensive the reform laws may be, and there will always be people who take advantage of it. The amazing thing, according to many women who had always heard about the smoke-filled rooms fueled by greed, is that there is so little of it. "You keep going back and people keep giving," congresswoman Connie Morella said about her own fund-raising, "and they don't want anything from you either. You know, you just feel like oh, some will, but it is amazing how many don't. They're good people."

In fact, Morella, like some other women candidates, felt that part of her fund-raising success could be directly attributable to her sex. "I think women have no more trouble raising money than men, and in many instances because they can be more personal they probably succeed more. I think a woman can joke around even more than a man can on the phone. I mean, someone says, 'Ah, Connie, everybody is after me for every campaign. I don't have any money.' So I say, 'Oh, come on, you can squeeze a little bit more out. You know that we have a good chance to win'—but I can say it kiddingly." Another fund-raiser who has moved into the senior councils of her state party as a direct result of her ability to shake the money trees agrees wholeheartedly and points out that she has coaxed and teased more than one contribution into the campaign coffers. "They like it," she said frankly. "So it's a game—I flatter them, and they preen a little. It's kind of flattering to be asked for a big contribution, to be considered one of the guys with the big bucks. I guess if I didn't really like them, it wouldn't work, but as it is, it's just a little bit of fun for everybody. I bat my eyes, even on the phone, and they eat it up, and I get the money."

One of the reasons that the nationally known major fund-raisers are wealthy men is that the major donors like to deal with a financial equal. As every candidate can testify, you can't send out a kid to get the thousand dollar donations. The game just doesn't work that way. But for a woman, however, the rules are subtly different. A woman doesn't have to have the same financial resources as long as she's a social equal—nicely dressed, knowing some of the same people, able to approach the donor on a more informal basis. She may be able to get people to donate who otherwise would only come through if the candidate himself did the soliciting—and the less fund-raising the candidate has to do, the more time available for doing other kinds of campaigning. A few years from now, when women come closer to having equal opportunities in the business world and are a more routine part of a man's professional world, that distinction may disappear. But at the present, in the middle of all the disadvantages women have coping with the money side of politics, there are still some roles that men can't play.

By and large, however, women in politics, candidates and staffers alike, are learning the facts about the system that the men have known for years, and using those facts to achieve a more credible presence on the political stage than women have ever had before. As Stephanie Solein said about Washington, "Money is what makes this town tick, and we've learned it the hard way."

In politics, as in many other fields of endeavor, money is the language power speaks. What women are finally beginning to prove is that the language is not sex-specific.

5. Women among Men

It was one of the first big events of Reagan's 1984 reelection campaign, and the president and Mrs. Reagan were being ushered to their places on the gigantic podium facing the crowd. The first lady's radiant public smile froze momentarily as she looked around the podium at all the beaming politicians—the beaming *male* politicians—who were going to be surrounding the president, chosen for their local importance to bathe in reflected glory. But this was the year of the gender gap, the year when the Democrats had a woman on the ticket, the year when the Republican party was going to need to broaden its appeal to women, and on that commodious platform not a single women was to be seen. It was the Republican establishment in all its masculine glory. The wife of the president—accredited only by her relationship to a man—was going to be the sole woman there.

Nancy Reagan blew up discreetly but unmistakably. Nobody may have noticed the omission before, but they noticed it then. Indeed, Mrs. Reagan was so furious that campaign staffers carefully found seats for themselves at a safe distance, out of earshot of irate whispers. Immediately after the event came a memo from campaign manager Jim Baker, ordering that from then on 50 percent of the people on every dais would be women, no matter what. It wasn't always easy: in some of the particularly chauvinistic areas the powerful men who had to be excluded in favor of women well down the totem pole put up a fight to try to retain their position, but every time, when Mrs. Reagan swept her glance over the platform, the women were there. The men running the presidential campaign

102

who simply hadn't noticed their absence before had been educated, at least temporarily.

■   ■   ■

Few men begin to understand how hard it is for a woman to make her way in the political world.

"Sometimes there are men who are honestly oblivious," explained Monica McFadden, formerly executive director of the National Women's Political Caucus. "Let me give you a perfect example: California's senator Alan Cranston. It does not compute in this man's mind whether the person sitting across from him is male or female. You're either qualified and competent or you're not. If you aren't, he will pay no attention to you. If you are, it doesn't matter. But there are all the others though who don't know because we're invisible to them and what they see is a male world and if a female voice pipes up they don't hear it. Those men range in age from eighteen to seventy-nine. I know a lot of men I've sat near, where I can say something and the man next to me can say exactly the same thing and he's the one that's heard. Why? Because I'm a woman. The pitch of the voice is wrong or whatever."

Among male politicians, just as among the male population in general, there is a bedrock level of a very few individuals who honestly believe that politics and government in general is something that women ought not to mess around with. Seldom do they give much indication of having their minds open to intelligent discussion on the topic: their opinion is apparently integrally linked with their view of the essential nature of mankind and the universe. Most of them are older men; many of them have come far enough to learn that it is imprudent to say what they think openly, at least in public, which is probably as far toward understanding women's ambitions as they're ever going to get. Basically, that unconvertable bedrock level is not the problem. (For one thing, according to pollster Harrison Hickman, there is a balancing 8–10 percent of the population who prefer to vote for—or, presumably, pay attention to—a woman.) According to most women, the problem lies in the vastly greater numbers of more aware, more sympathetic men who nonetheless have no appreciation of the extent to which women have been closed out of political power. ← STOP

"There are still massive perceptual problems," Celinda Lake of the WCF said. "We had an interview with my home governor, from Montana. Montana ranks fourth lowest in all of the states in terms of women appointees, and that's ridiculous. This is one of the first states to have suffrage, there are lots of women in leadership, we had the first woman in Congress. We're not talking Mississippi here—there's no excuse for it. And he said, 'Well, you know, the sex of an applicant just never even enters my mind.' I'll bet that's right, but that's the point, I said. We need you to look out of the room that's all male, and say we must have missed something here."

The central difficulty is that, with a few notable exceptions, it is women who are most troubled by the underrepresentation of women in political life. The men who have been there all along are used to things and like them the way they are. They know it's no picnic getting to a position of significant political power—they have, after all, fought their own battles—and it is very difficult for most of them to understand how much more daunting the obstacles are for a woman. For them, the all-male gathering, whether it's a party caucus, a committee meeting, or an informal get-together after a late session, isn't meant to exclude women, it's just the normal course of affairs. It probably doesn't even occur to them to notice that it *is* all male. That's not what's on their minds. They're trying to get a job done, not worry about such trivial concerns (to them) as the gender of the participants. Most of them have never paid any attention to whether or not there happen to be any women present. In fact, there usually are, but only as a kind of living wallpaper. Women traditionally have attended most formal meetings at some level of service capacity, secretaries, perhaps, or more recently as AAs (administrative assistants) or LAs (legislative assistants)—support personnel, not the decision-makers.

Jeane Kirkpatrick, formerly the ambassador to the United Nations, writes of sitting in the Situation Room in the basement of the west wing of the White House, at one of the regular foreign policy meetings of the Reagan administration, attended by the president and his most important advisors. She was the only woman at the table, of course. She remembers wondering if there had ever been another woman so close to the center of decision making in U.S. foreign policy. Not under Carter, she knew, not under Ford or Nixon, not under Johnson. "There are people who come and go in the room," she wrote, "and among them is almost invariably a woman or two—fetching and carrying papers to the people who are sitting at the table."[1] But are the people at the table paying any attention to the fetchers and carriers? Not very likely.

Being invisible is one of the most exasperating aspects of being a woman operating in what has always been a man's world. It's hard to get a grip on. As one woman who has had a long career in politics said gloomily, "It's not that they get up in the morning and say, 'We're going to be nasty to women today.' Damn it, sometimes I think that would be an improvement. Most of the time they just never think about us at all. It's like if we're not right there, we don't exist. If you point it out to a man, if you show him that most of the time the meetings, the committees, the appointees, whatever, are all men, he looks at you in innocent amazement, and most of the time he *is* innocent, in a way. It just never occurred to him that there weren't any women there. And unless the meeting was about something that specifically concerned me—policy I've been involved in, something on my turf—he still doesn't see why not having a woman there should bother me!"

After nearly twenty years of feminist agitation and increased female participation in politics, more and more women are in some of those meetings. Not in all of them of course: since Jeane Kirkpatrick left the United Nations in 1985, there has been no woman in the highest counsels of the Reagan administration. Sometimes this may work to their benefit. As Dr. Estelle Ramey, a feminist physiologist who has taught in Washington for twenty years, pointed out, "The Iran-contra scandal has one advantage, however: no women are involved—not because women are holier than men, but because no woman is allowed to get her nose in the tent."[2] But even in those organizations where there are women, some men fail to pay attention to them because as men they are so geared into a masculine context that it doesn't cross their minds that a woman might have something distinctive to contribute. Virtually every woman who has worked on a man's campaign or as a staffer has her own war stories to tell. One of ours has amused us for years. In 1982 Ronna Romney was the cochairman of Republican Richard Headlee's gubernatorial campaign in Michigan. Headlee also had a woman, Mari Egbert Patterson, as his campaign manager. There were numerous other women working on the campaign at one level or another. And yet one bright day Romney walked in on a meeting between Headlee and one of his most senior (male) aides. Together, the two of them were trying to work out the definitive strategy for dealing with an increasing problem of getting their message across to women. In trying to work out the tactics by themselves they were not deliberately snubbing the women on the campaign—it had simply never occurred to them to ask them.

Now if men thought just like women, it wouldn't really matter whether a woman was included in that discussion or not. However, in the experience of most women involved in politics (or in any other sphere of life, come to that), in some ways men don't. Men and women simply have different ways of looking at some things. To determine whether these differences are innate or learned might be interesting, but in a practical sense such a debate is probably close to irrelevant. What matters is that women can bring a distinctive new perspective to political life, based on their experience of being women in our society. Even the men recognize this sometimes. When Marian Bergeson, now a California state senator, ran for the school board in Newport Beach in 1964, there were no other women on the board. She reported there were mixed feelings about having a woman run. Back then, she said, "We did great things to get men elected to office, but women had not been participants in that fashion and so running for the school board raised a few eyebrows." However, she was told the superintendent had said, "Well, I think we should have a woman because it might be nice to have someone who knows something about kids."

Recently, however, the whole question of women's experiences leading them to different conclusions than men might draw has become a major issue for political tacticians. In 1980 for the first time in polling it became obvious that women supported candidates in different proportions than men did, and were attracted and put off by different issues. The gap in percentages between men and women was dubbed the "gender gap," and whether or not the gender gap is alive and relevant depends on who is explaining it and which figures they use to support which particular argument. However, polls are consistent in showing that women are more opposed to war than men are; indeed, they are more wary of the use of force anywhere, whether in a foreign or domestic context. More women than men are opposed to the death penalty, and more women than men are in favor of gun control. Broadly speaking, women are more liberal on social issues, such as civil rights and social welfare policies. This may be partly accounted for by women's greater economic vulnerability: according to the 1980 census figures, women are concentrated on the lower half of the economic ladder, and women are more dependent on the government for assistance than men. It is also a matter of historical record that women have been more prepared to limit and control social vices such as drinking, drugs, and gambling.

What all of this may mean in terms of any single election clearly varies: in 1984, for example, when the Democrats hoped that the presence of Geraldine Ferraro on the ticket would sway women, the percentage of women voting for Mondale was indeed higher than the percentage of men (46 to 38 percent), but Reagan still took an absolute majority of women's votes: 54 percent.[3] The Reagan landslide was broad enough so that it swallowed up differences that might have been more decisive under other conditions. In 1986, a smaller gender gap *was* more decisive in assisting the Democrats to take control of the Senate. In Colorado, for example, where Democrat Timothy Wirth won with 51 percent of the vote, 53 percent of the women voted for him and 44 percent voted for his Republican opponent, whereas 49 percent of the men voted for the Republican and only 48 percent voted for Wirth.[4] According to CBS exit polls, the women's vote also made a difference in eight other states as well, in each case tipping the balance toward the Democratic candidate. As Ed Rollins, Republican strategist, put it, "We are back to gender gaps again, and I think realistically as Republicans we have got to watch it extremely closely."

Among elected officeholders, there also appears to be a relatively consistent pattern of male versus female opinions on current issues. Between 1981 and 1983, the Center for the American Woman and Politics conducted a project that involved surveys of men and women in elected and appointed office, and found that a gender gap continues between political women and men.[5] They reported three major patterns: first, across all levels of office, women have different attitudes from men, and the gap becomes more pronounced in attitudes toward women's issues; second, the gender gap is greater at higher offices and narrower at local ones, and women at higher levels are more liberal or feminist than women at lower levels; and third, black women holding elective office at all levels are more liberal than the majority of women or men serving at the same levels.

These results are borne out in practical, everyday politics, according to Ellie Smeal. "Well, the women who came into office—Republican or Democrat, it doesn't matter what their background is—end up being more supportive of us than a similarly situated man would be, because of their own personal happenings. Like a Paula Hawkins [from 1980 to 1986 a Republican senator from Florida, considered conservative on most issues] would vote with us on social security, or vote with us on child abuse or something like that, and feel an identity, could see that some things were not fair. You wouldn't expect that, knowing her background. I can find sympathetic women that you would be very surprised by who would help us, both on the Republican and Democratic side. They see a lot of things they don't like."

This is not to say that all women plump down on the liberal end of the scale, or that there is necessarily a women's bloc of liberal votes in the state or federal legislatures. The Congresswomen's Caucus, formed in the late 1970s, had to be reorganized in 1981 as the Congressional Caucus for Women's Issues, including men whose stand was broadly speaking profeminist, when the more conservative women who swept into office with Reagan and the predominantly liberal Republican and Democratic women who had been in Congress already couldn't come to sufficient agreement among themselves to make the caucus an effective force.

Wherever they are situated along the ideological spectrum, women officeholders can hardly be oblivious of the fact that although as women they are in the majority in the population at large, in the legislative halls, they are part of a tiny minority. Inevitably, they still do bump up against what they themselves describe as gender differences less associated with ideology than with attitude and style. Lynn Martin, a Republican congresswoman from Illinois, is the only woman included in the Republican House leadership and has been described as "one of the boys"—a tribute she reportedly feels a little ambivalent about. She sees herself very definitely as a woman with a woman's approach to some things; she wisecracked during the fiscal 1987 budgetary deliberations, when she was arguing against restoring funds for the general revenue-sharing program (on the grounds that the federal government with its massive deficit didn't have funds to share), "Maybe girls learn to say 'no' easier than boys."[6] More seriously, she said of her work on the Armed Services Committee that she thought a woman's point of view might provide a useful new angle. "If I may be allowed one sexist remark, I think men tend to become enamored of weapons systems—and that can be very expensive—rather than asking how they fit into the pattern for our defense. I think women are less emotional about those choices."[7]

For all the additional illumination that a female point of view may provide, if a woman expects to be effective with the men surrounding her, it is impolitic to beat them over the head with her female wisdom. Men in politics (and elsewhere) seem to remember the aggressiveness of feminist politics of the 1970s unhappily, especially the confrontational style associated most generally with Bella Abzug—fairly or not. As Mitch Daniels said, when he was political director at the White House under Reagan, "I think it will be interesting to see what the most effective style for women is in politics. I wouldn't try to prejudge it. There are women, and I see them more on the Democratic side, who are just emulating the style of the men from whom they are trying to take a fair share of power, and by that I mean profanity and all that. There are others who try to do it through no-nonsense professionalism that still preserves an element of dignity that some men don't worry much about. I think that style is probably going to be the model of the future because I don't think it's necessary to overcompensate and to be sort of Bella Abzug, in fact I think it's probably counterproductive in the end. My guess is that men probably respond to firmness in a woman and it may only detract from her effectiveness if she overlays an excuse for the man to dismiss her point of view, namely that she's acting like Bella or something." It can of course be argued, and many articulate women do, that a woman's style should surely be less important than the substance of what she has to say. Men are clearly allowed a greater latitude of style without attracting criticism. However, the practical fact is that in order to carry a point of view, any officeholder—particularly any legislator—has to be persuasive, and part of being persuasive is achieving sufficient rapport so that the person to be persuaded listens to your argument.

What this means is that one of the primary problems for women officeholders is to work out just where the line lies between firmness and the kind of overcompensation that puts men's backs up. As Michigan state representative Shirley Johnson put it, "There is a frustrating side to it. You know, a man can get up on the floor of the House and debate an issue, and he is strong, and he is hard, and he is emotional, and he is tough, and isn't he wonderful? And let a woman get up there and give you a good debate and be strong and be hard and be tough and have the right emotional tone, and *she* is strident. He is terrific, but she is a strident bitch, and that's the attitude."

Certainly a lot of the difficulty still is that there are not enough women around for a generalized pattern of expectations to emerge: each woman still has to prove herself from the beginning, and her behavior, for a lot of onlookers, applies not only to herself but to all other women. Marian Bergeson, in her pioneering days as a woman school board member in California in the 1960s remembers talking to a member of another school board at a conference and asking if they had any women on that board. "Well, no," he told her, "we tried one once and it didn't work out." Unfortunately, the experience of dealing with a successful woman doesn't seem to transfer very easily from one arena to another: the men on each school board, on each city council, in each state legislature, and so forth seem to need convincing individually that a woman can be a competent peer.

Certainly the political world is aggressively masculine. Mitch Daniels, with quiet amusement, pointed out that a lot of the metaphors of power come from explicitly male activities. "When people talk about or think about campaigns or fighting the legislative battles, contesting decisions, it's all either sports metaphors or military metaphors: we're in the fourth quarter, we're launching an offensive—that kind of thing. After all, both sports and war are competitive at base, all politics is competition, and all of those have been typically male pursuits."

Sometimes there is even an element of hazing, fraternity-style, in the relations between legislators. One woman state legislator told about the veiled struggle between two other women in the state assembly who came into the legislature at the same time. They overheard a male colleague in their caucus predicting that a male newcomer was going to end up with the freshman of the year

110

award. Each of the women immediately decided that if anybody was going to be freshman of the year, *she* was, and each went to considerable trouble to be seen to be unfailingly prepared, to be outstandingly cooperative, to ingratiate herself with the leadership, and so forth. One of them was apparently being viewed with greater favor by the party whip—thus frustrating her rival no end—when both women discovered that there was no freshman of the year award. "It was just a little behind the scenes game that is played by the men. In our state nobody gets a freshman of the year award—it turns out that freshman of the year means asshole of the year," said the woman state legislator, who had come along later enough to be let in on the joke by the now-wiser assemblywomen.

This kind of humor is not the only way in which men in politics operate differently from women, according to Susan Bryant, an experienced campaign consultant who has been involved in political campaigning since 1964 when, as a college freshman in Galesburg, Illinois, she dropped by Charles Percy's gubernatorial campaign headquarters and got hooked. After more than twenty years of working with male and female politicians, she says, "Women are more likely to take people at face value. Somebody says something, they say, 'Hey, I assume you're telling me the truth.' That gets us into trouble, because men do not assume that. A man assumes that when another man has said something, he in fact is not necessarily telling the truth. He may be, but he isn't necessarily. So the first man might not be telling the truth either, if that's the standard. We, however, believe people are telling the truth. I have now learned to say, 'Look, I am very straightforward. I do not play games. When I say something, that's what I mean. If it bothers you that I'm so straightforward, I'm sorry, but at least you know where I stand. And I expect you to do the same.' "

It is hardly news that women not only perceive themselves but are generally perceived by men as more truthful and honest and consequently less likely to be involved in corruption: polls and studies have shown that those have been political stereotypes right from the beginnings of women's campaigns. After all, it was the belief that women would bring a new era of honor and respectability to politics that fueled a lot of the suffragist action in the first place. Women have been heavily involved in most of the major reform movements: the agitation against drinking, drugs, the fight for gun control.

Cynics would suggest that the main reason women remain untouched by major scandals or corruption is that they are still outsiders in the political game, not sufficiently in the loop to be trusted by male conspirators. It is hardly surprising that back in the early 1970s there were no women Watergate defendants or that more recently only one woman, a secretary, testified at the Iran-contra hearings. Whether women, once admitted to the closed rooms, will prove more upright and less likely to bend laws for their own principles or profit than their male peers remains to be seen. So far, by and large, the doors are still shut.

Although not many women would wish to have become ensnarled in either the Watergate or the Iran mess (or the less apocalyptic scandals along the way), encountering those stubbornly closed doors is exasperating enough so that there is a definite satisfaction when women themselves are in a position to do the excluding. Susan Bryant obviously relished the moment during Julie Belaga's 1986 Connecticut gubernatorial campaign when the women clearly were in control. Elizabeth Dole, Secretary of Transportation, offered to help with Belaga's campaign, and Susan Bryant, who was acting as a consultant to the campaign, was on the scene working with the campaign staff, many of whom were men. "Liddy Dole came in to speak for Julia at an airport rally," she said. "When they got in, there were a couple of things Julie had to tell Liddy privately, to make sure they had the right speech. So they went to the women's room. I was standing outside with all the other crew from the campaign, and I said, 'Well, boys, with all due respect I am now going to the conference with the candidate and the Secretary of Transportation, and I don't believe any of you are invited.' And off I went into the ladies' room."

And then there was the sweet revenge of Connie Binsfield, a Republican Michigan state senator. A woman of considerable common sense as well as seniority (she's been in the state legislature for more than twenty years), who held the post of deputy majority leader at the time, she was justifiably annoyed when she was excluded from the party officially greeting Vice-President George Bush when he landed in Michigan on Air Force Two. It's the kind of petty one-upmanship that happens to both men and women in political life, but probably more frequently to women because they are perceived by many of their male peers as semioutsiders who can be snubbed more safely. In this particular case, the men had misjudged their snubbee. Working through another woman politician, Binsfield was able to arrange to take a quick trip to Washington and fly into Michigan *with* Bush, so that on landing, she had the inestimable pleasure of surveying the faces of the greeting party as she came down the steps of Air Force Two behind the vice-president. On any absolute scale that kind of thing isn't of supreme importance, but it can be very satisfying.

Not all of the incongruities women find in making a place in a man's world have to do with variations in behavior between males and females: sometimes just plain physical facts are unavoidable. Kansas senator Nancy Kassebaum is small and fragile-looking, with a gentle voice. That works fine in the confines of her office, or in a small meeting, but may not be as effective on the Senate floor. "I was talking to another woman who had worked on my campaign in '78 and is now an elected official herself, and she said, 'You know, several of us got together and we realize we're not as strong in debate on the floor.' I know that I'm not either. My strength really lies in trying to work behind the scenes. I'm never going to be a great orator. I think that's where men have an advantage. I always told Tom Eagleton that I wished I had his voice, a great voice. You can be commanding just with that voice."

For Anne Stanley, a longtime political strategist who is also a small woman, it's not so much the voice as the size that makes a difference. "If I could change anything about my life in politics, I'd be bigger," she said. "Taller. I think people would take me more seriously. I'm short—five-two—and I always feel that's a drawback because a lot of this game is *presence*. I wish I were about five inches taller at least. When you're short, you don't communicate the same presence, or at least it's harder. People have a tendency to put their little arms around you and do those kinds of things."

Maryland senator Barbara Mikulski is even shorter than Stanley—in fact, at four feet eleven inches she is reportedly the smallest person ever to serve in the United States Congress—but everybody who deals with her agrees that her forceful personality more than makes up for her stature. She has a good time kidding about it: when a Baltimore newspaper reported she was four feet ten inches she had her press aide call them up with a correction, on the grounds that at her height, she needed every inch she could get.[8] As a practical matter she carries around a metal suitcase to stand on when she speaks to crowds, and when she presides over the Senate, she stands rather than sits as her colleagues do. In her office, where she is on her own turf, her furniture is designed to her scale, which means a tall man sitting on her couch may find his knees closer to nose level than he is accustomed to see them—a neat reprisal for all the overstuffed chairs the senator herself has been swallowed up in.

Of course, not all political women are short, any more than all political men are tall. (Former Texas senator John Tower, who measured five feet five inches, liked to say, "My name is Tower, but you can see I don't."[9]) Mari Maseng, former director of public liaison in the White House, stands an even six feet in her stockings and agreed without hesitation that it was an advantage. "Are you kidding?" she said. "It's definitely an advantage. I remember when I was a fledgling reporter, and I was going to interview a mayor from one of the cities I was covering, and he was so angry at me about something I'd written that he started shouting and stood right up from behind his desk. So I stood up from the front of his desk"—her hands flew, pantomiming the medium-sized mayor's confusion at discovering he was the one being dwarfed—"and we both sat down. It's great. A lot of women don't have that opportunity to tower over somebody. When I was a teenager my mother always told me one day I'd be glad."

■　　　■　　　■

Most of the time, fortunately, women politicians are neither towering over nor being towered over by their male colleagues. One way or another they have jobs to do, and whether the men around them are used to seeing those jobs being done by women, the work has to be accomplished. "There's nobody with whom I don't want to work," Mari Maseng said of her job in the White House. "Anybody who's willing to help me get the ball from here to there is who I want to work with. Anybody who'd help me with something I'm just learning to do is even better. It used to be I'd let people have their own turf, but I'd really protect mine. Now I understand that there's a lot of people willing to get my ball part of the way there, and I might as well let them do that because I know the only thing that I'm being judged on is that it gets there. If they start taking it off in the wrong direction, that's different." She obviously got it in the right place often enough, because as public liaison director she was the most visible woman in the White House; according to Mitch Daniels, she was the only woman regularly attending the morning senior staff meetings. She was not part of the innermost circle: Reagan, like the presidents who have preceded him, has had only men as his most intimate advisors.

At a less exalted level, Vera Katz of Oregon, speaker of the state house of representatives, like many other women state legislators across the country, has worked out her own style of getting along with the men. She came into politics obliquely, drawn into Robert Kennedy's presidential campaign in 1968. When he was assassinated the week after the Oregon primary, she and some of the other volunteers felt they simply couldn't walk away from the issues he had championed, and so they formed what they called the Kennedy Action Corps to carry on working on specific programs. For Katz, it was lobbying the Oregon state legislature to establish a detoxification center for the homeless and inebriated in the skid row section of Portland. Giving her time strictly on a volunteer basis—she was a housewife with a small son, teaching part-time at that point—she learned how the legislative process worked. Once involved, she stayed involved. Eventually, it turned into a full-time occupation. She was elected to the state legislature in 1973, and moved rapidly up through the hierarchy until she was elected speaker in 1985. Although she is a Democrat and functions within the House as a Democrat, in her early political years her activity was only loosely party oriented, focused much more on an issues group called Demoforum, which brought together Democrats around the state who were not affiliated with the party but were concerned about similar issues. "In other states, people are very party oriented," she explained. "Here it was purely issues."

Possibly it is as much her less partisan background as the fact that she is a woman that shapes her approach to managing the affairs of the Oregon House. Certainly her dislike of party discipline techniques in common use elsewhere is plain. "Power brokering is distasteful to me," she said flatly. "It's not the way I operate. It's abusive. Power brokers play on special privileges, and I am very much a conciliatory individual. If we can't sit down around this table and come to an agreement on an issue, then who can? That's our task, to *do* it, rather than pushing people around and using those kinds of techniques, intimidation techniques and threatening techniques, removal from committee, or removal from financial assistance, those kinds of things. I don't use them and I don't want to be in an environment that does."

Although she has been widely acknowledged as a successful speaker, getting elected wasn't easy. "When I decided to become speaker, this office was empty," she said. "The gentleman who had been in office is now sitting in the senate, so I became a candidate. I raised money. I didn't raise a lot of money but I raised enough, and I helped some candidates. It was going to be very close. It took 101 ballots. We started at 2:30 in the afternoon, and we went until 9:00 the next morning without a break. There were two of us. I was seven or eight votes ahead all the time but I had to have thirty-one votes because that's what you need on the floor. It finally broke when somebody else put their name in, and that's when it happened.

"I always ask myself, why did it take that long? What problems did they have? I think number one I was a woman. Deep down in my heart of hearts, I think probably it was also that I was Jewish, but I don't know that for sure. Three, I was not a very partisan Democrat. I mean, I work for Democrats, I raise money for Democrats, I was sensitive to it, but I was also able to work with Republicans. It's a battle at the campaign but when it comes here we are going to work together. They were a little nervous about that. A lot of those reasons. Most of them were men in the caucus, and they probably felt a little uncomfortable with the fact that a woman was going to be in this office. It took me almost the entire session to set a comfort level, and when it was all over it was one of the best sessions that we have had in ten years. I worked with the senate president—the first time probably in the long history of this legislature that the house and the senate had such a working relationship. It was the shortest session in ten years, and we got nothing but kudos and praise for the way we managed to run the legislature."

Katz may have wondered why it took her colleagues so long to give her the thirty-one votes she needed, but they came further than almost any other state caucus in the country: she is currently one of only two women speakers. (Deborah Anderson, in South Dakota, is the other.) In Oregon, the state legislature meets every other year; in 1987 she had only thirty-one Democrats to work with, the slimmest possible majority—which means, among other things, that she really has to know where everybody is for every vote. Out of the sixty members of the House, there are currently ten women, six of them Democrats. In some ways, working with the women is easier, she said. "There are some women who are far more sympathetic and understanding of the conflicts and the problems I face as a speaker. They won't make the same kind of demands that their male colleagues would make, because they know that if I could provide them with what they wanted, I would do it. If I can't, they understand it and they will wait. They know that their turn will come and they won't play those power games. Not all of them, but a good many of them. I appreciate it so greatly. It is something that is unspoken, but it is there. You just hope that someday you can turn around and do for them what pleases them."

At one level, her experience that women are easier to work with is unsurprising. Women, after all, have been trained all their lives to wait their turn and work well with authority figures. It is her contention, however, that women are even better qualified than men for leadership skills. "Look," she said, "we have a leadership program, and we have people coming from Boston or California or wherever to train us on how to run meetings, on how to get to 'yes'—well, all the techniques are women's skills. You listen, you don't allow this argumentative behavior to go on. You try to separate process from substance so that you don't argue substance when you are really dealing with how are we going to get it done. You realize that you are there as a facilitator. You are there to align people, to empower others rather than always to empower yourself. As speaker, I can't fire anyone. I can remove him from a committee, but then I have a revolution on my hands. I have to work this way." She grinned and said with obvious relish, "I figure, well, shit, if I can run this outfit, I can run any corporation."

Vera Katz is clearly not alone in her observation that it takes time for men to get used to working with a woman in command. Women politicians everywhere discover that it takes a while for men to get used to having women as part of the political decision-making process at all, let alone at the top of the pole. Wilma Goldstein, Republican activist, believes part of the difficulty is that men and women typically have different approaches to working together. "When the tension gets high," she said, "men just get more hostile, but the women want to talk about it." When men talk about women being "too emotional" or growl about getting stuck in "touchy-feely meetings" with women who are trying to figure out what's going wrong they may be referring to women's desire to be more open about interpersonal relationships. Some men perceive women as making a mess of administration—or just generally being flaky—whereas actually the women are just doing the same job in a different way.

Women attack this problem in different ways. Pat Schroeder of Colorado, in her eighth term in office, is one of the women who has been described as flaky by some male colleagues, who apparently overlook the fact that she's been in Congress (and functioning with considerable success) longer than many of them have. Schroeder is a forthright woman who often chooses to assault the system head-on—although to what degree her methods are those of a woman in a man's system and to what degree they are simply a reflection of the chosen style of a strong-minded, independent member of Congress is of course open to debate. "There are some people for whom [being elected to Congress] is the biggest thing that ever happened to them, and they live in fear it'll be taken away," she said, speaking of her congressional colleagues. "I always looked at the job as if it was a fluke that I ever got it, and if I got it, I was at least going to try and do some things that make a difference. When you're doing that, you're operating on the edge, and if you go over the side, so what? At least you made your mark while you're here. I'm not going to go through all the aggravation and the long hours just to be a team player because I've really felt that there were lots of things that needed to be done. So if you work those things out and decide what it is you are really trying to do, then I think you don't get into the other stuff as easily.

"A lot of people come here and don't know what they want to do, except they want to get real active and they may want to run for the Senate, or they may want to run for this or for that, and what they *know* they want is a political career. I don't know that I want a political career yet, really. I know there are issues and things I really care about. If you remember seeing some of the movies, they portray people finding an issue that will help their career, whereas I do it the other way around. I may take the issue that heightens the career, but I feel strongly about the issue and think that it needs to be picked up and articulated. So I have members who get very angry with me because they say that you're supposed to compromise, dummy. 'What's the matter with you? You get too involved in this stuff. When are you going to grow up, when are you not going to be so naive?' "

Many of the men in the House haven't figured out yet what they expect of the women in their midst. Probably a lot of them would be most comfortable if the women would behave precisely like male congressmen, except for wearing skirts. There are certainly male legislators as independent-minded as Pat Schroeder, but her refusal to be buffaloed by the institution's periodic pomposity and general pretensions of grandeur exasperates some who would be much more tolerant of a man's refusal to play the game. In the deliberate majesty of the Congressional office building she is visibly relaxed and comfortable with where and who she is. Her office is large and airy, her furniture is comfortable, and she curls up in a big leather chair, sitting on her feet, while she talks. She is well prepared on the issues she cares about, but she clearly is not about to take herself or her colleagues too seriously. She has a wonderful gift for the apt phrase—it was she who first described Reagan as the Teflon president, a metaphor that might not have occurred to a man.

Not all women in Congress, or in public office anywhere else, are necessarily Pat Schroeders, of course. In Congress, Lynn Martin of Illinois on the Republican side and Corinne Boggs of Louisiana (known universally as Lindy) on the Democratic side are both women who work smoothly within the system and have been rewarded by it: Lynn Martin is vice-chairman of the House Republican caucus, and Lindy Boggs was the permanent chairwoman of the 1976 Democratic National Convention and is a member of the powerful Appropriations Committee. Unlike Lynn Martin, who initiated her own political career, Lindy Boggs came to Congress as a legatee. Her husband, Hale Boggs, was the House majority leader when he was killed in a plane crash in 1972 while he was campaigning for another congressman in Alaska. His wife had been his campaign manager in their home district of New Orleans and had been widely recognized as one of the most knowledgeable political wives in Washington. (It has been remarked that given the intricacies of Louisiana politics, campaigning in New Orleans was an assignment that permitted little political innocence.) She had long been a Washington insider who knew everybody: she has known every president since FDR in the years before each became president and has been close to several of them. The night after John Kennedy's assassination, she and her husband were invited to the White House by Lyndon Johnson, who had the job of assembling a new administration in spite of the national paralysis of shock and grief. Many women have taken over their dead husbands' seats in Washington, but Lindy Boggs, unlike many of them, has had distinct success in her own right. In 1984, during the national speculation over the likelihood of a woman on the Democratic ticket, she was sometimes named as a possibility along with Geraldine Ferraro and Dianne Feinstein, although her age—she was sixty-eight then—was an obvious liability. Throughout her independent congressional career, as during her years as a congressional wife and partner, she has made it her business to get along smoothly with the men around her.

The dynamics of a woman working with a man, smoothly or not, may still be fundamentally different from that of two men working together. Connie Morella, congresswoman from Maryland in her first term, said, "Things are different with men and women in politics. Women lobby differently, for example, because they don't always have the opportunity for the kind of access that men have. Women do have some access, but for instance in Annapolis [the Maryland state capital] a lot of the lobbying took place at the Hilton Hotel late at night over booze. Now a woman has got to be careful and she doesn't want to overbooze, and so there is that fine line. There *is* a line and it doesn't help you to go over it, and you wouldn't be comfortable doing it. There are always some women who are 'like one of the guys' kind of thing, but it just has to be something you are comfortable with personally, and that is honest for you. Most women, I think, do their lobbying through homework, through planning a strategy and then meeting one on one, and it might be over a cup of coffee or it might be an early drink—but I am just saying that they don't always have the free access in terms of reputation."

Reputation—at least in terms of moral propriety—has always been a matter of concern to women in public life; it is only recently that men have had to worry about it, as Gary Hart discovered to his cost. It was a long matter of common knowledge that many male politicians led active extramarital lives (John Kennedy and Lyndon

Johnson are two names that come immediately to mind, but the pattern is hardly restricted to deceased presidents); however, until now, a man's private life was considered off-limits, except for the delectation of Washington gossips. With the revelations about Gary Hart and his adventuring with a Florida beauty, the lid came off.

Geraldine Ferraro believes that at least part of the reason was the freedom the press discovered when every detail of her financial and family affairs, past and present, suddenly became fair game in 1984. "Don't tell me they didn't know about what was happening with Gary Hart in 1984," she said. "What I think people have not connected is that the Gary Hart stuff is all the result of my campaign. What happened in 1984 was that the press found out that they could go anywhere. They could go after my father, who has been dead for some forty-odd years. Nobody turned around and said, 'Where is your shame? Why do you pull a man out of the grave? When do you stop beating up on an eighty-year-old woman? When do you stop?' I'm a great supporter of First Amendment rights. I believe in freedom of the press, I believe that's what our country is about—these freedoms of religion, of separation of church and state. The Bill of Rights is an important thing that was written by those guys who knew what they were doing. I really think people have a right to know. They have a right to know about my finances, they had a right to know when I was in Congress if there was a conflict of interest. How was I voting? Was I voting for the real estate industry? Take a look—find out. You're entitled to know that. But are you entitled to know every detail of my parents' lives? Does anybody know about Ronald Reagan's father? And none of us care."

One concern of some women in politics is that ambitious male politicians in the post-Hart era will begin to worry that even perfectly platonic professional relationships with female aides and colleagues would look bad under press scrutiny. "It's opening a whole new can of worms," said one. "Of course you have one-on-one meetings from time to time—who doesn't? Whether you are a man or a woman, getting a chance to talk to the candidate when nobody else is there to interrupt or force his own agenda is pure gold. But who can blame the guys—particularly if they have national ambitions—if they get nervous about it now? Everyone is jumpy about everything, and if it means relegating your contact with women to nice safe general meetings, so be it. And there we are back addressing envelopes or whatever. Maybe it will all blow over. Pray God it will all blow over."

Clearly the rules are changing. As Ruth Messinger, New York City councilwoman for the West Side of Manhattan, put it, "It's probably true that women in office or positions of prominence are assumed in fact to lead a more circumspect life and probably would be a great deal less likely to flirt with those things that have come under public attention. There seem to be at least some men in the business who flirt with it all the time and on the theory, at least before the Hart matter, that nobody was likely to talk about it and that people would sort of conspire or quietly agree to keep it secret. So I think a lot of people in politics, especially people who have something that they think that the media might focus on, tend to keep it very quiet. The few who don't are probably men and probably they felt they could get away with it. I don't think that anybody's going to think that they can get away with it so easily any more."

Or as Ferraro said, "I was asked [about the Hart affair] if a woman would have been treated any differently, would she have been treated any worse if it had been found out she was having an affair. I said, 'How could you be treated any worse than Gary Hart was?' I mean, he's out. What are you going to do, put a scarlet letter on a woman's head? A woman would have been treated the same way. But all that stuff, that's a result of the '84 campaign."

Michelle Laxalt would say that keeping a discreet distance from the Washington social round and consequent temptation is less a matter of maintaining a reputation than of plain tactical intelligence. She has been around Washington since 1974, when she came with her father, former Nevada senator Paul Laxalt, one of President Reagan's closest friends. She spent the better part of ten years working on Capitol Hill, and in 1984 established her own lobbying firm. "Women can be seduced by what they feel is a closeness to power when in fact they're another young girl, a piece of meat, on Capitol Hill, and I think it takes a lot of them a long time to recognize it," she said. "It may help them at the front end, but it'll kill them in the long run. And it'll kill all of us."

It's more than simply not being taken advantage of, she went on. "The only advice I would give to a girl who has come here and wants to make a career is that she keep her eye on the ball and recognize that a career does not mean a cocktail suit. And that is where I think women in this town very clearly fall into two categories, the workers and the partyers. I don't disagree that work can get done giving dinner parties. But before someone determines that she wants to move into a career mode in Washington, D.C., as a female, she should know herself well enough to know where she wants to go. This is not only a power town. This town also has a higher incidence of alcoholism than any other town in the United States of America. The alcohol circuit in this town is atrocious. I hear about the business that's done at the cocktail parties, but I don't buy that. I just don't think you get business done in the barrooms. I happen to think that people do not think clearly when they're drinking— they may be very agreeable to what you're saying, and the next day you call to seal the deal and they have memory block. Everybody has a different approach. The way I deal is I work during business hours or when the Congress is in session."

Michelle Laxalt is not the only woman to decide that some ways of doing business are counterproductive. June Roselle has raised money for Detroit's powerful Mayor Coleman Young for fourteen years and is one of his most important political appointees, but for somewhat different reasons she figures that as a woman, she does better to do her talking with the mayor on a one-to-one basis, rather than joining in the late-night meetings at his official residence with the male inner circle. "If I were to call up the mayor and say I really think I should be in at those meetings, I think he'd probably put me in. But then they'd all be uncomfortable. Because most of them are older men, and they talk foul, and they look at me as so prim and proper. I mean, the mayor does not swear in front of me, and if he does, he says 'Excuse me.' Again, it's the age. He looks at me as the mother of these children [she has five], and as a very respectable, genteel type of person. I think he likes that idea, that I am like I am, and that I'm his fund-raiser because he thinks people are always so surprised when they meet me that '*you* work for Coleman Young?' I think he likes that. But again, there is something to that old boys' network. I'm sure that when they sit over there they're drinking and talking about where the city should go and there are many, many serious conversations going on. But I imagine I'd be very uncomfortable in it."

For all her success in handling the Oregon legislature, Vera Katz knows what June Roselle means. Talking about the solid friendships she has formed with her women colleagues in the legislature, even across the aisle with Republican women, she said she particularly values those close relationships with women who understand, as nonpolitical women can't, the pressures and rewards of her career. "I mean we have a real relationship that I really don't have with my male colleagues. I am still somewhat of an odd person for them. It's hard for them to come in here and crack a beer open at five o'clock, and there is beer here, at least there was beer in the refrigerator. They have a difficult time about it. You know I am not prissy. I use four-letter words and I can hold my own with the best of them and I can tell off-color jokes and laugh at them, but it's still not the same. It's not the same."

■　　■　　■

If it's not the same, one of the persistent problems for women making their way in the political world is to figure out what the differences mean. Mona Charen, a White House staffer for two years during the Reagan administration, raised eyebrows all over Washington by writing an article in 1986, after she left the West Wing, which was titled "What the White House Women Think of the White House Men." Most of it was naming names and giving examples of what she saw as male staffers scurrying around in pursuit of power, and their consequent timidity about taking any position that might even remotely be considered controversial. Published in a Washington magazine, it created a major stir. "I got a lot off my chest," Charen, who went on to be a speechwriter with the Jack Kemp campaign, admitted with satisfaction. "There are so many people who said, 'It's exactly true: I can't believe anybody said it.' " But she began the article describing a bright, beautiful, single woman staffer in her twenties who worked in the White House for five years and was never asked out by a White House man. Charen's point was that the men there were not as masculine and powerful as myth has it, but instead are so intent on pursuing their own careers and protecting their own vulnerabilities that they never notice the women around them, which she considers unfortunate.

Another single White House woman would, and has, taken issue with her on that. Mari Maseng said, "I told Mona I didn't like the way that article opened. The first thing out of the box there's 'There was this very pretty woman there and nobody asked her out.' So what? I don't want these people to ask me out. I spent my entire career getting them to take me seriously. I don't want them to think that I don't go out with someone else, but they don't ask each other out. When we're leaving senior staff meeting in the morning, I want to be arguing about trade legislation, not whether or not we're going to go to the movie or dinner."

Margaret Tutwiler, another single woman who is also a former White House staffer, says the absorption in business goes both ways. Having moved over to the Department of Treasury with James Baker when Baker and Donald Regan switched jobs at the beginning of Reagan's second term, she says it's less a problem of the White House as such than it is a reflection of the intensity of high-level political life in Washington. And it's not just men who are single-minded in concentrating on their careers; a woman working in their world has to be the same way. "I do not live a well-rounded life," she said flatly, in her high-ceilinged, elegant Treasury office. "Almost every job I have taken on has traditionally been a man's job, and I personally enjoy responsibility and seek responsibility, but with that comes a price. I am in this office anywhere from ten to fourteen hours a day. I was in the White House the same amount of time, if not longer. It does not allow much time for what I would call cultivating a personal life, and that does takes time. Half the time I do not feel pretty. I do not have the time to go home and get all dressed up, and I know that side of the street very well because I was raised on that side of the street. I love that part of life, but I keep putting it on the back burner." She has been in Washington since Reagan came into the presidency, and she clearly feels that whether she meant to or not, she has made some irrevocable choices. "No one who was a woman ahead of me ever sat me down and said, 'You're going to take on this next job, this next additional responsibility, but you are paying a price and at some point is it going to have been worth it to you?' " she mused. " 'Do you want to be a fifty-five-year-old woman in Washington who has a closet full of scrapbooks, who has an incredible wall of photographs, an unbelievable window on history? Is that what you want?' "

In politics, as in any other career, most women carry dual

responsibilities. As Tutwiler explained her own life, "When we leave here at eight-thirty at night, I go home, and I either make my own dinner or I've made it up on Sunday. I take my own car to the station and fill it up, I go to the cleaners—I mean, I have another job. When a Jim Baker or a Dick Darman or many of these men leave, that's it. They're leaving. They don't really have that other job. If I am going to entertain, and I am going to have maybe twenty people for dinner, I have a lot of work to do *around* my job. It's hard. It looks glamorous, it looks fabulous, if I had it to do all over again, yes, I would do it again. I have had a fascinating experience. I traveled for four years around the world with the president—a president of the United States. We just met in Saudi Arabia with the Crown Prince in a real meeting. Not a ceremonial meeting, but a real substantive meeting. I wouldn't give up the experiences I've had, the exposure that I have had to what I call a man's world. A real world. But I also know it has not been without a price, and the older I get—I am thirty-six—the more I recognize I really have paid for this."

Tutwiler, now the Deputy Secretary for public relations, was the deputy assistant to the president for political affairs in her White House days, and before that executive assistant to Jim Baker, then White House chief of staff. She speaks out of her intimate experience with the pressure that comes with pursuing a political career near the top of the totem pole. The men there, who've had their own challenges getting there and feel they've played by the rules, are disinclined to offer special privileges to a competitor who happens to be female. If a woman has more out-of-work responsibilities than a man, that's her problem. Ed Rollins, who is now a political consultant in Washington working on Jack Kemp's presidential campaign but has been Reagan's campaign manager and political director in the White House, sees the whole issue as basically simple. Is a woman willing to play the game the way it's played, or not?

Rollins bluntly said that Faith Whittlesey, one of Maseng's predecessors as director of public liaison in the White House, was "a total disaster for a couple of reasons." The first, he said, wasn't really her fault: she came to the White House from her previous job as ambassador to Switzerland. "To be out of the country for two years and then brought into the White House is like being shown a freight train going down the track at one hundred miles an hour and being told to jump on it." But then, he went on to say, "She compounded that by having children. [She has three; she was widowed at thirty-four.] I mean, Jim Baker would say we need to have a six o'clock meeting, and she would say, 'Well, I can't stay after six. You know I have children, and I have to get home to my children.' Or you would say we'll meet at a 7:00 A.M. breakfast—'well, I can't because I have children.' I think that is very admirable, but as Dave Gergen finally said to her, 'You know, these people are working from seven to eleven at night, and no one asked you to be an assistant to the president.' If you want to play in that league, you have to play by the rules of that league, and I don't mean to be totally unsympathetic. I guess I am the greatest promoter of women going." (Faith Whittlesey, just before she left the White House to return to her ambassadorial post in Switzerland, said her priorities had to be that way: "I think the highest priority in my life has been my children, and that's the most lasting contribution we can make to the world. I think the most important job a woman has is to raise her children in a way that they will be productive and make a contribution to the society, and if they are emotionally disturbed because of a lack of attention from a parent, then all of our labor has been for nothing. I would say that in terms of the kind of career I've had, I would have preferred to have had more time with my children, but I am the sole support of those children and I really don't have a choice.")

In all fairness, Ed Rollins is every bit as hard-nosed about men placing primary emphasis on their family responsibilities. "That's the big question about a Joe Biden today," he said, "who's got tremendous political people around him." Senator Joseph Biden of Delaware, who was one of the candidates for the 1988 Democratic presidential nomination, is well-known around Washington for commuting nearly four hours every day to go home to his family in Wilmington: his wife and baby daughter were killed in an automobile accident a month after he was elected to the Senate in 1972, leaving him solely responsible for his two sons. He remarried in 1977. "Joe Biden's got the commitment to his kids that he made when his wife was killed, that 'whenever you need me, I'll be there.' Climbs on a train every day and goes home. And I've had friends of mine that are very key Democratic players, saying 'Well, if he *means* that, that he'll be with the kids, he's unelectable.' That's kind of a sad commentary. But as I lay out Jack Kemp's schedule for the next year, and I'm going to put him in Iowa fifty times, and I'm going to put him in New Hampshire fifty times, you basically try and give him one Sunday a month to be home—that's not enough."

The men like Biden who actively place primary emphasis on their obligations to their children are still as rare in the political world as they are outside it. Much more often it is the political woman who has to make the hard choices between the seven o'clock meeting and being at home. Most women have family responsibilities, and so do most women politicians—they come outfitted with children and husbands and fathers, and sometimes all these connections are politically irrelevant and sometimes they aren't.

For Michelle Laxalt, for example, her relationship to her father is one of the things that brought her to Washington in the first place. Had her father not been elected to the Senate from Nevada, she might have remained out west as she had up to that point: until she came to the capital, she had never been east of the Mississippi. Certainly her family connection helped her get started working—her first job was working for the chairman of the Republican Senatorial Committee. From there on she took over on her own, fund-raising for James Buckley in New York and then went back to Washington to work for a succession of senators and governmental agencies. By the time she opened her own lobbying firm, she was well-established in her own right. Nevertheless, enough people think of her as her father's daughter so that she has to take deliberate steps to make it very clear that she isn't the quickest way to reach him. "It used to be that my response—as my mother would say, 'my kidding on the straight response'—would be no, I don't lobby my father. It's too easy for him to say no. But the fact is that I write into my contracts that I do not lobby Senator Laxalt nor any of the subcommittees on which he sits. I did that at the front end because I don't consider myself stupid, but by the same token, I didn't want any appearances that there was any wink, nod, or anything. In a couple of instances I dropped clients who didn't take the written word real seriously. It wasn't hard for me to do that. I don't sell my family."

Maureen Reagan is another daughter in Washington whose political career has been undeniably shaped by the career of her father.

It is perfectly true, of course, that presidential sons have had their own problems in escaping the shadow of their fathers—back in the thirties James Roosevelt, for one, had his initial Washington career indelibly marked by the fact that his father was FDR. But women still have a tougher time being considered independent of their families. It is not particularly surprising that in 1978 Muriel Humphrey, who had succeeded to her husband's Senate seat after his death, upset people when she dared to vote independently on a matter the administration thought was important.[10] The Carter people sent in Mondale to reason with her; they dug up old letters Hubert Humphrey had written to prove he would have voted differently, but she refused to budge. As was pointed out at the time, Hubert was no longer the senator. Muriel was. But she was Hubert's widow: she wasn't supposed to see things differently.

And it's not surprising that Elizabeth Dole resigned her responsibilities at the Department of Transportation so that she could accompany her husband Robert Dole, Senate minority leader and presidential candidate, on the campaign trail. It would be more surprising if Robert Dole resigned his to accompany her across the country. There have not been all that many married couples in which both parties have achieved considerable political prominence, but when it happens it's usually the wife who is more careful in measuring her words lest an unintended slip imperil her husband's career.

Jill Ruckelshaus had to step with particular caution. She has had a long and distinguished political career on her own—among other jobs, she was chairman of the presidential commission for the observance of the International Women's Year in 1975. When she met William Ruckelshaus in 1961, she had just finished graduate school and he was a new graduate of Harvard Law, working in the attorney general's office in Indiana. His first wife had recently died giving birth to twin girls; when Jill married him, the girls were fourteen months old. In subsequent years their careers accelerated, they had three more children, and by 1973 her husband was Deputy Attorney General, and she was working on women's affairs with Anne Armstrong in the White House. It was at that point, on October 10, in the middle of the Watergate investigations, that Attorney General Elliot Richardson resigned rather than go along with Nixon's unwillingness to surrender the tapes, and Nixon fired

William Ruckelshaus and Archibald Cox, abolishing the Special Prosecutor's office.

"I stayed on for a while," Jill said. "Billy and I made that decision together. I enjoyed what I was doing—I thought it was useful. I thought the decision to fire Elliot Richardson and Bill and Cox was just foolish, and I didn't want to quit automatically and make it look as though there was pique involved. Both of us thought that would in some way vitiate the message he and Elliot had made—a message about legality and constitutional points and personal morality." But the experience necessarily changed her own point of view about her job. "I lost a lot of confidence in the judgment of the people who were running the White House," she said. "I did leave about six or seven months later."

In other ways her relationship to her husband has affected and continues to affect her career. She says almost reluctantly that she doesn't believe she will ever run for office. "I love the issues, and I like campaigning," she said. "I think the reason I won't is that I am a little bit inhibited. This isn't a good answer for a feminist, but I am a little inhibited about my husband's career. I am much more liberal than he is, and I am too sensitive about peers and about criticisms of me reflecting on him. I just am not comfortable with that."

The problem has come up before. "I was on the Civil Rights Commission for several years, and the Civil Rights Commission got into a lot of trouble with the Reagan adminstration. I was essentially fired along with Mary Louise Smith during the time that we were in Washington. Billy was back there doing something the president had asked him to do, and I was doing what I had been asked to do by another president, and it caused me a lot of personal anxiety— and yet I could not do it the way I believed in doing it. I know that there are women and their husbands who have dealt with this in what appears to be a much more forthright, personally autonomous way, but for me—and I can only do the thing I am comfortable with—I decided I don't mind taking the heat for me, but I am not happy if I think I am bringing criticisms to Billy because of things I do."

Exactly what the web of personal relationships may do to influence a woman's political career clearly varies from one woman to the next. As Jill Ruckelshaus points out, other women handle what she sees as her difficulties differently. Other women deal with political husbands, or fathers, or brothers, or uncles, in their own characteristic ways. Susan Molinari, New York City councilwoman from Staten Island, is the daughter of congressman Guy Molinari, who is a strong right-to-life advocate. Susan herself is prochoice. The issue has caused problems: "When I announced [my candidacy]," she said, "the right-to-lifers on Staten Island naturally assumed that that was my position. When they found out it was otherwise, they wanted to call my house night and day, they said I needed to have counseling, they would taunt me at every event I was at, and really kind of took it out on my father, who is probably one of the strongest proponents that they have. It's an argument Dad and I had many times prior to this point. But finally, when I entered this race, it just wasn't one of those issues you discuss much any more." As she puts it, a sixty-year-old man and a twenty-nine-year-old woman look at things differently, and they agreed to leave it at that.

The one thing that all women in politics have to face is that the problems of meshing family relationships with political relationships—when those problems arise—are real ones, with no easy ideological script to supply answers. When it was only men who moved in the political arena, many of these complications simply never arose. The position a politician's wife, or daughter, took on public issues was generally a private affair, debated around the dinner table if anywhere. As more and more women enter the professional political world, the complications caused by the juxtaposition of individual integrity and family solidarity seem unlikely to go away. Men and women in the same line of business tend to fall in love and marry each other even if they don't always see eye to eye on the issues, whether the public is prepared for married politicians to present a divergence of opinion or not.

Ambition, principles, and mutual consideration may well combine to make an interesting domestic political stew for more couples than the Ruckelshauses.

■   ■   ■

"A rising tide raises all ships, and every one of us who climbs the ladder a little higher makes every one of the rest of us more important," said Maureen Reagan, cochairman of the Republican National Committee and daughter of the president. "That's what a boys' network is, and that is what a girls' network is. The fact that Nancy Kassebaum becomes a more important person in the Senate makes everybody who knows her a little more important because we have access and she is our friend. And that's what it is all about."

The increasing numbers of women in leadership positions make it possible for other political women to make an end run around the men already in place. June Roselle, who has watched the city government of Detroit expand the opportunities available for blacks under the administration of the city's first black mayor, thinks that it will take a woman at the top to open doors for women. "I always say you'll never see real importance for women in city government until you get a woman that's mayor. To see what a black has been able to do for affirmative action is amazing. It hasn't made anything go down in terms of quality or anything. It's just that the importance of being there is so strongly obvious."

Where women have moved into the top positions, whether in city government or elsewhere, they have demonstrated that Roselle may have a point. Dianne Feinstein, mayor of San Francisco, has made a difference in her city. In 1969 when she ran for the city Board of Supervisors, she was told that there was only one seat for a woman on that board, and it was already filled. "One woman's seat on a board of eleven supervisors, with a population of this city that is 53 percent," she said. "I challenged that, and I was elected." She got more votes than any of the other candidates, which meant she was the board president. There was still the other woman on the board: "And then I was told, 'well, two women can't get along,' and of course we became fast friends and we got along very well." When she was swept into office in the aftermath of the dual assassination of Mayor George Moscone and supervisor Harvey Milk in 1978, she took the reins into her own hands and things began to change. Eight years after she had become mayor, a majority of the Board of Supervisors were women. "I have appointed a woman as treasurer," she said, "I have appointed a woman as city attorney, both of our congress people are congresswomen, and we have gone from zero department heads [out of fifty-two] to ten women who are department heads."

Similarly, having Elizabeth Dole at the head of the Department of Transportation in Washington made a significant difference in the number of women employed by the agency. "Transportation of course is very much still a male-dominated area," she said during her tenure. "I asked when I got there, 'How many women do we have in our work force?' and I was told 19 percent are female. And I said, 'Now, back in 1967 when we established the department, how many women were in the work force?' And do you know what the answer was? Eighteen and a half percent. They had come up a half a percentage point from 1967 to 1983. So we put together a ten-point program and really went after it, in terms of helping women to enter and improving their skills and abilities to move up the ladder and so on. It's been working very well. We're almost to 23 percent female now, which doesn't sound like a lot, but we've got a workforce of one hundred thousand, so it takes a lot to move up even one percentage point." Once the women are there, issues important to women are more likely to be taken up: as Dole explained, "Recently the senior staff at DOT—men and women—got interested in a day care center, so that people who have children could bring them to work and be with them at lunch time and all, and they got out and raised the money. We now have a day care center at DOT! Those little kids are wonderful—it's working just great. We recently had the Walt Disney characters, you know, they all came in for a seatbelt function, and we had the children from the day care center there, and they loved it. They saw Minnie Mouse, and Mickey and Donald Duck and all the rest—so we have a lot of fun with them."

The women moving into the new executive responsibilities are bringing a lot of things with them—a fresh perspective, determination (because no woman who isn't determined is going to make it), conscientiousness (for the same reason), practical idealism, and common sense—and they are bringing other women along as well. If the only way to prove that women can handle the political responsibilities is to let them handle them, as the small number of women leaders move up, they are giving other women the chance to prove it. As Maureen Reagan said, "That's what a girls' network is," and that's what it's all about.

6. Other Women

For Hattie Caraway, getting along with women colleagues during her senatorial career was no particular problem.

In 1932 Caraway, an Arkansas Democrat, became the first woman elected in her own right to the Senate. She initially took her seat as her husband's successor: he had died during the previous term. An unobtrusive soul, she spent most of her time in the Senate knitting and doing crossword puzzles. Huey Long, the notorious Kingfish of Louisiana politics, had campaigned for her (he told her to give up her bright-colored dresses and wear somber black in respect for her dead husband), and once she had won the seat, reportedly she got her instructions on how to vote from the same local political bosses who had orchestrated her campaign. She apparently fulfilled their expectations satisfactorily and was reelected in 1938. She was most noticed by Washingtonians for her habit of coming to work on the streetcar, carrying her lunch with her in a brown paper bag, and for introducing the same bill, unsuccessfully, in practically every session— Senator Caraway wanted a parachute provided for each airline passenger. Otherwise, she didn't speak up much. "I haven't the heart to take a minute from the men," she was quoted as explaining. "The poor dears love it so."[1]

Nobody took Hattie Caraway very seriously as a senator, not even, it's tempting to speculate, Hattie Caraway herself. She was a useful tool for the men around her—presumably having Caraway succeed her husband saved a lot of tedious argument about who else would. Would she have put down her crossword puzzles if there had been a Nancy Kassebaum or a Barbara Mikulski present to act as a role model or rival?

Possibly. Possibly not. Maybe she figured she was doing her part just by being there. Margaret Chase Smith, elected in 1948, ten years after Caraway's reelection, was also the only woman in the Senate for much of the time she was there. However, she chose to play the game more the way the boys do. Originally, like Caraway, she came to office as a widow: her husband, Clyde Smith, died in 1940 at the end of his second term in Congress. She went on, however, to become a full-fledged politician in her own right. In all, she served eight years in Congress and then four full terms in the Senate. Like Hattie Caraway, she was not much for making speeches from the floor of the Senate, but unlike her, when she did stand up, she had something important to say. Her first real speech in the Senate, in 1950, was to condemn the junior senator from Wisconsin, Joe McCarthy, for his tactics of character assassination in his so-called crusade against Communism—thus becoming the first senator, Republican or Democrat, to speak up publically against him in the Senate. She joined in the 1960 week-long attempt to break the filibuster against the civil rights bill, sleeping on a cot in her office like her male colleagues, leaping up and dashing down the halls to answer the periodic roll calls. During one noteworthy overnight session she showed up in a red dress at 3:50 A.M. and a green one at 5:45 A.M. —apparently when the quorum bell clanged, she groped in her office coat closet and grabbed the first thing that came to hand.[2] Margaret Chase Smith lived in a man's world, and worked by men's rules.

Smith was accustomed to being the only woman around. With the numbers of women politicians increasing (fairly rapidly at the state and local level, much more slowly at the national), women today have to come to terms with working with each other. For some of them, there is a latent sense of comradeship, a feeling that their identity as women in some ways underlies their professional relationship, whether or not it happens to be the operative principle at any given moment. For others (often older women who made their way back when being a woman in politics was even tougher than it is today), gender is regarded simply as irrelevant, and whether allies or opponents are male or female makes no difference except that a militant young woman is somewhat more annoying than her male counterpart. But like it or not, political women are inevitably grouped together in the eyes of the world, and they have to come to terms with that one way or another.

There are those who say their very sparseness in the political mass is what makes the majority of women turn, at least to some extent, to each other. In particular, the initial impact of entering a legislature with its own peculiar customs and procedures can be daunting to almost anybody, male or female. The women have an additional hurdle: it is perfectly obvious that, for a long time, nobody ever planned on women being there at all.

Take the minor but exasperating business of toilet facilities. Everybody has to go to the bathroom from time to time, men and women, legislator or not. The need to go to the bathroom is always foreseen for the male officeholders but the need for equivalent facilities for women is all too often not. It was just a few years ago that the men's room in the New York state assembly chamber was divided in two to accommodate a women's room. Up until then, women legislators using alternative facilities elsewhere ran the risk of being late and being locked out of the chamber during an important vote.[3] In California, it is not surprising that the original plans for the state capitol building (erected in 1874) did not incorporate any facilities for women senators. It was irritating to many women that when the building was renovated over a six-year period ending in 1982 it took women senators to point out that the newly drawn-up renovation plans *still* didn't make any arrangements for the women who are here to stay in the senate. The authorities who initially worked out the requirements for the refurbishment apparently were oblivious to the omission. New York and California are not isolated glaring examples. It happens all the time.

Such confrontations with the unyielding masculinity of their surroundings do tend to foster womanly solidarity, at least initially. Kathy Stanwick, project director for the Center for the American Woman and Politics at Rutgers University, has been in a position to observe many women legislators, particularly at the state level. "You have some common ground once you're in office," she said. "One of the things that happens is that even if you view yourself as a Republican first, or a Democrat first, and a woman second, or as a legislator first and a woman second, it changes a little once you get into the institution. Remember, these are institutions which have been defined, created, and operated on premises that were developed by men. And, by the way, the institutions are still overwhelmingly dominated by men. I think when you get in there, it's difficult. Any new legislator, in any position, feels like an outsider. And so what you do, what the men do, is try to become more comfortable with your colleagues—your like-minded colleagues, or in this case, with other women."

How the women go about getting more comfortable with each other and their surroundings varies from woman to woman and place to place. Like people anywhere else, women in politics discover other women who become real friends. One woman legislator described a dear friend who happened to be of the opposite party, a confidant in thin times and thick, and added, "We share information sometimes—if either of our parties knew about it I think they would probably be very unhappy with both of us. But there's a difference between talking things over and using that information independently. We understand that."

Friendship comes where it comes; what most political women describe as their feelings for other women in their line of work is something partway between the intimacy of real friendship and the professional friendliness that is a hallmark of successful legislators and politicians in general—a businesslike purposive friendliness that is made up of courtesy, tact, and respect but that does not automatically imply a particularly personal relationship. Women can handle that and generally do with their male colleagues, but for most women, the relationship with other women is a little warmer.

Susan Bryant, a long-time Republican campaign consultant, feels that part of the reason is basic male-female differences in the quality of friendship in general. She talked about powerful men who discover, once they are no longer so powerful, that a lot of their erstwhile friends no longer have much time for them. "They forget that their friendships are based on power, and not on real true in-depth feeling. I'll tell you, that's the difference between the men and the women. Because when women feel they have friendships, they have all of the loyalties, and it's based on emotional needs, it's based on emotional support. The guys don't seem to have that. There are differences between men and women, and I think that's one of the differences."

This business of common loyalties often extends across party boundaries. In the world of realistic politics, Republican women like their male counterparts tend to spend more of their time, and form closer relationships, with other Republicans, and likewise the

Democrats tend to hang together. The nature of partisan politics in the United States underlies and reinforces it. Even so, occasionally an important issue that overrides party loyalties, or a particular friendship independent of issues, unites politicians of opposite persuasions. The main difference with women's latent sense of solidarity is that the issue that unites them grows out of their common experience as women functioning in the political arena, banging up against very similar frustrations. It doesn't seem to matter whether a woman's political persuasion is Democratic or Republican. She encounters obstacles that are much the same. The institutional preference for the status quo that keeps women isolated may be eroding around the edges, but it is far from gone.

According to several observers, what happens to the women is a gentle movement toward a more egalitarian attitude on women's issues. Celinda Lake, of WCF, looks at the process from her perspective as a pragmatic feminist. "The women who are kind of conservative or moderate Republican through liberal Democrat feel a certain bonding with each other," she said, "independent of knowing that they will disagree on things, but knowing also that they all are making sure that the women get to be committee chairs, or things like that. That's something that they all agree on. And knowing that you can't compare a liberal Democrat to a conservative Republican, I still see that the women conservative Republicans are much better on the things that women care about than the conservative male Republicans."

As Monica McFadden, a campaign consultant from the Democratic side and former staffer at the National Women's Political Caucus, sees it, this identity rises out of a sense of common experience and common purpose as women. "I have an awful lot of good Republican women for friends," she said. "Anne Stanley [a Republican campaign consultant], for example—she and I are friends. I can call Anne up—I mean, we're not the closest friends, but I can call her up and talk. I think she's funny and she thinks I'm funny, because we disagree on a lot of stuff. Same thing with many of the women. I guess the thing is that I have a certain amount of respect for them regardless, because of the fact that I may disagree with them, and a lot of times I do, but in their own way they too are fighting for the same common goal many of us are as women. Now a lot of Republican friends will argue over whether or not society has an obligation to open doors for them. And the Republicans say, 'Oh no. It's your job to make it on your own.' But they are willing to say that at least it has been helpful to them that others have helped open the door. And my point is, okay, you guys say there aren't programs needed, I'm the one who's going to say, yes, there are programs needed because you're lucky enough to have the door open for you—not everybody is. But we share that same thing: damn it, women have a place in this society."

Sometimes solidarity shows up right in the thick of the campaign. One woman consultant says she just plain enjoys campaigns, has spent long years out on the trail, and explains with zest, "It's like a team. Our team against their team. I'm sure it's the same kind of thing that attracts people to the military." But when a woman candidate, suspecting that an outside group was trying to play her off against her woman opponent, asked the consultant if she should call the opponent's camp to check, the consultant told her, "Yes, call them up. This is not war. You can talk to the manager of the other side."

What it adds up to is a more personal interest taken in the triumphs and defeats of other women, and the sense that they are somehow linked to your own, whether you are working from the same ideological principles or not. Senator Nancy Kassebaum of Kansas, talking about her experiences of speaking on the Senate floor, remembered the woman reporter who once told her that when she got up to speak she had immediate attention from all the women in the press gallery, and that "You don't realize, Senator, how many of us just really are cheering and hope you don't fall on your face." And it was not only the Republicans there who were doing the silent cheering.

Or Jan Meyers, Republican congresswoman from Kansas, who first won her seat in 1984. She campaigned as a Reagan Republican, and yet her face lights up when she talks about Geraldine Ferraro, who was running on the Democratic presidential ticket the same year. "I think it was a very positive thing for women, I really do," she said. "In the first place, just the fact that we would have a woman nominated as vice-president was a tremendous breakthrough. It will never seem quite as unusual again. That was very positive. The second thing was, she did have enormous difficulties and she handled herself very well. She didn't fall apart, she didn't get nervous, she didn't cry—she handled herself extremely well. So regardless of whether you agree or disagree with her politics or her philosophy or anything, I think it was a tremendous thing for women."

One of the obvious expressions of this conviction that women have interests in common, apart from partisan differences, comes in the formation of women's caucuses in legislatures across the country, taking in women from both parties. However, there does come a point where the connection as women is not strong enough to hold across basic policy disagreements: Gerry Ferraro reported that the Congresswomen's Caucus under the Carter administration had "spoken in one voice on women's issues, regardless of party affiliations."[4] With the arrival of the more conservative women who came in with Reagan, the unity collapsed. According to Ferraro, Republican Margaret Heckler, caucus cochairwoman, vetoed any criticism the caucus leveled at Reagan, which infuriated Ferraro and her liberal colleagues. In the end, the caucus split, became the Congressional Caucus for Women's Issues, and opened the membership to men. There are now about five times as many men as women in the Caucus, it is an influential and liberal voice on women's issues, but it no longer functions as it originally did, as a connection between disparate women.

Seeking to bypass the divisiveness of issues, in some states legislative women choose to get members from both parties together on a quasisocial basis, for regular lunches or dinners. Barbara Roberts, a Democrat and now secretary of state for Oregon, remembers that when she was in the state house of representatives and Republican Norma Paulus was the secretary of state, Paulus had a dinner every legislative session for all the women legislators, "so there was some kind of bonding that existed even with the women who were outside of our feminists' concern areas. It was enough of a link that at least it always afforded us politeness and communication, and even those women who may have disagreed strongly with us on issues of abortion choice, they were respectful, and I think we liked each other. That is a wonderful asset in the political process, to like someone and not feel uncomfortable with them as a person, even though you disagree with their politics." Roberts did suggest that although the bond between the Oregon women was very strong in the late 1970s and early 1980s, "stronger than the partisan bond, really," that was no longer true, "partly because women are so much a part of the system now that people don't make the distinction about male and female." In Oregon, where a woman is the speaker of the house of representatives, a woman is secretary of state, another is commissioner of the bureau of labor and industries, and yet another took 47 percent of the vote in the 1986 gubernatorial race, perhaps she is right, and the barriers *are* coming down, and with them the most compelling motivation for women to stand shoulder to shoulder together, even across party lines.

Optimistic as she may sound about the situation in Oregon, Barbara Roberts would still stop short of declaring the battle for political equality won. Most women still find their closest allies and supporters among other women, as women political activists have traditionally done since the days of the suffragists. This is especially true of women on the same side of any issue, where they are working together for the same goals and principles. Wendy Sherman, for example, who was campaign manager for Barbara Mikulski's senatorial campaign in 1986, says directly that she came to work on the campaign because she believed in the importance of Mikulski's vision of what could be accomplished and because of her personal ties to the candidate, not because she wanted a job as a campaign manager. "I am Barbara Mikulski's campaign manager because of Barbara Mikulski," she said flatly. "I'm not a professional campaign manager she hired."

By general agreement, Mikulski is as tough as they come. Wendy Sherman is more soft-spoken, but still no pushover. The campaign Sherman ran was nonetheless in some ways very much a woman's campaign. Wendy Sherman was good at making it all work. Pollster Harrison Hickman, who worked on that campaign, said, "We worked with twenty-five or twenty-six campaigns [in 1986] and Wendy Sherman was the best campaign manager we worked with." One of the things she was concerned with was the way people felt about each other, working under the boiler-room pressure of a major campaign. It's not something the male political pros talk much about, but it helped the Mikulski campaign hold together under heavy attack.

"Coming in, we knew who the top team was," Sherman said, "and the strategy group had worked together for quite some time, so we knew each other's foibles. On the campaign—and I'd like to think that this is one of the skills that I did bring to it—people knew each other's downfalls, but we tried to create an atmosphere to be in it together and sort of make up for each others' failings, to tease each other about them and to laugh about them rather than start destroying each other with them. Nobody is ever in any organization all the things that you hoped they would be. You either can let yourself be bothered by that to the point of it being destructive or you can understand that nobody's ever going to be all that you want them to be and as a group put all the pieces together."

The stereotypical woman is assumed to be more humane, generous, and responsive to others than her male equivalent, and maybe her virtues are not entirely fictional. Mary Matalin of the Republican National Committee said she feels as if the traditional women's virtues are creeping into the male workplace. "Maybe I'm just hearing this vis-à-vis the Committee," she said, "but what I think has happened is that we've been allowed to behave more as women. You used to have to behave as men: you had to be mean, you had to be tough, you couldn't be nurturing to your staff—and we get to do that now. Maybe it's because there are more women there, but you get to be kinder to your staff. We get to work in an atmosphere more rife with consensus and well-being—we're allowed to compromise and there is not all this black-and-white, turkey stuff. People want to work together. I am finding that as we are allowed to behave the way we naturally would behave with our families or whatever, the men are mellowing out a bit too, at least in our building."

It's worth remembering that Vera Katz, speaker of the Oregon house of representatives, talked about the more comfortable level of cooperation she received from most of her women colleagues ("they know that their turn will come and they won't play those power games") and obviously felt that their attitude made her work, and hence that of the house itself, go forward more smoothly. It may well be that the special relationships women politicians forge between themselves have something to add to the political climate as a whole.

．　　．　　．

When there were just a handful, it was probably easier to generalize about women politicians. As their numbers have increased, there have come to be exceptions to practically any rule anybody can come up with. Women politicians come in as many varieties as their male counterparts, and spread out rightward and leftward all along the political spectrum. For some of them, obviously, being a woman and thus part of a tiny political minority has more significance than it has for others. Helen Delich Bentley, for example, is currently a Republican congresswoman from Maryland. She spent twenty-four years of her working life on the Baltimore docks as a reporter and maritime editor for the Baltimore *Sun* and was later appointed by Nixon to the chairmanship of the Federal Maritime Commission. Dockland anywhere is a rough place, and Bentley is a brusque, blunt woman with a legendary vocabulary when pressed. (She has a white poodle named Bleep.) She has been the only woman doing the things she does since she was eighteen years old, running political campaigns in Nevada in the 1940s. This does not strike her as particularly important. "I never paid much attention to that," she says dismissively, and goes on to subjects she finds more interesting.

On the other hand, there is Nancy Kassebaum of Kansas, who emphasized in her first campaign for the Senate in 1978 that she would be a "fresh voice" in Washington, and Robert Dole, the senior senator from Kansas, toured the state for her pointing out that as the only woman in the Senate, her "fresh voice" would be heard more than that of other freshmen senators. Ten years later, Kassebaum takes obvious pleasure in the progress made by other women who started out in politics working on her campaign. "When I ran there was only one woman in the Kansas senate, Jan Meyers, who ran against me in the primary and is now, of course, in the House. And now there are six women in the Kansas senate, several who really got active and started in my campaign in '78. That's really what's interesting to me—to see women who had never been involved before and are now on city commissions and have gotten involved in school boards and so forth. That really has been rewarding."

Sometimes a woman who is not a politician herself may find herself in a position to give another woman a helping hand in the political world. Pat Schroeder of Colorado looks back at her earliest days as a congresswoman in Washington and suspects that a politician's wife may have been the one who eased her onto a committee that she would probably never have been assigned to otherwise. Her first choice for committee assignment was the powerful Armed Services Committee, for which she was anything but an automatic choice. Not only was she a woman, but this was 1972, when the Vietnam War was a painful issue, and she had run her campaign as an environmentalist and antiwar activist. She was not what the chairman had in mind, and he made his opposition plain. Pat Schroeder was assigned the committee regardless. She didn't know enough about congressional politics at the time to appreciate how remarkable the whole sequence of events was, but she's figured it out since, along with a theory of how it happened.

"I don't know for sure how it all worked," she said. "At that time, Ways and Means [Committee] made the choice, which meant really that Wilbur Mills [then Ways and Means chairman] pulled all the strings. I think what happened is that Wilbur Mills's wife was a very close friend of Elliot Janeway's wife—Elizabeth Janeway, who's written lots of books and is really a very savvy lady. And somehow (I found all this out after—*I* thought I got on the committee because I flew airplanes and all that), somehow Mrs. Janeway and Mrs. Mills heard about my campaign and were very interested in it. Apparently they just beat the stuffing out of Wilbur Mills, agitated him to no end, saying, 'Give this woman what she wants.' Because it was the first time anybody ever got on the committee over the objection of the chairman. I think the guardian angels were Elizabeth Janeway and Mrs. Mills. I even got this phone call—I think it was just before I was elected—I got this phone call from Wilbur Mills, wondering what he could do [to help]. I thought, what? You're calling me out here in Denver and I haven't a prayer? What *is* this all about? When I put it all together—well, now that I've been here a while, I know how very extraordinary that was."

Of course, it would be misleading to imply that all is sweetness and light with political women, hands clasped across the aisle and solidarity under all circumstances. Political women are politicians, and like any other politicians, their loyalty to party and partisan principles is not lightly put aside. Democrat Monica McFadden talked with warmth about her Republican political friends, but she also said, "Don't let any Democratic woman tell you she's really bipartisan. Phooey. She's not. She's a Democrat. And if it came down to a choice between a Republican woman and a Democratic man, she'd probably vote for the Democratic man."

Geraldine Ferraro campaigned against Republican women for Democratic men. In 1982, as a result of the redistricting following the 1980 census, incumbent Democratic congressman Barney Frank of Massachusetts was running against incumbent Republican congresswoman Margaret Heckler. Ferraro went to Massachusetts to campaign vigorously for Frank, primarily because Heckler was a firm supporter of Reaganomics, and Ferraro felt the Reagan budget was a woman's issue. She even made a TV commercial, pointing out her conviction that Frank cared more about the significant issues affecting women than Heckler did. She also campaigned in the New Jersey senatorial race for Democrat Frank Lautenberg, opposing Republican Millicent Fenwick, who had been a fellow congresswoman. However, as Ferrraro points out, she had supported Lindy Boggs's daughter in the Democratic primary. "Barbara Boggs Sigmund was the mayor of Princeton," she explained. "I've never gotten into a primary, but I supported her and did some campaigning. Only after the primary was I supporting Frank Lautenberg." As she saw it, Fenwick's record was unquestionably better than Heckler's, but even so, Fenwick had voted for most of the Reagan policies Ferraro didn't agree with—and she certainly would rather have one more Democratic senator than one more Republican, whatever the gender.

In her book, *Ferraro: My Story*, she reports her intervention led to sparks flying in the Members Dining Room during the lame-duck session of Congress following the election. Ferraro was having dinner with her Democratic women colleagues when Millicent Fenwick reproached her vigorously, declaring that what she had done to Peggy Heckler was a disgrace.

Ferraro says she told her she was sorry that Fenwick felt that way, but that she felt equally strongly that she had to support her own principles, that she disapproved very much of the president and his policies and thought Peggy Heckler was supporting the wrong issues.

Although she didn't bring up Ferraro's involvement in her own campaign, Millicent Fenwick, according to Ferraro, replied sharply, "We'll do that against you someday."[5] And for all their enthusiasm for the *fact* of a woman running, certain Republican women all across the country nevertheless campaigned vigorously for the Reagan-Bush ticket against Mondale-Ferraro. Pat Schroeder, a spirited advocate of women sticking together, was dismayed by the numbers of women of all political stripes who chose not to support Ferraro as the campaign wore on and the questions about her personal life multiplied. "Women felt they had to assert themselves: 'I'm not for her and I'm a woman.' Why would we do that? Couldn't we be at all happy about an image going to the next generation of women that they could set their sights higher?"[6]

In California, as in other states, the women's caucus steers away from issues that are likely to create dissension, according to Marian Bergeson, a Republican state senator. "The caucus concentrates on issues where we can find agreement," she said. "Child care, domestic violence, insurance problems—you know, all the various issues, particularly those that are strictly concerning women and children. Then on other issues we don't try to get involved. It is obvious that we have our various persuasions, that because of our constituencies we probably would not find a lot in common."

One recent issue that divided political women—although not in the same proportions as it divided the rest of the population—was the battle for ratification of the Equal Rights Amendment. Support of ERA remains one of the criteria for support by virtually all the women's PACs, but with little prospect of meaningful legislative activity, it has become more a statement of loyalty than anything else. As Monica McFadden put it, "Right now ERA becomes a litmus test and code for a whole set of attitudes."

When the campaign was at its height, however, in many places it was an extremely divisive issue. In 1977, Carmela Lacayo, then Democratic vice-chairman, blamed the ERA fight in part for the fact that as a result of the 1976 elections the number of women in Congress fell. "There seems to be a tendency in this country to divide and conquer women," she said. "Because of lack of unity and tremendous infighting among women, their political energy is dissipated. It traditionally was channeled toward election of viable women candidates."[7]

Even earlier, in 1974, Jeane Kirkpatrick reported that women state legislators found that carrying the Equal Rights Amendment in their legislatures—a labor undertaken in the cause of female solidarity—sometimes cost them dearly in terms of their relationships with their male colleagues. Said one such woman, "I got persuaded to carry the Equal Rights Amendment. I don't know how much of my credit I used up on that one. The men really didn't want it. They don't understand what it does and doesn't do, and they are afraid that it is going to do something that it shouldn't do."[8] For such women, who became acutely aware of the costs, it seems likely that there was a small sigh of relief once the battle was over, the issue became more or less symbolic, and the press for equality of women moved forward through less controversial channels.

Unfortunately, the issue that succeeded it in terms of creating problems for and among women politicians is the abortion controversy, which is, if anything, even more divisive. Most women in politics, functioning in a man's world, were sympathetic to ERA. They could see what it was all about, were prepared to dismiss as ridiculous or irrelevant the most-dire-case consequences imagined by ERA opponents, and, with some exceptions, when they were opposed to the constitutional amendment they were influenced as much by their constituents' attitudes and traditions as by their own hesitation. Taking a prochoice or prolife position involves taking a stand on a much more personal and private affair, requires arguing basic moral positions, and means that a pragmatic politician, female or male, has to face the inevitable fact that most of the opposition, whichever side is taken, will be committed to its stand as a matter of conscience and resistant to conversion. Whatever ERA came to mean to its supporters or opponents, it didn't literally mean life or death, whereas the very question of life and death is absolutely central to the abortion debate.

What most women politicians hoped, as the issue began to rise to a boil, was that the debate would not necessarily intrude as a dramatic theme in every campaign. Pat Schroeder, a committed feminist if there ever was one, suggested emphasizing other aspects of feminist policy on women's reproductive rights when she talked to would-be candidates under the auspices of the National Women's Political Caucus back in 1973. "You must also guard against being pushed into unreasonable or irresponsible extreme positions by your erstwhile supporters," she warned. "I was the only major candidate running in Denver last fall who would attend and speak at an abortion panel hearing held at a local college. But I was criticized by some women there when I tried to emphasize my support for birth control and family-planning programs, rather than an 'abortion on demand' policy. It is all too easy to become a 'kamikaze candidate'—crashing and burning on one or two emotionally packed issues."[9]

Eleven years later Gerry Ferraro was practically pilloried in public for her prochoice position, which she had carefully not emphasized, particularly because she was a practicing Catholic and felt compelled to look at the issue differently in her private and public lives. In her book written after the election, she explained, "Personally, I have always been against abortion. But my election as a public official who would set policy had forced me to face the issue, to take a stand, one way or the other, on legalized abortion. Could I, in good conscience, make the decision to continue or terminate a pregnancy for somebody else? Coming down on the side of choice, concluding that the decision had to be between a woman and her own conscience, had been very difficult for me."[10] It was also very expensive politically, not only because of votes lost from people who disagreed with her, but because so much precious campaigning time had to be diverted from themes the Mondale-Ferraro team needed to emphasize into frustrating circular arguments about her prochoice stance and the place of the church in secular politics.

The increasing presence of single-issue activists and the conflict in state Republican party organizations between the generally more moderate established party leaders and the religious far right, only recently a significant presence in mainstream politics outside the South, keeps the abortion issue on the front burner for many women politicians across the country. As Celinda Lake of the Women's Campaign Fund, a prochoice, pro-ERA PAC, pointed out, prochoice women are particularly vulnerable to pressure tactics. "It's a real threat to these women, because women candidates are hit much harder. After all, it's supposed to be women who are keepers of morality and they really get hit hard by these right-wing candidates."

On the other side of the issue, women like Congresswoman Mary Rose Oakar, a Democrat from Ohio in her sixth term, find themselves isolated from the primary sources of finance from the women's community. Oakar is solidly liberal on economic issues, active in several women's organizations, and yet is opposed to abortion, and therefore ineligible for assistance from PACs like the WCF, who agree that she is genuinely a woman's advocate in every other way. According to Kathy Stanwick, who has spent years following the development of the PACs in the women's community, the decision about handling the abortion issue hasn't come easily to any of them.

"I think one of the things that's very interesting about the abortion issue is that it's one that's torn apart all of the women's PACs from time to time," she said. "It's particularly a sensitive issue when you're dealing with supporting candidates. You have candidates who are just terrific on a whole bunch of other issues and then what happens if they're wrong on that issue? And I know that in the late '70s the Women's Campaign Fund board of directors almost had an organizational split over that issue. It's very difficult. All the PACs have grappled with the issue. It's *very* difficult when somebody is running in a particular kind of district for them to take a prochoice position."

The issue remains unresolved and, one suspects, unresolvable. Mary Rose Oakar announced in 1986 that she was going to organize a PAC that would support women candidates who are liberal on economic issues and presumably supportive of equal rights, leaving the abortion issue out of it. More than one political woman said that she waited hopefully for the day when enough votes had been counted so that the issue would recede and a woman could follow her own conscience and let other issues monopolize the headlines.

Even if the abortion debate magically vanished, there would still be plenty of dissension about how the goal of electing more women can most usefully be pursued. Again, it is a particularly sensitive issue for the women's PACs because they are in the business of endorsing candidates and deciding how much of their limited resources goes to whom. One continuing problem for bipartisan groups, given the conservative climate of the Reagan administration and the Republican party as a whole, is finding viable Republican candidates who are "good on the issues," which means pro-ERA and prochoice. Furthermore, there are many in the women's community who felt that the Republican economic programs introduced by the Reagan administration early in the first term were plainly antiwoman, and electing more Republicans simply gave more votes to the administration and its allies at the state level to pursue policies of which they disapproved.

In 1982, the PAC affiliated with NOW decided that being feminist was more important than being female, and further, in Congressional races, being Democratic was critical to avoid a Republican majority that would give vital committee chairmanships to conservative Republican men. These conclusions brought them to support a longtime Democratic congressional incumbent in New Jersey, James Howard, against a Republican woman challenger, and in the senate race to support Democrat Frank Lautenberg against Millicent Fenwick, as did Gerry Ferraro. Fenwick was then a Republican congresswoman and had voted for some of Reagan's policies, but was otherwise a fairly liberal Republican. In her race Fenwick was underfunded—she could spend only $2.6 million compared to Lautenberg's $6.4 million—which crippled her in communicating with the voters in New Jersey, a state in which media buys have to be made in both the expensive New York City and Philadelphia suburban areas. Even so, she managed to get 48 percent of the vote.

For the Washington-based WCF, which only endorses and funds women and makes a determined effort to remain truly bipartisan, the difficult decisions about choosing to fund a good man running against a less acceptable woman don't arise. If a woman does not meet their criteria, they stay out of the race altogether. Woman-woman races are another story. "There aren't that many, at least there have not in the past been that many woman-woman races," Celinda Lake said. "Now it's going to start to be increasingly more of a challenge." The three all-woman races that held the nation's attention in 1986 were the Nebraska gubernatorial race between Republican Kay Orr and Democrat Helen Boosalis and the two Maryland races: the senatorial contest between Democrat Barbara Mikulski and Republican Linda Chavez and the congressional contest between Republican Helen Delich Bentley and Democrat Kathleen Kennedy Townsend. In terms of women's issues, in all three races the choices were clear-cut. Both Nebraska women were prolife, so neither was supported; Kay Orr is now governor. In Maryland the prochoice, pro-ERA PACs viewed both Mikulski (who won) and Townsend (who didn't) as clearly superior in their stand on women's issues to their Republican opponents.

In the future, the problem of women challenging women incumbents is one that will clearly have to be addressed. In the past, many women have backed away from those contests. In the early 1980s, at a series of conferences sponsored by Rutgers University's Center for the American Woman and Politics (CAWP), California state legislator Teresa Hughes talked about "an unwritten code of ethics" that prohibited woman legislators (who with increasing frequency contribute to other women's campaigns) from giving money against a woman incumbent. At that time, Hughes said, "I did not give any money against any incumbent women candidates of the opposing party. And I think if we have that kind of understanding among women, we can go a heck of a long way and we still don't do anything to get us into the bad graces of our own political party."[11] As time goes on, and there are more women incumbents to challenge, it seems inevitable that the issue will arise more and more often. After all, it is only logical for an ambitious woman to figure that if her district has elected one woman, it might well be inclined to elect another.

What almost all politically active women would agree, in spite of all the disagreement about credentials, specific issues, and tactics, is that it is crucial to get more women into the political system, however it's done. As Sandy Smoley, then a Sacramento County Supervisor, said in the CAWP conference, "I'd rather have a woman who *is* a woman and feels like a woman than a man who says he thinks like a woman. In order to think like a woman, you've got to be a woman. And I'd rather put my money on a woman. Because when the chips are down, her thought processes are different. She approaches problem solving differently. She *is* different."[12]

■　　■　　■

With the women's PAC community well established in the late 1980s, it seems odd to realize that only ten years earlier women were debating vigorously among themselves whether or not there should be women's PACs at all. Although the earliest women's PACs were mainly supportive of feminist candidates, PACs sponsoring women now cover a much wider range. There are strictly partisan PACs affiliated directly with the major parties and PACs that are equally strictly partisan but independent of the party structures. There are PACs associated with various vocations—the American Nurses Association PAC, for example, or the Business and Professional Women's PAC.

The oldest of the PACs set up specifically to fund women is the Women's Campaign Fund, which began in 1974 as an outgrowth of the women's political movement that had started in the late 1960s—an obvious recognition that if the movement was going to encourage women's participation in politics, it was necessary to provide money for women candidates. The most direct, and largely untapped, source of funds was other women, most of whom—even the growing number of business and professional women who earned considerable salaries themselves—still believed that a ten dollar donation was very generous. Educating women about the facts of political financial life has of necessity been an important element in WCF activity and, indeed, the activity of all PACs drawing contributions primarily from women. Many of the women who were originally involved in organizing the NWPC (which now has a PAC of its own) were also involved in the organization of the WCF, and the two organizations have very much the same general focus: both are committed to bipartisanism, and both support women who believe in social, economic, and political parity for women.

In its first years, the WCF was fairly small. According to Kathy Stanwick, who has followed the development of the women's PACs closely, it took three or four years for the WCF to become known to women who were thinking about running for office. By 1980, the WCF had a solid reputation, not only in the women's political community, but in the Washington network of other PACs, so that when a woman came to Washington in search of funding she would automatically be referred to the WCF.

During the years in which the WCF was establishing itself, the ERA campaign was also in full tilt and in perpetual need of additional funds. Even so, when national NOW delegates gathered at their conference and president Ellie Smeal proposed setting up a PAC of their own, she ran into considerable resistance. "You might not believe this," she says now, "but in 1977, the first time I ran for president, I fought like hell to get permission to form a PAC through our national conference. It was unpopular, it was viewed as 'politics are dirty and campaign fund-raising is dirty and if the feminist movement gets into it we will just get like the rest of them.' It doesn't seem possible that ten years ago this was an argument, or that I had a close vote coming through a conference to get my PAC started." Once NOW got into PAC development, they did it in a big way: NOW has two national PACs, one that gives to federal races and one that gives to state and local candidates. There are also seventy-five PACs affiliated with state or local chapters of NOW.

By the late 1970s, the visible success of the WCF was making more people think about the possibilities it suggested. As Kathy

Stanwick explained it, "Here was a bipartisan group, and the candidates that received support from that group had to adhere to certain issue positions, had to have a certain kind of a perspective on women and women's role in society. So then what happened is that both the Republicans and the Democrats recognized that there were many of their candidates who perhaps wouldn't necessarily qualify—Mary Rose Oakar, for the Democrats, is a perfect example. So what they did of course is they began their own political action efforts."

The parties' fund-raising, like the WCF and the early NOW efforts, was targeted primarily at the national and statewide races, and with limited resources this meant that very little trickled down to the state legislative level. The next step, therefore, was the formation of state and local PACs, to fill that gap. Staffed by volunteers, many of them started out with more enthusiasm than pragmatic experience and believed it would be possible to carry out broad agendas and give enough money to influence races all the way from the city council to Congress. They learned otherwise fairly promptly.

"I was personally involved in setting up the PAC here in New Jersey," Kathy Stanwick said, "and we quickly made the decision that we should target our resources to the state legislative level, and a number of the other PACs have had to focus, or target, their activity as well. I think you have to make the decision that if you really want to be able to make a significant difference in some people's races you have to make a commitment to contributing some large sums of money, because clearly that's what's going to make a difference. That's one aspect of it. I think the other aspect is that most of these organizations do not have staff. It's based on voluntary activity. You've got very very busy professional women, and to do the kind of research it takes to really understand the dimensions of what a particular race is all about requires an awful lot of work."

A lot of work it may be, but involvement in a women's PAC appears to be one of the fastest ways to educate women in the methods and working rules of practical politics. For one thing, any woman who starts learning about campaign finance rapidly discovers how absolutely vital money is in political efforts. There is no getting around the fact that the best candidate in the world isn't going very far without sufficient resources to enable her to get the message out to the voters. Given present-day media costs, this means that adequate fund-raising for women at any level is vital, and fund-raising for the major races has to be extremely sophisticated. One of the great successes of the 1986 women's campaign season was that the women candidates, and the women's PACs that supported them, clearly had grasped that point. In general, candidates across the board were more experienced than their predecessors had been, and one of the things they had learned from their experience was to be realistic about costs and fund-raising. In 1986 women candidates were financially viable to a degree they had never been before.

"We tell our candidates they should spend 60 percent of their time fund-raising," Celinda Lake said matter-of-factly. "It's an incredible prioritization. This country spent a billion dollars on campaigns in 1986—it's an incredible allocation of resources. But I guess one of the things we feel as an organization is that we can't change the scale, we just have to win by it."

The newest development in women's PACs has been the organization of two political action committees that are very different from each other in focus and structure but that have both started out on the principle that it takes big money to make a significant impact and that women can raise the big bucks.

The first of the committees, originally organized in 1984 but making its first significant impact in 1986, is the Hollywood Women's Political Committee, made up of seventy-two women, among whom are such luminaries as Jane Fonda, Sally Field, Whoopi Goldberg, Barbra Streisand, and other women working "in the industry" whose names may not be as recognizable but who are powers behind the scenes—movie and television producers, directors, executives, lawyers, and agents. As Susan A. Grode, an entertainment lawyer who is on the HWPC policy committee, put it, "This is not a group of ladies who have lunch."[13] Although the membership of the HWPC is all female, it accepts contributions from men and donates to men's campaigns. Each member pays dues of fifteen hundred dollars yearly (members under thirty pay five hundred dollars). The money goes to liberal causes and to Democratic candidates, in 1986 primarily to Democratic senatorial candidates. In fact, in 1986, the women of Hollywood became the single largest contributor to Democratic Senate candidates, dispensing more than $2 million. Some men were skeptical of the group's credibility in the early stages, but such extravaganzas as Barbra

Streisand's "Regain the Senate" concert, which brought $1.5 million into the treasury in one night, converted the disbelievers. "When you're effective, there's respect," Grode observed blandly.[14]

HWPC gave large donations to both Barbara Mikulski and Harriett Woods of Missouri, along with other donations to men who were Democratic Senate candidates—and refused donations to three other men who did not share the group's prochoice position. "We're not against these people. We want them to win their seats," said Bonnie Reiss, another entertainment lawyer and policy committee member. "But we're very careful that the people we give money to are consistent on our issues."[15]

HWPC demonstrates that women have taken the point that major donors command attention and respect, while the other new women's PAC shows that women are learning it's not only how much, but also *when*, that counts in political donations. EMILY's List was founded in 1985 by Ellen Malcolm, drawing together a membership primarily made up of business and professional women who would pay one hundred dollars to join and pledge to donate one hundred dollars more to at least two women Democratic candidates running for the Senate. In 1986, there were fifteen hundred women who contributed altogether $350,000 to Mikulski and Woods. The significant thing about the contributions from EMILY's List, according to Ellen Malcolm, was that the money came in early. (The acronym, after all, is Early Money Is Like Yeast.) "When women candidates have significant money early in their races, they can then go to traditional sources of campaign support from a much more powerful position," Malcolm explained. "With that early money, women's candidacies are more viable. Although women can't contribute the total of $4 million it takes to run for the U.S. Senate, women's money up front can enable women candidates to raise that money from traditional funders."[16]

EMILY's List, for example, contributed 20 percent of Barbara Mikulski's early money: the members contributed twenty-five thousand to both Mikulski and Harriett Woods during the first three weeks of February, when the money was most needed. "In the early days of Mikulski's campaign, even though the polls showed her 20 points ahead of her primary opponent, Congressman Mike Barnes, the conventional wisdom among the 'old boys' was that Mikulski couldn't raise the money to win," Malcolm said. "We all worked hard to raise as much money as Barnes so that Mikulski could prove her financial viability, and she did raise as much as Barnes on her first quarter FEC report."[17]

Out of the dazzling high-stakes spotlight of the new women's PACs, the old established firms like the WCF serve a slightly different function. Their job is not only to come up with money, but to temper the enthusiasm of women making their way through the system with instruction in the practical realities of politics. "I think you started out with a great many idealistic people who were very cause-oriented," Stephanie Solein, formerly political director at the WCF, said thoughtfully. "The idealism is still there, but I think we've realized that we've got to be pragmatic and sophisticated, and play the way the boys play or we're not going to ever be a part of it."

Once they choose their candidates to support, Celinda Lake says they stick with them. "That's one of the things we tell our candidates," she said cheerfully. "We set priorities and we say, you know, if this were AMPAC or something, if they don't like you they can leave you because they've got sixty other candidates competing for their money. There aren't that many women running. We've got nowhere else to go, so we're going to be in this to the end. It's going to be a toughlove program." In the course of their toughlove, they educate, counsel, refer their candidates to other PACs who can come up with more money (in fact one of their most valuable services to candidates is to open doors to other financial sources for them), inevitably argue some, and send out the checks that help keep the whole show on the road—and at the end of the election cycle they count their successes, their bruises, and so far, discover each time they're a little further ahead than they were after the last election.

Looking back at the 1986 election, Celinda Lake remarked bluntly that the results were mixed. "Some good news and some bad news," she said. "I guess realistically the victories were that we're holding our own in Congress, which is very good. We're a prochoice, pro-ERA PAC so we were very pleased with the strength of those candidacies and the fact that the five new members are all good on our issues at a time when it's supposed to be an impossible context for those issues. We were very pleased with the viability of the races the women ran, the amount of money they raised, the kinds of campaigns they put together, the seasoned politicians that they demonstrated that they are."

Increasingly then, many of the women in politics are learning how they can most significantly give support to each other and how to shape a framework for mutual action. In some ways it's a less cozy framework than it might have been in the early days, when most women were political innocents, and believing in the same things seemed to be the only important issue. Women politicians have become much more knowledgeable now and much less willing to spend time messing around with amateurs dabbling at the game.

"I met with Dianne Feinstein in San Francisco a couple of years ago," Stephanie Solein said. "One of the things we were talking to her about was our recruitment program, and she said, just promise me one thing, that you are going to identify women who are in this for the long haul. We don't need any more flashes in the pan. We need women who understand that if they are going to be taken seriously in politics and they are going to be successful they've got to get into it and make it a career and chart their course. Men have understood this since the beginning of time."

The current crop of political women is starting to learn that too. It is satisfyingly appropriate that their most effective guides are turning out to be other women who have figured it out themselves and can point out the handholds on the slippery slope that they themselves are climbing.

7. The Retrospective View

There are a lot of different ways of looking at the political world—two of the most obvious being from the outside in and from the inside out. But perhaps one of the more intriguing perspectives is the view of those who have been on the inside and are now out, whether temporarily or permanently, by choice or involuntarily. There are quite a few women among those experienced outsiders now, old hands watching from the sidelines, looking back with more detachment than would ever have been possible when they were actively engaged, maybe even with a flash of nostalgia now and then. They knew the excitement and insecurity of being in the game; they were there. When they look back, they see their political lives illuminated by their own idiosyncratic light: the things that got to them, the giddy successes, the odd details that memory tenaciously retains—maybe the pattern on the wallpaper or the drapes in a room where they doodled on the edge of papers and discussed the possible ramifications of insignificant, or crucially important, issues.

Jeane Kirkpatrick remembers a mouse.

It was obviously a very enterprising mouse; it had found its way into the Situation Room, in the basement of the White House West Wing, where the door is locked even to those with White House passes. Kirkpatrick was there as ambassador to the United Nations, sitting with the others at the small table in that rather small room, at one of the fairly regular meetings of the foreign policy makers of the United States: the president, the secretaries of state and defense, the head of the joint chiefs of staff, the national security advisor, and the director of the CIA. It is less clear why the mouse was there. When Jeane Kirkpatrick noticed it, it was slowly making its

158

way across the floor. Somebody else noticed it about the same time, she remembers. "A mouse?" someone said. "In the Situation Room?" But there it was. And she remembers thinking to herself later, "It might be that that mouse was no more surprising a creature to see in the Situation Room than I was."[1] For not only was she the only woman at that table then, she was the only woman who had ever had a place of her own there.

Jeane Kirkpatrick occupies a curious position on the American political scene. She is one of the very few women in politics whose name is recognizable to the general public, but among women politicians she is an anomaly—she came straight from the amateur ranks, as a professor of political science at Georgetown University in Washington, to a cabinet-level presidential appointment as the U.S. Permanent Representative to the United Nations. It is a career path far more typical of a man than of a woman. Most women politicians have put in their time at the lower levels before getting anywhere near significant policy-making power.

Throughout Reagan's first term, Jeane Kirkpatrick was America's voice in the world community, and she takes understandable pride in being the first woman ever to have had a significant official voice in shaping American foreign policy. She might have been secretary of state instead—most knowledgeable observers believe that she would have liked to have been. Under another conservative Republican administration, she may yet be. As far as that goes, when the Republican field of presidential hopefuls was gathering, she was mentioned fairly often as a credible possibility herself. What is odd about it is that her career as a public servant was actually very short: her four years' service at the United Nations was the only time when she was not in private life, as an academic, a wife, and mother. She has never campaigned for office. It was only in 1981, when she was fifty-five years old, that she stepped onto the stage of world politics.

She is quite frank about her reaction to living on that stage. From her comfortable corner office in the American Enterprise Institute for Public Policy Research, a conservative Washington think tank, she looks back at her public life with some distaste. "It is certainly true and I would happily say on the record that high politics is a harsher, dirtier, more devious kind of enterprise than I thought," she said. "I don't mean that everybody behaves badly. I do mean

that the competition for position includes more people who do
some sleazy things, some downright dishonest things, than certainly
in any other activity that I've ever been engaged in. I think this is
particularly unpleasant to women. I don't think I'm the only person, the only woman, to find it very unpleasant, either."

She found herself in an overwhelmingly male environment. As
she quickly discovered to her surprise after her appointment, not
only was she the first woman appointed to head the United States
mission to the UN, she was the first woman to be a chief of
mission of *any* Western country. "These facts alone," she once
wrote, "make it clear that the United Nations, like the Situation
Room, has been a male preserve. Male preemption of international
affairs is so ubiquitous, so 'normal,' so taken for granted that it is
invisible even to most women accustomed to thinking unthinkable
thoughts about sex roles."[2]

"I think high politics is as male as a locker room," she said later,
in the quiet of her office, above the noise of Washington traffic in
the street below. It was then over three years since she had left the
UN. "I speak now as the mother of three sons, so I know quite a bit
about locker room environments. I lived in a locker room environment with my husband and three sons through their teen years, and
the culture is, I suspect, not very attractive to most women. Now
that is to say that women differ from men in some significant ways.
I don't know—I can't prove it, but I think it's so. I also think that in
our culture, in our times, maybe even the women who get to high
places in politics don't *need* power in the way that some of the
men who hang in and compete do. I don't mean 'fire in the belly.' I
mean need power. I think needing power is something different.
'Fire in the belly' is about anything that you care deeply about. It's
not necessarily the drive to succeed and to reach the top—it may be
any one of a hundred other things that one cares about. I don't
know why (and there's a lot about this that cannot be proved: I'm
not even sure that it's true—I hold these views very tentatively) but I
think, for whatever reasons, there are fewer women who seem to
need power than there are men. So women can resign—leave
power—and not feel the enormous sense of loss.

"Believe me, people are always saying to me, 'Don't you miss the
UN and the excitement?' My response is, 'Are you kidding?' The
answer is no. I don't miss that kind of excitement. That kind of

excitement—many aspects of it were fascinating. It was a fascinating experience. I've never learned so much in five years in my life. But, also, it was tremendously draining, consuming, just plain tiring and frustrating."

Jeane Kirkpatrick is a strong woman with a fine mind. Her husband, a professor and political scientist himself, has said that her intelligence was one of the things that drew him to her in the first place: she was knowledgeable. "I could discuss things and get an intelligent response from her," he said. "She's a handsome woman—and that's not without significance—but the other was the real attraction."[3] It was the strength of her political arguments that attracted Ronald Reagan's attention to her in 1979 when he was a presidential candidate. As well as being a professor at Georgetown University, she was a resident scholar at the American Enterprise Institute and a prime mover in the formation of a new political group now most generally known as the neoconservatives. Reagan was impressed by one of her articles, and she became a foreign-policy adviser in his campaign. When he was elected, he asked her to take the ambassadorship to the UN. She was still then a Democrat—in fact, she had been the vice-chairman of the committee on vice-presidential selection in 1972 and a member of the credentials committee for the Democratic National Convention in 1976. Nonetheless, foreign policy was her specialty, and Reagan wanted her voice as one of those advising him.

For the other men in her new political world—who are probably, on balance, about as bright as any miscellaneous group of executives anywhere, but not noticeably more so—the overwhelming fact about her was, and continues to be, her intelligence. It apparently renders her "genderless," some men have suggested admiringly—a back-handed compliment, if there ever was one. Whether or not they agree with her opinions, her supporters and adversaries concur in the recognition that she comes to her conclusions thoughtfully. Like anyone who thinks seriously about issues, she is known to change her mind. She gets a little testy when challenged about it. "I am *not* opinionated," she has said. "Opinionated means having an unchanging, narrow frame of reference. I form opinions slowly and revise my analysis along the way."[4]

She was a thinker, a scholar. To go from the academic world—in which, it's perfectly true, she had a considerable reputation, but it was still a reputation in a private world—to the publicity of the front pages, where everybody not only wanted to know every personal detail about her but apparently felt they had the right to know, was disconcerting and exasperating. "It was very interesting to go from private life to public life, from being a very private person into a very public role," she said in retrospect. "I took over in January, 1981. The president appointed me before the inauguration, so I went through the two inaugurations. There was a lot I didn't know about what I was going to and there's a lot I was reluctant to believe. I did not understand then, quite frankly, why people in public life should be as interesting to the public as they turn out to be. I still don't. I wrote in a book recently that I thought we Americans both underpaid and overfeted public officials."

She paused thoughtfully, looking back. "I found it difficult to lose privacy," she said. "I found it difficult to understand that I really was not permitted private opinions while I was in that public role. I could *say*, 'This is strictly a personal opinion,' but in fact it got attached to the Reagan administration, to the president. So it required a very intense level of discretion. What I found most shocking about dealing with the press was that very often there was less interest in what one meant, or what one thought, than in what one could be tricked into saying. I learned very quickly that dealing with the press is like walking through minefields. I think I became more skillful at it, but it's not the kind of communication I like best. I find it very pleasant to return to being a private person," she said comfortably.

Quite apart from the obligatory dealings with the press, working at the United Nations is tremendously demanding. Kirkpatrick is matter-of-fact about it. "I can tell you it takes a sixteen-hour day and a seven-day week and a fifty-two-week year," she said. "It takes all the time there is." Jill Schuker, who was counselor for press and public affairs to Kirkpatrick's predecessor, Donald F. McHenry, agreed. "People keep saying nothing is like politics, but nothing really is," Schuker said, years after her stint in New York. "I felt that particularly when I was at the State Department and at the UN. In fact, I talked to Jeane Kirkpatrick about this, because she was coming into the UN as I was leaving with Don McHenry. I remember one conversation we had—we were talking about what is life like at the UN—and I said the thing about international politics is that someone is awake somewhere making trouble twenty-four hours a day. There is some part of the world that isn't sleeping regardless of what you're doing: it's always in process somewhere."

Not all of Kirkpatrick's adversaries were international. As she has said, flashing a sense of humor that people who have encountered her only on a formal basis may not have expected, "Becoming ambassador to the United Nations was quite an ordeal. I remember people chanting and waving death masks. And that was just the White House staff."[5] Some of her colleagues were unprepared to deal with a woman as a peer and chose to try to undermine her position. Other difficulties had nothing to do with sexism, stemming instead from frank differences of opinion about policy. It was no secret that she had her disagreements with other members of the cabinet, George Shultz and Caspar Weinberger being most frequently mentioned. She is in no doubt that part of her difficulties were gender-based. As she has written, "I think sexism is alive in the U.S. government; it's alive in American politics. It's alive at the United Nations; it's bipartisan."[6] In the end, she got tired of the wrangling and struggling, the long hours and the constant pressure, both on stage and behind the scenes, and she left. The men remained.

"That's also interesting to me," she said, musingly. "The number of women who make it, make it to high levels and who quit. Leave. Resign. The percent of women who say at some point, 'I've had enough of this,' is, I think, probably significantly higher than men. I can't prove this. I met Juanita Kreps since I've been out of office. She was President Carter's secretary of commerce. She quit, just as I quit. I look at the congresswoman from Prince George's County [part of the Washington suburban area in Maryland], Marjorie Holt, who was one of the congresswomen who had enough seniority to have achieved some position of influence there, who quit. Edith Green, a Democrat from Oregon years ago, was the only woman in the Congress who was chairman of a major committee. She quit."

Plainly Jeane Kirkpatrick is, and sees herself as, a trailblazer for other women who will come along later. She doesn't see any other women there now. As she said flatly, "There isn't [any other woman] in the foreign policy apparatus. I was the first and the last. It may be a long time before there's another." As evidence, she pointed to the "bubble" at the 1986 Reykjavik summit. "High-security communications in embassies overseas (or for that matter, in New York we had one) take place in special security areas that are encased in plastic and air," she explained. "You remember Maxwell Smart, when they said, 'Come on, chief, let's go into the bubble.' There *is* something like a bubble. It's a room, it's permanent—at least the facilities that I'm aware of in U.S. embassies are permanent—but it is inflated by air, so it's a plastic room that's a foot off the ground. You don't touch the ground, you don't touch the walls, it can't be bugged. Everything is translucent so you can see everything that's there at all times and you can talk without reasonable fear of being overheard. And at Reykjavik, although George Shultz had a woman there, she was not inside the bubble. This is a fact. The bubble had limited space, there was only room for six people in the bubble or something. No woman, I'm told by very good friends who *were* in the bubble, was ever in the bubble."

It is perhaps an interesting example of the difficulty in determining what really is going on in Washington circles to note that Rozanne Ridgway, Shultz's assistant secretary of state for Europe and Canada, who was at Reykjavik, said very matter-of-factly that she was indeed in the bubble and that it was no big deal. "They are small," she said, "and certain people went in in shifts. I've been the woman in the bubble now for about twelve years or so." She added that the bubble is unfortunately no longer completely secure. "The bubble is old technology. It represents what we know about Soviet espionage techniques. The new embassy in Moscow, to the extent that I can talk about it, represents a level of technology we have not seen before. So the conclusion has been that it would not be possible to fully protect yourself through certain bubble technologies. You just have to get rid of parts of the building."

Whether women are currently in or out of the bubble (or its even more secret successors), Kirkpatrick sees some evidence that the tide of male exclusivity in the political arena is sluggishly changing. Take Gerry Ferraro, for example, and her place on the presidential ticket. "I think it put women forward," she said. "I really do. I think that every time a barrier like this is broken, it moves women forward. Geraldine Ferraro broke the barrier at the vice-presidential level, and it's broken now. It's not a hypothetical question any more to talk about a woman for vice-president. It's only hypothetical to talk about a woman running for president, because no woman ever did it, no serious woman. Yes, Shirley Chisholm did it, Victoria Woodhull on a free left platform, but not seriously. Under normal circumstances a woman who desires to be vice-president would have to run for president—just as a man who desired to be vice-president would have to run for the presidency."

Whether Jeane Kirkpatrick herself would be that woman continued to intrigue party pros on both sides of the line as the vast field of declared and semideclared presidential candidates jockeyed for position. What she said at the time was firm, carefully phrased, and ambiguous. "I am not a candidate and I don't intend to become a candidate, and I don't rule out being a candidate. And that's all true at the same time," she added. "If I were to decide to run for president it would not be a symbolic race. It would be a serious race in which my intention would be to win the nomination, no question about that. Otherwise, I wouldn't do it."

．　　　．　　　．

Jeane Kirkpatrick was closer to the center of power—at least as far as foreign policy goes—than any woman before her, and so when she looks back at her years as a public servant she looks back at a political landscape that is different in some ways from the scene other women remember. Still, there are undeniable similarities.

Take the matter of privacy, of feeling that there are eyes constantly watching you, waiting to catch a slip. Kirkpatrick was stepping through what she called "minefields" with the national and international press; Betty Heitman, former cochairman of the Republican National Committee, was expected to carry out her job with suitable decorum in front of the no less critical eyes of Republican activists across the country—and even the public at large, as her successor Maureen Reagan discovered when she spoke out about her opinion of some of the central figures of the Iran-contra scandal and found she was suddenly front-page news. It was a burden Heitman gratefully put down. "It's a nice feeling not to feel like you have to watch every word you say and everything that you do for fear that you will reflect poorly on the party," she said, her voice still carrying the flavor of her native Louisiana. "There's a great deal of pressure knowing that."

On the other hand, as Carol Bellamy pointed out, there is celebrity and celebrity. Once accustomed to being recognized, it can be even more disconcerting not to be. For eight years she was president of the New York City Council, a familiar figure in the city's convoluted politics. Then, in 1985, she took on Mayor Edward Koch in the mayoral Democratic primary and lost. She began a new career as an investment banker, and settling into her unaccustomed status as a private citizen, happened to travel through New York's La Guardia airport. "I was clearly recognized at the security gate," she said. "The first woman looked at me and said, 'Don't you play tennis?' And the other woman said, 'No, she's the Brooklyn district attorney.' So one thought I was Billie Jean King and the other thought I was Elizabeth Holtzman!"

Obviously, there's a difference between resigning, as Betty Heitman did, and losing an election, as Carol Bellamy did. (Jeane Kirkpatrick's resignation probably forms a third category—by most reports, she had hoped to have been offered another major appointment when she left the UN and only returned to private life when nothing sufficiently interesting was forthcoming.) Most politicians, male or female, would clearly prefer to be able to choose the time for an exit themselves. Even so, the final decision may not be an easy one to make. Margaret Hance, who was the mayor of Phoenix for ten years, felt she had to get away from town altogether to see things clearly when she was contemplating the possibility of retirement in 1983. She was close to sixty and had been in public service ever since 1971, the year after she was widowed. In many ways she felt she'd had enough. "You kind of wish you could go out to dinner without having everyone look at you," she said, but in spite of that, giving up the challenge and prestige of office wasn't a simple business. "It was tough to reach the decision not to run again," she said frankly. "I remember I decided to make up my mind while I was away from the office. And at a convenient time I was head of a delegation of mayors to Israel, at the invitation of the mayor of Jerusalem—so I made my decision on that trip. Having been worried about it for some months, it was great to get away and get the distance between me and the office so that I could reach what I hoped was a good decision. It was really a great relief when I made the decision and came back and announced it. I remember the press conference—the media just couldn't have been more surprised. They all assumed I was announcing I would run again, because I hadn't had any real opposition in the last two elections. It's always fun to surprise the media," she added with relish.

For Betty Heitman, the decision to leave was much less anguished. She was just plain tired. Even so, finally walking away was not unalloyed liberation. "There was sort of an empty feeling, because I'd done it for so long," she said, remembering. "I'd been in Washington almost ten years, and I was really active on a full-time basis prior to that, so there's sort of an empty feeling when you walk away. Plus, you know, you miss the people you've been working with. But by the same token, there's a great feeling of pressure removed, of things being more relaxed—particularly initially."

Political women, like successful women in any field, tend to have high energy levels and are accustomed to fitting in a day's worth of achievement and aggravation before ten o'clock in the morning, which makes the sudden lull after the rush of campaigning or the jam-packed schedule of public office even more disconcerting. There is also the cold reality of making a living. For Carol Bellamy, who gave up her position as president of the council to enter the mayoral race, there was no time to waste facing things. Once she had lost the election, she said, "It was a matter of it being November, and me being out of a job as of December thirty-first. And worrying also about my staff—making sure they all had jobs."

Political life is by its essential nature an insecure business. The electoral cycle determines everything: a two-year term means one election is barely over before everybody has to begin gearing up for the next one. A four-year term is a little better, but there are no guarantees issued, and incumbents do lose. Even the leisurely schedule of the senatorial six-year term means that election day does eventually come and with it sometimes a changing of the guard. Senator Nancy Kassebaum of Kansas, who originally favored a constitutional limitation of two terms in the Senate, said that former senator Charles Percy of Illinois told her after he was defeated in a reelection bid for a fourth term, "Oh, Nancy, I thought many times about what you said about twelve years being long enough. Loraine [his wife] used to say the same thing. I wish I'd listened!" A change of presidential administration means instant unemployment for hundreds of Washington appointees, as (on a smaller scale) does a change in the governor's mansion in state capitols across the nation. Being out of a job is something that can happen to anybody, and does.

Still, it's not very pleasant when it happens to you. "I don't know that I felt bitter," Bellamy said, remembering back to her defeat. "I mean, it was clear to me before election day that I was going to lose this race, so it certainly didn't come as a shock. But it's the pits. We all like to win things."

When they don't, most politicians find it almost impossible not to run a mental tape of the campaign backward and forward, trying to identify the fatal flaws, mourning the might haves and the if onlys. Bellamy chooses to keep her meditations to herself: "I don't want to be one of those people who say, well, gee, it could have been won if this happened, or that happened, but you always see things you could have done differently."

It takes resilience for most political women to figure out realistically what part being a woman played in a defeat—or in a victory, come to that, but a victorious politician is usually caught up in the demands of the job she was elected to do and has less time to mull over the might-have-beens. Republican Norma Paulus won her primary and ran a tight, competitive gubernatorial race in Oregon in 1986. She came heartbreakingly close to victory, but wound up with only 47 percent of the vote. She says being a woman had a lot to do with it. "Each side made a lot of mistakes," she said. "But when everything else is said and done, the bottom reason I didn't win was because I was a woman, and there are a whole lot of Republicans, older Republicans, male and female, who simply would not vote for a woman for governor."

What happened to Arliss Sturgulewski, a Republican who lost the Alaska gubernatorial race the same year, is cited by many observers as a typical example of what happens to too many women politicians: she defeated former governor and Secretary of the Interior Walter Hickel in the primary, and then he entered the general election as a write-in, reviving the primary factional emotions just enough so that she lost by 4 percent. It was a classic case of raw frontier politics, but Sturgulewski herself sees it less as a matter of the voters rejecting a woman than as a consequence of the fact that, being a woman, she had followed a typical woman's pattern in the way she came into politics, and she simply wasn't prepared for the no-holds-barred struggle she encountered.

"My beginning was the League of Women Voters," she said simply. "I came through—in a sense—the do-goody good government kind of things: boards and commissions, public service. I didn't come up through the party structure. I didn't come up through the hardball political way, so I've always found myself a little askance at how hardball politics can be many times, because that is not how I saw it. My attitude came out of a public service attitude, and I think that's what happens with the League of Women Voters. It's a training in issues, and understanding the policy. Then you find that so much of political life is not necessarily public policy. There seem to be other goals and motives, and I am not sure . . . well, for me it was the right way to go, but I had to learn a couple of things. First of all, it was a very slow process, the building years that I went through, so certain doors are closed to me now in terms of my age. I also feel that I could have been more streetwise—I guess that's the word to say. I could have moved, in a sense, faster. I built very very slowly in terms of a political career, but then, there has always been a solid base out there too."

•　　■　　■

It is in the nature of political life that it is frequently the election at the end of a campaign which brings a career to a halt—whether permanent or temporary—but there is a lot more to politics than campaigning. Perea Campbell, who worked for congresswoman Lynn Martin of Illinois for four and a half years, finishing as her administrative assistant, was up to her neck in the practical daily political business of putting together the legislative agenda, coping with constituents and their convoluted problems, and getting through the ordinary workload of a congressional office. She had been on Capitol Hill for a long time ("I started out with Senator Richard Schweiker from Pennsylvania in 1972 or '73—I can't even remember any more," she said, pausing, trying to remember, then dismissing the problem), and she looks at the political process now with flat honesty and few illusions. Not only is she a woman there, she is a black woman, and a Republican at that.

"In general, this whole area is a fantasy land," she said, with a certain sour amusement. "We don't deal with real reality. We deal with perceived reality and hope that things work out for the best." She has watched a lot of well-intentioned legislators argue and scheme and compromise, and she has observed that sometimes what comes out at the end has little to do with the intentions that started the machinery going in the first place. "We make laws. We don't really know how they are going to affect the people," she said, out of her years of case work, of finding out on a person-by-person basis just how some of the laws did affect them. "To me that's proven, now I have done case work, grants, and contracts. Meantime Congress is the body that makes the laws, but then we give the agency the authority to make the regulations to implement the law. They are the ones who are dealing with reality. We are not. So we are making a law and we really don't know how it's going to affect these people. We are just hoping that the intent gets across.

"Take an agency," she said. "By and large the agencies are very, very good. They do their very best to carry out the intent of the congressional law, okay? But then you have some agencies—for example, let's take the big one. IRS. They are not in it for the people. They are in it to make money for the government. So their regulations are, of course, going to gear toward making money for the government. We don't really want to hurt the little man, we don't really want to hurt the big man, but we have to get our money. So that, to me, is where the perspective is that they come from in making their regulations. Whereas Health and Human Services is different. We have X amount of money to work with, so let's try as much as possible to put as much effectiveness as we can into this one little program so that we can use up all this money and benefit the people." Both the agency and the program are set up to carry out the congressional laws—but what Congress intended and what the program wound up being may be two different things.

Perea Campbell has been around long enough so that she has seen a lot of things change. When she first arrived, women staffers were present, but only on the periphery of the action. "Women were not included in any [strategic planning]," she said. "They just weren't. I never saw anyone fight to be included—so I can't say that they were excluded just because they were women," she added. "It just wasn't anything that was much thought about, I guess. That was my perception as a twenty-year-old. Over time and with the change of administration, you see more and more women being involved. They have to be involved because the men have no idea what is going on out here, for one thing. They try, but they really don't know. They want the women's vote, they want the minority vote, they want all kinds of vote. But they have to bring in someone who knows what that's about. The men here don't."

After sixteen years in politics, Campbell is ready to try something else. She is plain tired out. Part of it is the pace that political life demands: most of the time "the only time I ever really socialized was right after work because when I got home I had all this other stuff from work to do. Weekends were always planning time. I had to get ready for the whole week—that was always on the agenda too. I might get out and step totally out of character for a couple of hours on Saturday, and then the rest of the time was spent working or just plain resting." Part of it was feeling impatient with the way her life narrowed down to a continual absorption with the business of politics. "It started out kind of normal," she said. "It went from going out with different friends to going out only with political people. That's all you ever talked. Politics. Every party I went to seemed to center around what was happening here—and these were just Saturday parties, Christmas parties, party parties. They were always people that you worked with or in some way had something to do with politics." Much of what prompted her to turn away was plain burnout: a weariness that came from seeing too many hopeful intentions fizzle out or be so homogenized by compromise that practically nothing related to the original premise emerged at the end. "We all took it seriously at one time," she said, looking back at the eager young woman she had been at first. "I can remember that, and when I look back I think how in the world could I have wasted my mind like that? There were just so many other things to worry about—you can do so much, then [you have to] put it aside."

Perea Campbell is exceptional as a black woman in having been professionally involved in politics at all. Part of the reason is simply geographical. She grew up in Washington, D.C. Her family was never particularly political, but in Washington, the government is an obvious employer for an intelligent young woman with a college education. Her family was solidly middle class, and when she was looking for a part-time job while she finished college, her father knew of someone who needed a person to work on the Hill. They hadn't quite figured that she would turn into a Republican as a direct result. "My family was all Democrats," she said. "I thought I was a Democrat. I ended up in a Republican office the very first time I tried for a job, and I kept saying, 'I believe that. I don't believe this—I'm not a Democrat!' That's when I found out I was a Republican, and that's when I decided no wonder my parents always thought I was strange."

If women are thin on the ground politically speaking, black women are even sparser. Cardiss Collins of Illinois is currently the only black woman in Congress; of the 1,157 women state legislators now serving (of a total of 7,461 legislators) only 91 are black women—a miniscule 1.2 percent overall at the state level. There are even fewer Hispanic women than black women. According to the Center for the American Woman and Politics reports, black elected women are highly educated, more so than elected women overall, and are more likely to be lawyers. The overwhelming majority of them are Democrats.[7]

Barbara Jordan of Texas has been one of the most notable black women politicians. Nothing ever came easy for her: born in 1936, she grew up in then strictly segregated Houston. She went to an all-black college, Texas Southern University, and it was not until she went north to Boston University to law school that she first had to grapple with the problems of being a black woman in an environment geared to white masculine achievement. It was 1956, and the law school wasn't geared to women at all—there were about six hundred students in the entering class, of which six were women. As a black woman, Jordan faced twice as many hurdles as her white female classmates, but she and the only other black woman who started with her were the only women to graduate with their class. She returned to Houston after her graduation, and in 1962 and 1964 she ran for the Texas House of Representatives. Both times she lost, but she learned what she was up against. In 1966 she ran for the state senate and won. She was the first black woman senator in Texas history. In 1972, when her district was taken up in a newly created congressional district, she decided to run for Congress and won.

She stayed in Congress for three terms. She learned the rules and how to use them—the formal rules that determine procedure, and the informal rules that govern the way elected officials get along with each other. Take for example the business of trade-offs. It's the basic currency of politics. You ask a favor; if it's granted, you owe a favor in return. It may not be asked for right away, but when it is, both parties recognize the obligation. The politician, male or female, who welshes on such a debt finds he or she is locked out of the system the next time. On the other hand, as Jordan has commented, you always have a choice in getting into the trade-off in the first place. "I have discovered how to be discretionary in terms of who is permitted to use me and who is not,'" she wrote.[8] As an example, she told the story of a request from the White House that she go to New Jersey to help the Democratic candidate in his campaign for governor. As she saw it, the trade-off would be between herself and the White House: she didn't even know the candidate, so he didn't come into it. So for her, the relevant question was what she would get in return. "Well, I had already done my thing for Carter at the time of the campaigning and helping with the election. And I hadn't called in any of those chits at that point. I decided: I don't need to stockpile favors at the White House, so I won't go to New Jersey. That's just politics."[9]

She moved out into national prominence when she was a member of the House Judiciary Committee during the televised hearings on impeaching Nixon. In 1976 she was the first woman, and the first black, to keynote a Democratic National Convention. In 1978 she retired.

Everybody wanted to know why. There was speculation that her health had failed, but she insisted it was only a mobility problem, that she had had a bad knee for years. What she said was simply that she felt she no longer needed to be an elected public official to have a platform to say the things she thought needed to be said. "I was forty before I decided I really could turn my head and look in another direction," she said. "I decided there were other things that can be rewarding. It is not a sin not to work twenty-four hours a day, or thirty-six. I began including things that were enjoyable and pleasurable and found that it's not all one way or the other."[10]

She says she turned her back on politics with no regret. "It is difficult for a woman in politics. *It is very difficult for a woman in politics.* Look at Geraldine Ferraro."[11] Strictly speaking, Barbara Jordan has left professional politics, but she says that the work she is doing now, teaching younger students who will be the elected officials of the future, is a remarkable opportunity to have an impact on the generation that will come after her. Certainly for here and now it is the philosophy of politics that most interests her.

One of Barbara Jordan's colleagues in the House was another

173

notable black woman, Shirley Chisholm of New York. Chisholm came to Congress in 1968 from Brooklyn. A strong liberal and a tough fighter, she held her seat for seven terms. Although she ran for the Democratic presidential nomination in 1972, she was flatly realistic about her chances. "I just wanted to show that just because a person was not white or male they should not be underestimated," she said. [12]

She retired in 1982, because, she said, she was tired of proving herself to sexist colleagues and because she wanted to spend more time with her husband. She had first been elected to the New York state assembly in 1964, and eighteen years is a long time to be in public office. Perhaps it is particularly long to a black woman, who has to overcome all the hurdles the white women have, and then some.

■　　■　　■

In no way is burnout restricted to women politicians, of course. It's an occupational hazard, and virtually every politician, male or female, who has spent more than a couple of years in the game has watched it happen to colleagues. They all have spells of wondering if they still have the elasticity to get up and take off from the starting line the next time the gun goes. Politics is the business of cramping ideals into pragmatic reality, and by the nature of things everybody loses more often than they win. As long as you can regard the wreckage of today as raw materials for tomorrow's battles, you're still in business. Most people, however, find that the day comes when they'd rather sit down for a while and let somebody else lead the charge.

"Some people won't get burned out in thirty years, some people get burned out in three," Carol Bellamy said. She's been around long enough to know. "One of the reasons I left the [New York state] senate and ran for the presidency of the City Council was I thought to myself that too many of the debates each year were sounding like the debates of the previous year, and maybe I was losing some of the passion I thought you needed to have—that doesn't mean you have to be screaming, it just means you have to have some passion, you have to feel. One of the reasons I decided this time it was time to be either up or out is that I had been president of the council eight years. I thought I'd probably been a pretty decent one. But you need to get up in the morning and say, 'Boy, I'm going to—in my own stupid way—save the world today.' One of the things politics ought to have, although it doesn't have, is the ability to take a sabbatical. We'd probably get better officials if you could take a little time and then come back again. But you don't have that."

Betty Heitman, in her years as a professional Republican party worker, came to similar conclusions. "A friend from Louisiana told me, 'Betty, if you want to be in [politics] for the long haul, you have to pace yourself. You can't go full steam ahead all the time. We left a lot of bodies along the wayside because they've pushed too hard too constantly. You have to pace yourself.' Towards the end I got where I was not pacing myself. There was definitely a burnout. I really had a strong inclination not to run for election [as national party cochairman] in '84. I did run, but by the time this next term was up, it was time for me to do something else."

Anne Stanley has been actively involved in campaigning for twenty years, and active campaigning is a business that burns out most people in four or five. She's still at it, a consultant working on Kemp's presidential campaign in this election cycle. She's very familiar with the cliche that politics is a young people's game, and she thinks it's usually true simply because the rigors of a campaign take a lot out of you and the day comes when there's not that much left to give. This means taking a hard look at her own future. When asked if she thinks she's going to stay in the business permanently, she said, "Oh, probably not. I think you begin to wear out. Two things: one, you wear out and secondly, you don't like your life in a turmoil. And thirdly, financially it's got peaks and valleys. When I was twenty-eight years old I thought that was neat, that I never knew where I was going to be working next year. It's a little less neat for me now because I've got a house, I've got to pay for it—so the minute you start approaching commitments you think about what you're going to be doing when you're sixty-five. There are a lot of spinoffs I could do. I'm not sure I want to. What I like about campaigning, I think, is that it's high intensity and then it's over."

Politics is intense—and the same intensity that burns some people out is meat and drink to others, for a while at least. For exactly that reason, political Washington is a high-intensity town,

175

ingrown, gossipy, and obsessed. Jill Schuker, who has been caught up in it for more than twenty years, from campaigning with Robert F. Kennedy to working as Governor Hugh Carey's press secretary in New York, is now a senior vice-president in a prominent Washington public relations firm, where she can look at the city in which she's spent much of her working life with few illusions. "What I would say about Washington is that it's a very workaholic city," she said. "I've lived in New York City, and people work hard there, but it's different. What I think happens here is that you're always working. A lot of socializing is also working—the conversation you have at dinner is very political, is very business-oriented: the business of politics and Washington and government. I mean, you can go to New York and be involved in government there, and you'll find you can have dinner conversation that will center on the ballet. Not that you *can't* do that here, but it is much more unusual. You do have men—and women—who are hard-driving there, but here you have people who are just totally wrapped up in their careers."

Until the vote count comes out wrong—or maybe something internal just clicks—and it is apparent that the time has come to turn away and try something else.

■   ■   ■

"What I always say I'm going to do with my life—and everyone agrees with me—is that I'm going to march through the hills of New England in my sensible oxfords and shout obscenities at birds. That's how I'll end up," says Wilma Goldstein placidly when she contemplates her postpolitical existence. Then she laughs and suggests as an alternative fate, "or I'll be killed by a Washington, D.C., cab driver." Pending either of those interesting possibilities, she is using what she's learned from her long years of experience on campaigns to teach political skills to new recruits, at American University, working with one of the Republican party committees and at the bipartisan WCF. "For me, personally," she said, "one of the give-backs that you do, in particular if you like to teach, which I do, is to teach it as long as you can. But you can't continue to teach and keep your fingers out of the business." So she foresees her immediate future being a combination of teaching and getting involved in campaigns.

Other women choose other ways to go. When Carol Bellamy had

to decide what to do next after her attempt to replace New York City mayor Edward Koch was unsuccessful—having given up the presidency of the City Council to make her run—she chose to go in an entirely different direction, at least temporarily. She became a vice-president of a Manhattan-based investment banking company. Although she is a lawyer, when she went into the private sector after thirteen years as a public servant, she deliberately decided to try something new. "I'm [still] a lawyer," she said. "I'll go back into the law someday. One of the reasons I did investment banking was to add another skill. You've got to learn things. You stick your ego in a drawer and you go out and learn."

When Betty Heitman left the Republican National Committee in 1987, she had several other irons in the fire—she is still a consultant for the RNC, currently assigned to Lousiana congressman Robert Livingston's gubernatorial campaign, and involved in fundraising for state and local elections—but being nothing if not pragmatic after long years of being a professional politician, she figured she had to make her move into the private sector while she was still remembered, and, even if it meant she was working almost as hard as she had been at the RNC full-time, she went straight into a lobbying firm with her son. "Memory is very short," she explained. "People have advised me on my business—they said, 'Do as much as you can these first two years, because two years from now no one's going to know who in the hell you are.' And I'm sure that's true. I *know* it's true."

For all the aggravation and exasperation—not to mention plain old disillusionment—so richly available in political life, it seems to be extremely difficult to walk away from professional politics entirely. Barbara Jordan has done it; but Bella Abzug, who was in Congress with her, was still running for election in 1986 in New York's suburban Westchester County, where she won a congressional primary that few people expected she would—ten years after she gave up her original House seat to try for the Senate—and was then defeated in November.

What is the tremendous magnetism that holds people? It is powerful enough to draw the vast majority of political women even when they've been around long enough to recognize that there is an underside to politics, that not everybody is motivated by the highest regard for the greatest good, and that, in human affairs as in any

177

other arena, there is malice, narrow self-interest, blatant sexism, and probably most often, plain stupidity to be dealt with, among allies and adversaries alike.

Part of the answer has to be because of the power. Jeane Kirkpatrick may be right in maintaining that fewer women than men seem to have an overriding need for power, but women politicians, like their male counterparts, are in a position to see, close up, what power can do. Even Kirkpatrick herself, talking about power, doesn't sound wholly oblivious to the attraction: "Harold Lasswell, who is a very brilliant social scientist, defined power as 'to be taken into account in the policies of others,' " she said reflectively. "It's a very interesting definition of power. People with power get taken into account in the decisions of a great many people, and their views and their preferences and their likes and dislikes are magnified many times. They become important to many other people, and they are treated as such. That's what it is all about. One of the sources of that kind of power in Washington is proximity to the president. Another source of it is influence over processes and operations. It's also the ability to get things done, of course—to get things done that you want to get done and that need to get done."

For some women, like some men, that power becomes attractive simply for its own sake. This is just as true even if there is a notable lack of agreement on where power lies in the first place. State and local politicians on one side, and members of the presidential staff on the other, freely assert that merely being one of 435 representatives in Congress, for example, isn't being much of anybody at all, and yet people (not infrequently former state and local politicians or ex-members of the presidential staff) raise and spend hundred of thousands, even millions, of dollars in the effort to become one of those 435.

For some other women, the attraction lies less in the power per se than in the conviction that women have been shut out of the governing process for far too long and that women have something distinctive to contribute—not least about the ordinary issues of everyday living, about which the average woman knows as much as and probably more than the average man. "I never miss an opportunity to talk to women," Louise Slaughter, a first-term Democratic congresswoman from New York, said. "The economic issues are ours. There are some only we talk about because we live 'em."[13]

Once in the system, there is also the unique satisfaction of seeing that some of the things you're trying to do work. The political newcomer may start out with stars in her eyes, anticipating that if she is bright enough, and careful enough, and works hard enough at the job, she can change the world. The woman who's been around for a while knows the most she can realistically hope for is that some of what she's working for actually happens. It won't all come right—for example, few experienced women would completely disagree with Perea Campbell's observation that lawmakers can't completely predict how a law may actually work out in the governing process—but, with luck and hard work, enough may work to keep you going. Looking back at thirteen years of public service, even after a dispiriting defeat, Carol Bellamy takes a matter-of-fact pride in what she accomplished in the system. "It made me feel as if I'd made a contribution," she said. "We just can't be cold automatons all our lives," she added reflectively, then abruptly changed tone and finished cheerfully. "Anyway, I made a difference. I made a small, little difference."

It's hard to explain to someone outside the process how those "small, little differences" can be enough of a reward to be worth it all, particularly because the failures are often so much more visible. The public nature of political failure, when the votes are announced and more people voted for the other guy, is what most outsiders focus on. The intangible rewards of getting involved with the governing process, as imperfect as it may be, are much more private. As Jill Schuker, who has worked with state legislators, congressmen, administrators, and appointees over the course of her long career, explained it, "Because, happily, one has had the opportunity to serve in government, you also realize it is not only the 'politics' and the campaigning that is important and fun—and committing, and interesting—there's a lot to be said for being involved in the actual governing process. We're at the point now where we can really experience that and be involved in that part of it, where you are not just electing the person who's going to put together government that's going to make policies, but you can be part of that experience, too. The canvas on which you can operate is broader.

"I think what's important as well is the excitement of working with leaders—politicians—who you really know to be quality people, who care about what they are doing," she said. Longtime Democrat that she is, she made the point that the good people are on both sides of the aisle. "Obviously, there are many of them— people who care about governing, care about policy, and seeing how change can be effected. And I think for many of us who are at the front of the baby boom, much of the excitement is that we were part of a generation that did indeed see some very exciting changes that were really effective through a *political* process."

Again and again, these women looking back at the world they saw from the inside remember the people there, and the relationships they had with them, as being much of the reward for getting mixed up with what one woman called "the whole screwy business" in the first place. "I think working with people in politics, just by the very nature of the work, means you tend to get in more crisis situations," Betty Heitman said. "You get to know people better. Some of the people you travel with, so you're with them over long periods of time. I know it seems to me that the friendships I've developed, the political friendships, are every bit as close, and maybe a little closer, than the private friendships I had before. You lose a little bit of your awe of famous people when you find out that they're friends just like other friends you have, with the same virtues and the same failings. You just develop a sort of comradery, and it doesn't really matter if it's a vice-president of the United States or a senator or what."

For Margaret Hance, who chose not to run again for mayor of Phoenix in 1984, one of the satisfactions is that the friendships are still there years later. "One of the great rewards of politics for me is that I still have good relations now with—and am still good friends with—mayors across the United States," she said. "And then in campaigns, you *have* to make quick judgments—and you form friendships in a matter of six hours' exposure that last for years."

Or there's Susan Williams, who's been active in politics since the 1960s and at various times has been an assistant secretary of transportation under the Carter administration and one of Gary Hart's senior strategists in his 1984 campaign. Now settled in the private sector, she and a partner are running a Washington lobbying firm— but her political friendships can pull her right back into the middle of the fray. "We don't take any political campaigns," she said. "We made a real decision when we started the firm that we would not do that. We really concentrate on the substance of legislative issues. What politics we do is just for friendship. But," she added, "when a friend of mine, Brock Adams [the former secretary of transportaton under Carter], was going to run for the Senate [from the state of Washington in 1986], he called and asked for my advice, and I got very very involved in his campaign—went out to the state and all. He was a long shot, and now he's Senator Adams. So it's lovely to be able to use your talent and experience to help your friends and for issues you really care about." She got started on campaigns in 1969, and nearly twenty years later the enthusiasm is still there.

Looking back, political women see it all without illusions. Some of just about anything you hear is true: the good, the bad, and the indifferent. For the women who are willing to accept the whole mixture, it is apparently addictive. Very few women politicians are ever ready to say they have retired completely, however willingly they walked away from the arena. There is always another campaign ("I'm only going to help a little"), another need for fund-raising (I'm just going to make a few calls"), another candidate to counsel ("I'm not on the staff or anything—but we've talked a few things over").

"There is another world out there," Betty Heitman said, with the sort of mild surprise only a dyed-in-the-wool politician would appreciate. "It's hard to imagine that things can be done effectively on the outside when you're so busy on the inside trying to scramble around and put on programs and influence voter groups and that sort of thing. But I guess as much influence can be exerted—maybe more!—from the outside as when you're sitting in office."

She sounded convinced, sort of. But as a lot of political women murmur, very quietly, to themselves, it just isn't the same. No way. They've been inside, and they *know*.

8. Where Do We Get to from Here?

We were sitting around a table with our coats on, because it was Washington's Birthday and the heat in the WCF office wasn't on. In spite of the February cold, Wilma Goldstein was making us laugh with her dry tales of adventure as a working woman politician for the last twenty-five years or so. She's had quite a career. By 1975, she had already spent about ten years working in politics in Michigan and the general area, for much of that time helping to expand the political side of Robert Teeter's polling organization, Market Opinion Research. She'd even had a couple of years in Canada, working the political game there. But in 1975 she decided, more or less on the spur of the moment, that since the Republican National Committee was looking for a director of survey research, it was time to try Washington.

Friends told her she was nuts. In 1975 the Republican Party was still trying to pick up the pieces after Watergate. Wilma figured that was just about the right time to come: "What better time to come than when the party is a mess because then you get to put it back together the way you choose," is what she thought. She turned out to be right. She wasn't the only woman to join the Republican National Committee around that time—altogether there were about a dozen women who came in within six months or so of each other. There was no money and not much structure, and women were hired for jobs they might never have been offered if things had been more organized. Eddie Mahe, Jr., was then the executive director, and, according to Wilma, he said, "I don't know why in the hell any of you want to be here instead of home pregnant and in the kitchen, but I will tell you this: if you're going to be here you're going to be treated like everybody else." "And he did do that," she told us. "It doesn't matter whether he understands or not—he's the first to tell you he doesn't understand—but he decided he would treat us all fairly, and he would expect the same things from us that he expected from anybody else."

When you look at it rationally, Mahe's working rules were no big deal. He wasn't promising the women anything special, just that they'd be treated like the men, and they'd have to do their jobs the way men were expected to. It is a measure of the unequal conditions that women were used to that his willingness to start the women out even was perceived as a giant step forward. In 1975 a woman couldn't assume that would be the case. The ground rules offering equality had to be explicitly stated, and twelve years later Wilma remembered gratefully that he had stated them and, even more, that he had followed through.

However unenthusiastic he might have been initially when he opened the door, he opened it, and as Wilma told us later, he went through a lot of hassles with the other men when he kept his word and stood up for the women. It's not easy being a woman entering a world that the men have always accepted unquestioningly as their own private domain, but it's not always easy for the men who are prepared to give them a shot at it, either. Things haven't changed so much in the last twelve years that the whole episode can be put down as a quaint slice of history. No political woman in the late 1980s can take it for granted that she has a level ground to play on, and when the men give her a fair turn, she still remembers it.

So much for equality.

■　　■　　■

We've spent a couple of years talking to political women all over the country, going back over their careers with them, trying to figure out what it's like to be a woman active in the political system four years after Ferraro's spectacular breakthrough onto the presidential ticket, and nearly seventy years after women got the vote in the first place. A lot of what they had to tell us was different, one woman to the next, and a lot turned out to be the same. Sometimes the contrasts were dramatic. On one typical day we went straight from talking with Evy Dubrow, a lobbyist for the International Ladies' Garment Workers' Union (ILGWU) who came to Washington in 1947 and has been lobbying on Capitol Hill since 1958, to Elise Paylan, trained as an economist and now a devout supply-sider, who came to Washington directly from college in 1980 and seven years later was on the White House staff. Evy came to Washington as a lobbyist because the ILGWU decided they needed a full-time person there, and since 85 percent of their members were women, it ought to be a woman—and as the union president, who referred to all the union's women employees as his "girls" whether they were eighty-five or twenty-four, told Evy, "If we need a girl in Washington, the girl ought to be you." "The girl" has been there ever since. Thirty years later, Elise Paylan, crisp and efficient in her office in the Old Executive Office Building next to the White House, can say matter-of-factly, "If you're a woman, and you're just very straightforward and very professional, *especially* in politics, people will take you seriously." And nobody calls her a girl.

In a way, their different experiences reflect the changes that have taken place over what is a relatively short period of time. Women are no longer a curiosity in the political world. There are women as well as men on the local city councils, women in the state legislatures, women, occasionally, on the front pages making statements about the course of national policy. They are always in the minority, but they are there. It is very easy to forget that it wasn't that many years ago that the mere idea of a woman politician was outrageous to a lot of people.

Ronna Romney's mother-in-law, Lenore Romney, found that out in 1970, when she ran for the Senate in Michigan against incumbent Democrat Philip Hart. Nineteen seventy was hardly back in the Dark Ages, but even so many people made it plain that they wanted nothing to do with a woman senator. Lenore is an intelligent woman who had been active in community affairs for her entire adult life and was an articulate, gracious spokeswoman for the positions taken by the Republican party in her state. As long as the public knew her only as the wife of Governor George Romney, she had few detractors. Everybody told her she was wonderful, admired her gift for capturing crowds with her speeches (better at that than her husband was, some said), and generally treated her as a prized local celebrity. It was when she stepped out from behind her husband—George by then having been brought to Washington and Nixon's first cabinet as Secretary of Housing and Urban

Development—and embarked on a personal political career that everything changed. She ran for the Senate on the party ticket because she was asked to by the Republican leaders, for the sake of party unity, and she was astonished and appalled by the general public's reaction.

"I got criticized just because I was a woman," she said, still sounding faintly surprised by the experience eighteen years later. "People who had liked me so much would say, 'How can you do this, you a lovely lady, getting out there and boasting about yourself?' Up in the Upper Peninsula they would even say, 'We don't vote for niggers or women up here.' It was really very difficult. They said, 'Don't you have any men in the state?' And Hart was so condescending, so patronizing, really. It was terrible. He would bring me a flower, or a little bottle of perfume or something, and say, 'I wish I could see you in a drawing room.' You know how demeaning that was." Lenore Romney lost heavily, picking up only 32.9 percent of the vote, and retreated gratefully back to being her husband's wife. "I was glad it was over," she says now, with heartfelt sincerity. She never considered running for office again.

Certainly one of our primary conclusions after two years of talking to political women is that prospects have improved since 1970. Lenore's experience could almost be a measuring stick of how far women have come in the last eighteen years. What's made the difference? It seems to us that three major elements have gone into the change of climate.

The first is the fact that the electorate has gradually become used to the idea that women can function in political life without the whole fabric of society falling apart—or whatever it was the most sexist elements of that electorate were worried about earlier. In part, it was a result of Lenore and all the other women who ran political campaigns, the few who won and the many more who lost. The *idea* of a woman "boasting about herself" on a campaign platform became less of a shock, simply because it happened more often.

Those years were also years in which women moved out of the exclusively domestic environment into the larger society in hundreds of other occupations as well. When your experience includes women managers, women engineers, women physicians, women lawyers, and so forth, the idea of a woman city councillor, or even a

woman state legislator, seems considerably less outrageous. (That
people still have a hard time visualizing a woman senator, however,
has been amply demonstrated in many an election.)

The second element is closely allied to the first, but has more to
do with approved social attitudes. Aggressive male chauvinist piggery
is simply less acceptable than it once was. Feminist attitudes have
permeated far enough into our national consciousness so that except
in the most radically conservative enclaves the kind of things people
said to Lenore and to other early women out on the campaign trail
just aren't said anymore.

Note there is a distinct difference between saying those things and
thinking them, however. Whereas nobody with serious political
ambitions would dare formulate his views on electability of minori-
ties as "We don't vote for niggers or women," the view is apparent
in thoughtful political commentary on the realistic chances of Jesse
Jackson or, for example, Pat Schroeder being elected president.

There is also the disquieting suspicion that the new rhetoric of
liberation frequently masks the old exclusions. As pollster Harrison
Hickman remarked to us regretfully, "I think, at least on our
[Democratic] side, we have a whole new generation of candidates
who at least know how to talk the talk. There's not a Hollings or a
Glenn or a Mondale or a Hart whom you've heard suspicious things
from over the years and you need to hold their feet to the fire to
find out if they even are sensitive to these issues. But there's a whole
other kind of chauvinism that we may see come out in the course of
this [1988] election, which I think is actually worse—these people
talk the talk and don't walk the walk. They say all the right things
but when the big decisions get made in their campaigns, for the
most part, there won't be women sitting at the table." Harrison was
speaking of the Democrats, but from what we have observed of
political life in general, the Republicans are no better. Lip service to
the premise of women's political capabilities is much better than it
used to be; genuine effort on the part of the men already in place to
allow the women some space is at best only somewhat better. It is
still tough to be a woman in politics—but it's tough to be a woman
and ascend to the top of the management ladder, too.

Even so, there *has* been progress. Most of the time women are
measuring themselves against the gap between where they are and
where they think they might be if they happened to be men. It's

encouraging occasionally to look back and see the gap between where women were and where they are now.

The third element in the improvement of the political climate for women is a straightforward result of the fact that women have increasingly worked themselves into the system, and have done their jobs well. Women now have an established track record of considerable success. There have been capable women who made political marks: Margaret Chase Smith won the nation's respect over the years when she was America's token woman politician, Ella Grasso was a success as Connecticut's governor in the 1970s, and more recently, enough women have done a good enough job as mayors nationwide—all the way from little towns to major cities—so that even in the aggressively macho arena of Texas politics, there are women mayors flourishing all over the state. Geraldine Ferraro ran for vice-president and did a notable job of it. Republican and Democratic women alike were impressed and proud of the way she brought it off. Again and again, we heard the same formulation: "She handled it with dignity, like a professional. And damn it, she never cried." It went without saying for all of them that she had more than enough reason to.

Gerry herself pointed out to us that before her campaign there were people wondering if it was even physically possible for a woman to take the pressure of a full-blown presidential campaign. "I showed that a woman was physically capable of dealing with the rigors of a campaign," she told us, with understandable satisfaction. "If you take a look at the schedules, at my schedule, Fritz [Mondale's] schedule, Reagan's schedule, Bush's schedule, I did more than each one of the three of them. I probably did more than Reagan and Bush put together. Emotionally, no one in the history of this country has done a press conference like I did for two hours. What I had to do was get up there and just answer questions and show them that I was not going to break. The one thing that came out of that press conference was that people said, 'You know, if nothing else, you showed that you could handle emotional stress.' Take all the Reagan press conferences. He couldn't handle it. Take a look at Bush when he got rattled during the course of the campaign when they were asking questions. Watch what happened with [former NSC advisor] Bob McFarlane when all of a sudden he was put into the hot spot—he tried to take his life. And these are tough marines, these are veterans of the service. And a little five-four, 130-pound woman was able to deal with the whole thing. So that's what came out of the campaign. You showed you could do it. No one will question Pat Schroeder or Jeane Kirkpatrick or anybody else in the future as to whether or not they have something biologically in their system that is not going to allow them to address the problems that face them. For that alone, it was worth it."

All these successes—the well-publicized successes, like Ferraro's, and the less advertised successes of women who got on the town and city councils, who made it to the state legislatures, the handful who even got to Congress—are gradually supplying incontrovertible evidence that women can do it. Women politicians have gained a reputation for being honest, trustworthy, and responsive to their constituents. Most of them are. They *care*—at least that's what the voters believe, and quite frankly, we were surprised at the number of women legislators who have their home phone numbers listed in the local directory, presumably on the principle that being available to someone who genuinely needs them is worth the aggravation of dealing with the occasional nuisance at 2 A.M. One way or another, a woman incumbent may be as hard (or harder) to unseat as her male counterpart.

What this all adds up to is a more encouraging climate for women. There are a lot of women who would be hesitant to step forward as the first woman to do this or that, but who are quite willing to be the second, or the third, or the fifth. Each woman doesn't have to invent the whole fabric of a political life out of her imagination anymore: there are role models out there now for younger women, who can see how it's done and shape their own ambitions to match or surpass the goals they've seen achieved. They are educated as to the possibilities. Barbara Jordan was so fiercely motivated and ambitious that she figured out for herself how to travel the long road from being a young black girl in Houston who rode at the back of the bus and drank only from the "Colored" drinking fountain to being a member of the United States House of Representatives, where she participated in the lawmaking process for the entire country. There are certainly thousands of other black women, born about when she was, just as intelligent and just as capable, who lacked only that burning determination to be different from all the rest. But once Barbara Jordan had showed how it could be done, *that* it could be done, she opened a road for the younger sisters or daughters of those other women to follow.

Unfortunately, if our first conclusion is that making a political career is easier for a woman now than it used to be, our second has to be that there are still not nearly enough women doing it. We think this is unfortunate for a couple of fairly obvious reasons.

First of all, we think that the problems our government—and world government in general—has to grapple with are complicated enough and intractable enough so that we need every possible bit of human intelligence applied to work out solutions, and to exclude women from policy-making means you waste half of the available brainpower. It's perfectly true that not every woman is interested in taking an active part in government. Neither is every man. Rozanne Ridgway, speaking at a woman's conference on national security and the nuclear threat in 1987, expressed her conviction that women ought to be involved in very pragmatic terms. Ridgway is far from being a dedicated feminist politician—in fact, she says she isn't a politician at all. After thirty years in the foreign service, she is a civil servant who has become skilled at leaving the definition of policy to the politicians and serving as a resource for information before and implementation after. She maintains firmly that there is no such thing as a uniquely "woman's view" on national security issues. This does not mean she thinks that women ought not to involve themselves with those issues; what she pointed out from her vantage point as an exceptional woman who *is* an expert on national security is the dismaying fact that the vast majority of women never learn enough about those crucial issues to discuss them knowledgeably. Talking about the typical woman's ignorance about the difference between strategic and tactical missile systems, the global economy, our relations with our allies, and, naturally, the throw-weights Donald Regan was talking about, she said, "It is essential that women qualify themselves in these topics and not keep saying, 'Those are men's topics.' I'd like to see enough women understanding that only 50 percent of the population considers itself qualified to deal with national security. We are denying ourselves the talents of half the population."[1]

At the same time, whether or not there is a woman's view on national security (and there are other women, every bit as convinced as Rozanne Ridgway, who will argue that there is), there are defi-

189

nitely other issues on which women have something distinctive to offer, which brings us to the second compelling reason for women's greater participation in policy formation.

It is stating the obvious to say that men and women still play different social roles. From what we've seen, the different perspective women bring to government, based on different life experiences and different patterns of socialization, is just as vital as any other perspective. Just as Albert Gore, Jr., of Tennessee was pointing out to Iowa farmers that he was a farmer, too, in a manner of speaking, and thus could bring a farmer's perspective to presidential deliberations about agricultural policy, so it seems likely that Pat Schroeder, who raised two children while holding down a seat in Congress, has the perspective of a working mother to bring to presidential deliberations about the provision of child care, for example. "My family looks like the typical American family, with one or two struggling, working parents, juggling eighteen balls," she has said. "The average politician's family is more traditional."[2] Any woman who feels her husband just doesn't seem to grasp the complications of her life, trying to maintain the often-conflicting roles of wage earner, mother, and wife, is likely to feel another woman who has fought the same fight will probably represent her better in some ways than a man who has observed his wife's multiple obligations from a distance and believes he understands her frustrations—sort of.

It would be unquestionably sexist to say that a man can't be committed to issues like pay equity, provisions for child care, care for the aged, the growing feminization of poverty, or the complex problems of displaced homemakers, but all of those issues, and other issues like them, have always been more integrally a part of a woman's sphere of experience than they have been part of a man's. It may also be relevant to note that most of these issues have only been addressed at the national level since there have been women there to emphasize their urgency.

This is not to say that elected women want or ought to be confined to being advocates for women and specialists in women's interests. Barbara Mikulski wanted to get on the Appropriations Committee when she came to the Senate because it is one of the most important committees, but she also wanted that assignment to underline what she has often said: the fact that she's a woman doesn't have much to do with her aspirations as a senator. Barbara

Mikulski doesn't have to convince anybody of her commitment to women's issues, but she is also an experienced and respected legislator. Like Nancy Kassebaum, who is now in her ninth year in the Senate, she has a lot more than her woman's perspective to bring to the legislative process, and by and large their colleagues recognize and respect that. But their woman's perspective is a valuable asset in itself—just as Robert Dole's experiences as a handicapped veteran and Paul Simon's background as a newspaperman enhance their contributions to the legislative process. And since more than half of the U.S. population is female, it seems to us that without skewing the balance, their special interests could be represented by more than 2 out of 100 senators, or 23 out of 435 congressmen. *There ought to be more women there.*

Why aren't there? The easy, knee-jerk explanation is sexism, and undoubtedly there's a lot of that around, whether it's the nice straightforward old-fashioned sexism of courtly gentlemen who call all women "honey" and insist that you flirt with a woman, you don't do business with her, or the new improved version Harrison Hickman was talking about, where you talk the approved postfeminist talk but walk the same old exclusionary walk. But to denounce it all as sexism means that you can only attack the problem in the minds and hearts of a couple of generations of men, most of whom aren't paying a great deal of attention to the problems of underrepresentation of women in the first place. It seems more productive for us to look at exactly where the roadblocks seem to be positioned and to see what can be done about them before we launch into the project of changing the philosophical orientation of men who aren't listening to what we have to say anyway.

Oddly enough, one of the biggest problems is that not enough women consider getting into politics in the first place. Women who are astoundingly competent at merging the demands of a family, a job, and often impressive amounts of volunteer work simply never think about running for office, at any level. There seem to be a lot of premises that women as much as men take for granted and don't think about, and one of them apparently is that government is run by men. Some women who *have* thought about it are put off by all the horror stories about how women can't raise money, how women just don't get the support from their parties, or how substantial proportions of voters won't vote for women anyway (all of which are partly true and partly false), and they figure losing is almost inevitable and try something else. Ellie Smeal said it best: if you don't run, you surely lose. There is also the point that a woman bright and ambitious enough to make a mark in politics is almost certainly capable of making substantially more money in the private sector, and the private sector is increasingly open to competent women. It takes a long time to get rich being an honest politician, man or woman.

Another factor that seems to inhibit women from taking a shot at the political game is that, as women, we are not ordinarily raised to be risk-takers. We are taught to be cautious. Political life is exciting, but it's scary, too. In every election, somebody wins and somebody loses. Even if the woman is not the candidate out there in the spotlight, if she's backed the wrong horse, her career can be as dead in the water as his is. It is not only a matter of weathering predictable every-other-year or every-fourth-or-sixth-year crises. Between elections the business of a public officeholder is taking positions that are not going to be popular with everybody. Pat Schroeder talked to us about her deliberate policy of going out on a limb on issues that were important to her, saying that the only reason she was in Congress at all was to make a difference, and that having a political career was less important to her than making that difference. When, after Gary Hart was so unexpectedly swept from the presidential scene, she announced that she was thinking of making a bid for the presidency herself and would do so if she could raise enough money to fund a credible campaign, she put herself right out there where everybody could measure whether she succeeded or failed. As it happened, she had a very tough time getting underway, which surprised her but didn't stop her from trying. "I think it's very important," she told us in the middle of the effort, when her telephone was ringing continually, she was trying to put together a whole new fund-raising network, and was encountering rejections she had never anticipated. "I think when women lose, instead of falling back and saying 'Let's sit this one out,' women have to go back at it twice as hard." To get into the game, a woman has to be emotionally prepared to do her absolute best, throw everything into it, and lose. That prospect is authentically daunting, but not insuperable. Admittedly, many women may not have the determination and chutzpah of a Pat Schroeder, but even so, she's not the only woman around who does. Female resilience and persistence are legendary. It seems to us that more of the women who devote their considerable talents to business, volunteer activities, or professional organizations should think about the possibilities of an active political career and that more young women starting out should be aware that public service is as challenging and rewarding as any other career and more so than many. You may have to recognize the possibility of defeat, but winning feels terrific—and women do win.

Unfortunately, those fledgling women politicians need to start out with sufficient enthusiasm to sustain them past their initial bruising encounters with the old nemesis of politicians in general and women pols in particular: money. If women's unawareness of the possibilities of, or reluctance to get involved in, the political arena is a roadblock, raising the money is a Mount Everest, sitting square in the middle of the interstate. People have climbed Mount Everest, and women can raise money, but neither happens casually.

"Money is a bitch," one woman told us with feeling, and we agree. Money and the American political process are inextricably entwined. We also agree with most political commentators and participants that the dimension of political financing is completely out of hand. Candidates tear their hair, elected officials brood about possible reforms, and nothing much happens. Legislation has been drafted in both the Senate and the House to get control of financing at the federal level at least, and little comes of it. To the extent that the existing situation benefits anybody, it benefits incumbents, and so far a majority of incumbents have not been altruistic enough to abandon their advantages. So the costs of campaigning accelerate upward, and the pace of fund-raising gets more frenetic.

Women get hit hardest by the system. Given women's natural base of smaller donors, escalating campaign costs mean that women candidates running as fast as they can still have little chance of staying in the same place, let alone gaining on the pack. Over and over we heard that a woman candidate should spend about 60 percent of her campaigning time on fund-raising. There were those who said they spent 75 percent. That would leave only a quarter of the available time to spend on communicating with the voters, which is the ostensible purpose of the whole exercise. We say the system is nuts, but it's the system that rules the game, and if the women are going to get in, it's the system they have to beat.

A recurrent theme of women activists is that it's better than it used to be. Once a woman has won her primary and is accepted as a credible candidate, she can tap into the same fund-raising sources as her male equivalent can and raise the same kind of money. This may be true—and we were told it frequently enough so that we believe it is—but unfortunately, that just addresses the situation of a tiny minority of women office-seekers. Unless you're an incumbent, the starting line is a good way back from that point. The woman who has proved her credibility, and won her primary, has already won a couple of respectable battles.

Women typically raise less money from more donors. It is perfectly understandable that many women candidates look to other women as a significant source of funds, but women, at least up to the present, are an undereducated donor population. It is still only a small minority of women who recognize that the way you get a voice in our system is to provide financial support for the candidates you believe in. It's not a crude equation if you have to pay before they listen: it's simply a reflection of the fact that the candidates who hold the same priorities you do still have to get elected to have a chance to exercise those priorities—and it takes money to communicate with the voters who do the electing. There are still too many women who think a ten dollar donation is a lot of money. Part of this is a reflection of the fact that, twenty years after the revival of feminism, women still earn substantially less than men, and for many women, ten dollars *is* a lot of money to spend on anything but necessities. Even so, there are increasing numbers of affluent women who remain modest in their political contributions. Many of those women earn respectable paychecks themselves, spend one hundred dollars for a pair of shoes without batting an eye, but feel they have really done something significant when they write out a check for a ten dollar contribution to a campaign fund. They simply have no concept of how much it costs to run a credible campaign in the 1980s.

Symptomatic of the whole mind-set is the fiscal history of the Republican Women's Federation, organized in 1938, as the current national president, Judy Hughes, explained it to us. In its fifty-year history, members have donated countless hours in the service of the

Republican Party and its candidates: two million volunteer hours in the 1986 election, for example. Originally, the annual dues were set at thirty-nine cents, with the understanding that the Republican National Committee would subsidize the federation as needed. In the early 1950s, the dues went up to fifty cents annually, with the subsidy being continued. In 1979, the RNC decided to withdraw the subsidy, on the grounds that the women could meet their own expenses. In the federation convention that year, it was proposed that the dues be raised to three dollars a year for the national organization, with an additional one dollar for state dues.

According to Carol Josephson, a past president of the Michigan federation, the uproar was tremendous. The women were outraged. It is well known that Republican women volunteers are, in general, not an indigent population: they are, after all, the same women who were in a position to donate millions of hours of volunteer time. But to spend four dollars a year on a political organization seemed excessive to many of them. After all the arguing and lamenting, the dues were indeed raised (although the Michigan delegation, for one, voted against the change). Carol, looking back at all the fuss, thinks it marked a major step in the women's education about the realities of politics and money. "At the time it was happening we thought [the withdrawal of the subsidy] was awful," she told us, "but in retrospect it was the best thing that ever happened to the federation." The women learned something about money, but it's still fair to observe that few of them make the kind of contributions to candidates or party coffers that their husbands make—and that much the same thing would be true of their Democratic counterparts. Women are still much more geared to offering time than money.

At the local level, or even in a state legislative district, where enthusiasm and committed volunteers can go a long way in substituting for money, the fund-raising gender gap is less important, and we think that is demonstrated by the fact that at the local and state legislative level the percentage of women officeholders is highest. There is also the point that everybody has to learn somewhere, and getting involved in the fund-raising side of a campaign that costs only hundreds, or maybe a few thousand, is the way to begin learning what is required to mount a half-million dollar campaign. We keep hearing the voice of Celinda Lake, exhorting women to "raise more money than you need, give it away, do it for the party, do whatever, but get used to raising that greater volume of money."

Certainly women candidates are now much more knowledgeable about money, and that is an absolutely essential first step. There have long been wealthy women who were crucial figures in party fund-raising, but traditionally they were raising money for men. Their expertise hasn't seemed to transfer to the early women's campaigns. Money tended to be a marshy area. Nobody had much of it, mainly because practically nobody on a woman's campaign was linked into the male networks where the major donors were to be found. There was even a feeling among some of the purist feminists that the whole business of money was part of the murky underside of politics and women had cleaner hands if they didn't get involved with political fund-raising in the first place. Let the work be done by honest volunteers. The trouble is that increasingly campaigns rely on media, and you can't trade three volunteers for one thirty-second spot. You've got to have the money if you're going to play with the boys. It took the women a while to figure that out. Ellie Smeal still remembers she had to *argue* with the NOW national conference in 1977 for permission to set up a PAC under NOW auspices (and she still sounds pretty indignant about it, too).

Unfortunately, when women candidates don't raise enough money to be competitive, it cuts more than one way. First, and most obviously, if you don't have the money, you can't spend it, and that means less advertising, fewer materials to mail, posters to put up, and all the rest of it. But in politics money is worth more than what you can spend it on. Money is one of the very few measurable indications of a politician's strength, and consequently everybody watches the money. Gary Hart's presidential campaign finally crashed into ruins over a spectacular blonde, but it was already staggering as a result of major money credibility problems inherited along with the debts from the 1984 campaign. For much of the time we were interviewing, he was the Democratic frontrunner, but every time anyone mentioned his name, they also mentioned his debts.

In the same way, Pat Schroeder's struggle to raise the $2 million she felt it was essential to have before she formally declared herself a candidate was important not only because she would need to spend that money, but because she *had* to be seen as being capable of raising it to prove she was worthy of being taken seriously. And it was tough. We talked to her in the middle of the whole effort, and at that point she honestly couldn't predict which way it was going to go.

"There's just not enough hours in the day," she said, and added with a flash of vintage Schroeder candor, "I don't think I've talked on the phone so much since I was a teenager." Her problems were the classic problems of women politicians reaching for credibility. There is the problem of getting anyone to pay attention in the first place, since the media are so focused on the "genuine" (i.e., male) candidates. Take the initial "debate" of the Democratic hopefuls on the public television stations in the summer of 1987. As Pat explained it to us, "They invited everybody, including Clinton who is not announced, Gore who at that time was not announced, and Jackson who was not announced. We heard about the debate about ten days beforehand, and realized we had not had an invitation. So we phoned, and they said, 'No, it's too late.' I said, 'What do you mean it's too late?' They said, 'It's too late. You're not announced.' Well, we said, 'Tell us who else is there,' and when they told us, we said, 'Well, look, they aren't either.' 'Oh, but you don't have an exploratory committee,' and we said, 'Oh, yes, we do.' And then they said, 'We don't have time to do a video package'—you know, that little ninety-second thing they had on each candidate? I said, 'Are you kidding? That's a joke—I can do that in thirty minutes.' And then they said they had already handed out the seats in the audience and the program had been printed."

The problem is that that kind of episode is more than simply frustrating. It can be lethal to a fledgling campaign. As Pat said, how can she raise money unless she is publicly perceived as a candidate? "I've got enough to do trying to jump start this campaign without trying to find out where the next forum is and how the hell I get in," she pointed out. "I'm really frustrated. And then they tell me, 'Don't yell. Don't get shrill.' And I understand that too. If you're going to make a scene about it, then you're not being presidential. I can't believe it's all organized, it can't be a conspiracy. I mean I don't believe in that. On the other hand, I'm honestly amazed."

What Schroeder was concluding was that she was going to have to raise her money from women, whose standards for credibility would presumably be different. "It's either got to be women or it's not going to happen," she said—and in fact it was the women, at the NOW convention in July 1987, who supplied her with pledges for the necessary $5,000 in contributions of no more than $250 from each of twenty states, which would qualify her for federal matching campaign funds. On the other hand, women have also turned her down: when she asked, EMILY's List would neither give her their list nor do a mailing on her behalf. "Their answer is no, no, and no," Pat said. "They don't think it's a good time for a woman to run. They think everybody in the party will get mad. I mean, everybody's got different [reasons]. That women have already selected candidates, that I'm too late—I mean, they want their feminist credentials intact and they want their political credentials intact, and they think their feminist credentials will be attacked if they're not backing me and they think their political credentials will be attacked if they are backing me. So why don't I just make their life easy and disappear."

What Schroeder's campaign start-up problems may show most clearly is that money still is a bitch, even for a woman with Pat Schroeder's sixteen years of congressional experience, which has included collecting money for eight congressional campaigns. Her problems also show that women's PACs are getting considerably more sophisticated; being female and good on the issues is no longer enough. Other elements enter into their equations. There are no pat solutions to the problems of funding for women—perhaps the best course of action we can suggest is that any woman with political ambitions at any level make it her business to be deeply involved in the fund-raising side of a campaign so that she begins to know where the money is, be an eager student of any successful fund-raiser who would be willing to talk about his or her business to a fascinated listener, and use all the expertise available from the national women's groups, party and bipartisan. Too many women want to concentrate on issues and figure the practicalities will fall into place. They don't. The only sure thing in politics is the permanent necessity of finding the money if you're going to play the game.

The typical woman candidate doesn't have Schroeder's precise problems, of course—presidential campaigns are in a class of their own. At the lower levels, there is an expanding network that provides some money and a great deal of information about where more money can be found. There are educational programs, intended to teach politically interested women how important it is that they dig in their own pockets. There is much less naivete and much more realism. There are more and more women active in fundraising, learning where the money is, making the personal connections that will enable them to raise money for other candidates in the future, and perhaps some of those candidates will be women. And once a woman has won her primary, proved she has a chance, the traditional donors are there for her, as they have always been there for the men.

So some of the news is good. But money is still Mount Everest to a political woman unless she has deep pockets of her own.

Opening your eyes to the possibilities, finding the way to finance them—those are both practical, logistical problems. The third major factor that cuts back women's participation in the political process is more personal, and in some ways more intractable.

The typical pattern of a political career—which is to say, the pattern men have established—just doesn't mesh too well with being a mother and wife. Not all political women marry or have children, of course, but most of them do. Career women everywhere lament that what they need is a wife, but a politician *really* needs one. Most political life swings around the electoral calendar, rising to peaks of frantic intensity during campaigns. A wife not only keeps the domestic side of life ticking along whether her husband is campaigning or not, but also increasingly is a full-fledged campaigner in her own right, in effect doubling the candidate's availability. Being a political wife has become a career in itself, and even the wife who has an independent job usually respects the priorities of her husband's political needs. Nina Solarz, wife of New York Democrat Stephen Solarz, has worked throughout her marriage and is currently the executive director of a disarmament organization called Peace Links. She says, "But that doesn't mean I wouldn't drop everything if my husband needed me. If he had a difficult campaign or was running for higher office, I think I would be very old-fashioned and put my own career on hold."[3] Not that many husbands could, or would.

A husband just doesn't do the same job as a wife, out on the hustings or at home. Most successful ambitious women marry men equally or more ambitious and successful. Few of them are in a position to put their own careers on hold to assist in their wives' political efforts. Furthermore the average husband isn't fully house-trained anyway, capable of running the home with minimal input from his wife. Even political women who have domestic help usually find that they themselves are still the organizers who issue instructions and sort out the difficulties, not their husbands.

A retired husband is an advantage in that his schedule is more adaptable to that of his wife, but he still isn't as much use on the campaign trail as a wife would be. A political wife can appear on behalf of her husband, and everybody says she's wonderful. A husband shows up on his own to campaign for his wife, and everybody wonders why on earth he isn't running himself, if he's so interested. Presumably this attitude will change, but at the rate it's going, it's going to take a long time.

Children complicate everything. We now live in a society in which over half the mothers with young children work, so it would seem that the electorate would be accustomed to the idea that a mother of young children could undertake the job of holding political office, but unfortunately our attitudes haven't caught up with our realities. As Celinda Lake told us, "The young children thing is really unfair. If a male candidate has young children (and we know this from a study that Yankelovich did), people think that's great, because they think it shows that this is someone who is going to care about the future of our country. If a woman has young children—and this is true even among other women who are working outside the home and have young children themselves—they will ask how could she do it, who's taking care of the kids. Even among her peers she will undergo extra scrutiny."

It is not just a problem of what the voters think. A woman who is active in political life might well have a lot of days—and even weeks, during the campaign frenzy—when she sees her children only to kiss them good night when they are sound asleep. For most women, that just isn't enough. Wendy Sherman has a daughter who was three years old during Barbara Mikulski's senatorial campaign. She told us she tried to do her campaign managing on the phone at home at night, so her daughter wouldn't think she had disappeared entirely, and so that Wendy could at least put her to bed. It didn't always work out that way. Mikulski's campaign was a campaign Wendy was totally committed to, it was only a short-term thing, and she still felt guilty and personally short-changed about the scraps of time she had for her daughter. Wendy (and remember Harrison Hickman called her the best campaign manager he'd worked with during that election season) isn't planning on doing another campaign any time soon.

We don't see that kind of emotional tug-of-war fading away in the foreseeable future. Children need their mothers, and most mothers want to be more available for their young children than a high-pressure political career allows. There are increasing numbers of fathers who take over the main responsibility for nurturing; there are also, quite honestly, mothers who are comfortable with a more remote connection with their children, but we think it's unlikely that either of those options will be a choice for the majority. There will always be the rare woman, supercharged with energy, who truly manages to do it all at once—but again, we can't see superwoman being a realistic pattern for the majority of women politicians (or women anything-elses, as far as that goes).

This leads us to a kind of subconclusion: because of this third, most intractable obstacle, most women will continue to wait until their children are older before undertaking the kind of political commitment that means they must spend a substantial part of their time away from home. This is an inevitable consequence of the reality that while older kids may or may not enjoy appearing on a platform or going around sticking in yard signs or fixing their own microwave dinners night after night, at least they are old enough to know that the worst of it is only temporary. They don't cry because Mommy isn't going to be there to tuck them into bed, or live in the all-encompassing present of the small child for whom now is the only time there is, and Mommy can't come home tonight again.

This is not to say it can't be done. There are indeed women who manage to couple a political career with small children, and other women cite them with wonder and admiration. (Everybody always points to Pat Schroeder in this connection, but it's probably more realistic to note that no other congresswoman with small children has ever tried to do it for more than a term or two.) And of course there are a lot of different ways to be involved in political life—even different circumstances connected to different elective offices. If the geography is right, and if the woman can manage financially with the rather niggardly compensation the taxpayers are typically willing to provide—admittedly two fairly big "ifs"—being a part-time state legislator can fit comfortably around family commitments.

Fran Ulmer is a state representative in Alaska with two small children. She is one of the new younger political women who knew from the beginning she wanted to go into public service. She was born in Wisconsin, but when she went on vacation to Alaska she loved it and stayed. She now lives with her husband and children in Juneau, Alaska's tiny capital city. When she first settled in Alaska she worked for the state legislature and later on the governor's staff, but by that time she had her children (who are now six and eight) and decided it was time to concentrate on them. After a couple of years of staying home with the children and doing volunteer community work she took a chance, ran for mayor of Juneau, and won. At the end of her mayoral term her state representative decided to move up to the state senate, so she ran to succeed him and won that election too. Living right in Juneau, with the part-time legislative schedule starting in January when her children are in school, is a perfect arrangement for a young mother. "I imagine I'll stay in the legislature for some time because it fits my personality as well as fitting my personal life as a parent of small kids," she said. "Being in the legislature for a 120-day session is a pretty good arrangement. I am very intensely involved in the legislature when they are meeting, but the rest of the year it's a part-time situation—an occasional job when the committees meet during the interim, legislative council occasionally, meeting with constituency people occasionally, but it fits also being a parent very nicely. Better, actually, than being back in management."

For Fran, it all breaks perfectly. It would be a different story altogether if she lived in Anchorage or Fairbanks, with hours of flying time between home and her job. There are young women like Fran all over the country, for whom everything fits in neatly, and for them a political career is more than possible—it's terrific. After all, how many part-time jobs can stack up to that of state legislator (or town or city councilwoman) for interest and challenge? And the kind of experience they are gaining is not to be underestimated. Ten or fifteen years from now, their little children will have grown up, and those mothers will have had the time to work their way into roles of real leadership, ready to move up to statewide or

202

federal office, if their ambitions lie in that direction, or to wield power in the state house, if they choose to stay where they are. But we believe those lucky women who can comfortably blend family and elective office in those early years will continue to be a minority. So will the women who choose not to marry, or whose marriages come to an end, or who spend their twenties and thirties unencumbered by small children. For most women, the demands of an ambitious political career will have to wait a few years, until the most insistent needs of the family are outgrown.

We don't believe this is entirely unfortunate. For one thing, the typical middle-aged newcomer to public office knows her community and her fellow citizens with the kind of intimacy you only grow into after years of working together. Those women are generally responsive, accessible legislators. For another, mature women have quite likely acquired the practical virtue of patience. They realize that all problems are not going to be resolved by a week from next Thursday, no matter how hard they work at it, and so they're more willing to work with their eyes on the long-term goals. According to Wilma Goldstein, who has been training campaign workers for years, they have also mastered equanimity. "Middle-aged women are wonderful to deal with because so many things roll over their heads," she said. "Kids get all exercised about things and women don't. I say it's from all those nights you stay up with babies. Nothing bothers you after that."

There is also the point that an older woman is more acceptable to the voters. It still seems to be dismally true that a young woman is perceived as younger than a young man, even if they are exactly the same age. Voters like experience and maturity in their representatives—it's part of the same value placed on stability that serves incumbents so well—and even in these relatively emancipated days, a woman doesn't seem to be considered fully adult until she is older. Voters like to look at pretty young women, but by and large, they don't vote for them.

There is, however, a significant disadvantage to getting underway only in middle age. The average age of the men entering the House of Representatives in 1987 was forty-five. The average age of the women was fifty-four.[4] All of the women were well qualified, all of them had served in their state legislatures, all of them were competent, capable women. They came to a Congress in which seniority is no longer the primary determinant of leadership and committee assignments. Even taking all that into consideration, the younger men who entered the House the same year those women did will probably (everything else being equal) be moving into the leadership or other positions of real importance when the women are considering retirement. It doesn't have to happen—there is no compulsory retirement age from Congress—but nine years is a lot to give as a head start to a competitor.

Lindy Boggs of Louisiana is a good example. She came to Congress in 1973 when she was fifty-seven years old. By general consensus, she is a distinguished legislator in her own right. In terms of her background and experience, she was well qualified to be considered by the Mondale people as a possible vice-presidential candidate, but her age was against her. In 1984, she was sixty-eight years old. Had she been ten years younger when she came to Congress, she almost certainly would have had much wider horizons to her career—but most women get there at just about the same age as she did. By contrast, Pat Schroeder (the frequently cited exception), who arrived only a couple of months before Lindy did, at the beginning of the session, was thirty-two when she was elected, and sixteen years later could consider a run for the presidency.

Women will undoubtedly become more politically ambitious. The money problem will gradually be resolved as contributors get more used to contributing to women's campaigns. We wish we could foresee this structural imbalance between men's and women's political careers evening out soon. We don't.

■   ■   ■

It is plain fact that the rate of increase in the number of women in Congress, or the number of women governors, has been pitifully low, and those jobs get the most attention. What has struck us as most encouraging about women's participation in political life is much less publicized. There are two very different areas where women are playing a significantly more important role.

The first is a backstage revolution, where a whole new breed of women political professionals is maturing: a cadre of bright pragmatic women who are in their thirties and forties now, seasoned by fifteen or twenty years of practical, hands-on experience, and addicted to the rhythm and excitement of the political process. Many of the women we've been talking to over the course of the last two years have been members of that generation, and some of the most thoughtful comments we've heard have come from those women whose business is the practical day-to-day details of politics.

Young women have been involved with campaigns for a long time, but until relatively recently they were stuffing envelopes and handing out campaign literature on street corners, or serving as light entertainment for the candidate and senior staff. When the campaign was over they went back to their other lives. It wasn't until the 1960s and early 1970s that they started to stick around in any numbers, to take what they'd learned from one campaign and apply it to the next one, and the men started to notice that they knew what they were talking about. Those were years of ferment for women generally: what we were then calling women's liberation was beginning to bubble and seethe. We forget how far we've come. In 1963 her boss was fired and Wilma Goldstein was told that it was a pity she was a woman because she really ought to have had his job, and she accepted that quite placidly. Ten years later she wouldn't have bought it, nor would the other women out on the campaign trail, who were learning the ropes and beginning to direct other people around because jobs needed doing and in the general hustle of a campaign it was temporarily less important whether the person who knew how to get things done was male or female. Those women are now highly knowledgeable campaign professionals at virtually every level of American politics.

"It's a silent revolution, and almost no one talks about it," Celinda Lake told us, when we were sitting together, almost at the end of the interviewing, companionably going over all we'd learned since we'd talked to her last. "It's just enormous, the change. Even if they are feminists, in the sense of being strong on women's issues, that's not the activism they're showing. They're showing partisan activism. Women are not just making it through women's organizations. They're making it as politicos outside the women's movement. I think that's going to make an untold difference."

Celinda is one of that new breed of political women; so is Wilma. Wilma suggests cheerfully that her own motivation may arise from a persistent refusal to settle down: "I've always liked starting things rather than maintaining things, which may also be a key as to why I like politics," she explained. "I tell all my students that the reason I like it is that I'll die tired but I will never be bored. I think that's the drive. It has to do with people who are a little bit more used to immediate gratification—maybe there's some immaturity in this whole process, I don't know. But it's very exciting, and it's true that every two years we generally get to decide what we want to do when we grow up and we avoid the growing-up process for a very long time. And yet in all of that we handle an enormous amount of responsibility and major amounts of money and develop many skills that might be transferable for other people—like to corporations. But we last about six to eight months in a corporation, and we just go crazy."

Wilma is a Republican, but she has her counterparts on the Democratic side. They know each other after years of encounters around Washington and out on campaigns, but the two-party system being what it is, the closest friendships are generally on your own side of the aisle. One way in which cross-party alliances do come about is through working with the bipartisan women's organizations, like the WCF and the NWPC.

Celinda sees different career paths for women in the two parties. "Clearly there are more campaign professionals in the consulting branch on the Republican side. What that came from I think is because they nurtured a whole cohort of women over at the RNC and the committees. Eddie Mahe and some of those guys were really good about bringing women in, and you're just developing more of a cadre of campaign professionals, period, that came out of that committee. So that on that level I think the Republicans have done much better than the Democrats.

"The Democrats used their women consultants in a constituency-oriented way. They think, okay, women do women. But Democrats think of everything in a constituency-oriented way—'I'm going to add seniors to blacks to labor to women, and I'm going to win.' The flip side of that is that because constituencies are so strong on the Democratic side, in campaigns which have a far more fluid structure than consultants, you have women who have come up and been able to find places of entry. So you have these women who have been nurtured in the constituency, who have built up their skills in the constituency, and then moved over into serious campaign slots out of these women's organizations. So, for example, you have the head of the nurses a key advisor on the Gephardt campaign. You have the past head of NARAL, the National Abortion Rights Action League, a key advisor on the Dukakis campaign. You have Geraldine Ferraro's deputy campaign manager on the Dukakis campaign. Similarly along the line you have women in key positions who have moved over. So I think it really reflects the differences between the two parties, where you find the women in power."

The women pros we talked to got into politics from a variety of different directions. Long before she encountered the RNC and Eddie Mahe, Wilma was just looking for a job and happened to try the local Republican county committee. Jill Schuker got fascinated with government when she was in high school during Kennedy's presidency. She was one of many. For Susan Bryant, it was Charles Percy's candidacy in Illinois that made the difference. However they got there, they dug themselves in, learned what they were doing and that it was possible to make a living doing it, and discovered they had turned into professionals. Some of those original pioneers are still out on the campaign trail, and many are now campaign managers. Some of them are consultants, working with several campaigns simultaneously during any one election cycle. Some are now specialists, for example in polling or media. Some went into lobbying, either with established Washington lobbying groups or opening their own firms. Some of them worked for the national parties—probably more of them with the Republican National Committee and its congressional committees than the Democratic National Committee, primarily because the Republicans have had more money to spend on staff the last ten years or so. Some moved back and forth between the parties and women's organizations and working as staffers on Capitol Hill. Whatever they did, they ate, slept, and dreamed politics, and Washington became the place where everything important happens, with the bits and pieces of United States territory extending beyond the boundaries of the District of Columbia memorable mainly for the campaigns they had been involved in out there. They are completely political animals.

They are the generation of the firsts and the onlys—the first women to do this, the only women to do that. The firsts seldom were noticed outside the circles of other politicians, but that appeared to suit them just fine. They have quite deliberately chosen to stay out of the spotlight. As a group, they represent a fund of political expertise that women have not had before now. Increasingly, they are essential to running campaigns for women and men alike. They are as much part of the pool of talent available to campaigns as the men who are their colleagues and competitors.

Predictably, most of them lead a workaholic life-style. Many of them have never married. Remaining single wasn't anything most of them set out to do intentionally, but the timing has never been right—there was another job or another campaign coming up, and for the time being that seemed more important. Some who did marry found the marriages didn't last under the strains of a peripatetic existence. Women immersed in politics tend to meet and marry men in the business, and when both of you are under intense pressure, shooting off in different geographic directions for extended periods of time, it's hard to hold a relationship together. More than one person also made the point to us that it takes a peculiar kind of personality to want to spend your working life this way. As one national party committee staffer said about her ex-husband, a field man, "If you're good in politics, you can be as eccentric as you want to be. It's almost like the music business or something. Nobody cares how weird you are so long as you get done what needs to get done." Eccentricity isn't confined to the men. As another woman, a longtime campaign worker, told us, "I think you have to be a little bit whacko to stay in this game. What normal person wants to wake up in a different seedy motel every morning for weeks at a time?" Almost none had children, a circumstance they mentioned with varying degrees of regret. Of all the political women we talked to, these Washington pros seemed to be living closest to a traditional political man's life-style. They were clearly flourishing on it, but they are certainly a special breed. They have opened up a new career option for women, but it seems highly unlikely to us that more than a minority of women will ever get involved in it. The intensity is too consuming, and the inroads into a personal life too deep.

When they were getting started there was nobody there to tell them anything about it: they themselves are now the mentors and educators of the new generation of political women learning the ropes. They talk about taking life a little easier now, letting the younger people do the running around and have the nervous breakdowns when the whole campaign seems on the point of collapse, and then they grin and admit that if a personal friend asked them to get back into it, they probably would. A couple of women even talked about retiring, and we wondered to ourselves, retire where? It seems inconceivable that they would ever be happy outside the Beltway that rings Washington, away from the gossip and friendships that take over the function of family, and the lengthy, unprintable anecdotes about what really happened years ago, behind the scenes.

■　　■　　■

If Washington is the center of the universe for the new women political operatives, the other arena where political women are indeed making significant progress is everywhere else—out at the state and local level.

It's happening because for once the logistics are in favor of women out there. There is enough turnover so that there are open seats to contend for: not every race involves taking on an incumbent. State and local elections are usually much less competitive, which means the campaign costs less and can be conducted more informally, without the pressure and trauma of a major race. A state legislative or local district is more often reasonably compact in geographical terms, which means the travel inherent in campaigning or holding public office is likely to be less grueling and disruptive of the rest of a candidate or officeholders's life. They are closer to home, more in touch with the people who vote for them. It's possible to live a much more normal life. It's also helpful that the public is accustomed enough to the idea of women holding those offices so that each woman does not have to undertake the job of convincing everybody that a woman can handle it. Once elected, a woman will probably find there are other women already there who can offer advice, solidarity, and practical help.

This is even coming to be true at the mayoral level. The electorate, notoriously unenthusiastic about choosing women for executive positions, appears to be coming around to the idea that women can be competent mayors. Pat Schroeder suggested to us that part of the reason is that mayors don't come into what she calls the Rambo mentality. "We've had women emerge as mayors but I don't think you are going to see [women executives] at the national level until we get out of the Rambo craziness. What the mayor doesn't have to do is be commander in chief. People think of women as being competent now, thorough and all that, but they also think of them as being compassionate, maybe a little wimpy, as we're all into this Rambo business. Women just can't be Rambo."

She probably has a point in terms of sexual stereotypes, although as a practical matter Margaret Thatcher of Great Britain is undoubtedly perfectly capable of out-Ramboing almost all the men around her. But for whatever reasons, the numbers of women being elected as mayors of large cities are increasing steadily. Once elected, the women are being reelected. Margaret Hance, who served as mayor of Phoenix until she chose to retire, pointed out with pride that women do very well: "An interesting observation—to me at least—is that very few women mayors are ever tossed out by the electorate. They tend to serve as long as they want to and then retire. We rarely lose, which I think speaks very well for the way women run cities and should be a great encouragement for women down the line." But it's still hard for a woman to be elected governor.

Not all the advantages of staying closer to home are logistical. Washington is a very big pond with very few big frogs. The federal government is a leviathan that moves slowly and ponderously and it quite literally can take years for anything to happen legislatively and more years before you can see practical results. Compared to that, a lot of women (and men) feel that the state and local level is where the action is.

Several state legislators we talked to were convinced that they had a lot more say about what actually goes on than one congressman (or congresswoman) ever has. The decisions a state legislature makes have immediate impact on events in the state—the issues of education, roads, and budgetary priorities are much less remote than they seem in the nation's capital. "Congress?" said one state legislator dismissingly. "It's just a quagmire down there. I really have very little respect for that process at all."

Carol Bellamy would agree. She has heard the old line about the state and local jobs being the "farm team" for the congressional big leagues and is exasperated by it. "I'm wholly offended by that farm team business," she said bluntly. "I think these idiots in Washington could fall over a balancing budget and wouldn't know what it was. I'm not one of those people who think there's a pecking order of people who are smart: you know, they're smarter in Washington and a little dumber at the state level, and then total nincompoops at the local level. I want to see women mayors and I want to see women governors, and the way things are going these days, they will affect people's lives much more than women in Congress."

Margaret Hance told us that being a mayor was more satisfactory than any other political job around. When we asked her if she had ever considered running for anything else, she said she's already done the job she thought was most interesting. As far as she's concerned, statewide or federal office has little to offer in comparison. "The problem with being governor is that after being mayor, it is—in my mind—something of a comedown," she said. "I realize you're one of 50 instead of one of 115,000, but in the governor's office the governor does not make daily, hourly decisions. Mayors enact budgets and they enact law, but a governor is restricted to a few appointments and advocacy of special points of view. Then when it comes to Congress—in the first place, I'm too old for that. You have to start young because it takes many years to get in a position of authority, man or woman. Being one of 435 is not as exciting as being one of one. That's what's so exciting about local government, as a mayor or a council member. You can see your results immediately. You can see a bad development, or you can see a good development."

From what we've seen, the state and local opportunities are also promising for women because they utilize women's particular political strengths. Over and over again, women are commended for their responsiveness to their constituents, their ability to explain what's going on so that nonpoliticians can figure it out, their efficiency at hands-on operations. Once elected, a woman is perceived as more accessible than a man to the people who elected her, less a distant celebrity. People are less in awe of a woman, more likely to feel she will understand if they're in a mess and need help in finding a way out of it. A busy woman is still seen as more approachable than a busy man—probably because people all start out interrupting their mothers. All these virtues are particularly visible in local and state politicians, because they ordinarily live closer to their jobs and their neighbors who elected them see much more of them.

211

For all those reasons—the logistical reasons, the reasons growing out of the perceived differences between an individual's impact at the state and local level versus national office, and the reasons having to do with women's stereotypical strengths—we believe that it is at the state and local elected level that women will always be more numerous, that they will indeed eventually meet that magical 53 percent participation to match their numbers in the population at large. It would not surprise us at all if in time there come to be even more women than that, if women become a substantial majority in city halls and state houses. Naturally, if there get to be that many women in office we can't logically expect that all of them will be the top-drawer highly qualified candidates we are seeing in office now—at the moment the special hurdles women face mean that anything less than outstanding is likely to be washed out early in the selection process. Ruth Messinger of the New York City Council, which is currently roughly one-third female, remarked, "Despite how hard it is to get a woman elected, and no matter how few have succeeded, it never has been the case—and increasingly will not be the case—that they're all perfect. Just like the men." However, we would suggest that there have been more than one or two imperfect men in the American political system, and it still stands: we can probably cope with a few imperfect women.

There is no intrinsic reason why the same increase should not happen at the national level, but we don't believe it will. Here, at least for the foreseeable future, we think the practical difficulties are too overwhelming for more than a minority of women to overcome them. It's not that women can't run successfully. Some have and more will; we are convinced the numbers will continue to creep upward. But it will be a slow creep, and we doubt it will ever reach 53 percent. (For that matter, we doubt there ever will be 53 percent women chairmen of the board or CEOs of the nation's businesses.) As Celinda Lake put it, "The structural constraints are still there that still make it tougher despite the fact that many of the odds have evened out." Washington is a long way away from most of the fifty states; most younger women's family obligations make long-distance commuting difficult. Women will continue to marry and have children, and for the majority of women that will still mean that a full-fledged political career won't get underway until later or at least that their single-minded intensity might be interrupted. Older women will have shorter careers than their younger male peers. Congressional and federal campaigns are horrendously expensive and not getting any cheaper. The competition is stiff, and incumbents are getting ever harder to dislodge. Getting into the system is tough for anybody, male or female: it seems unlikely to us that more than a minority of women will ever be willing to take on all those challenges, particularly since a more comfortable option that can be just as rewarding (and according to many women, more so) exists at the state or local level. The Washington jobs are challenging and exciting, but the life-style is too consuming and too restrictive on a personal life for most of us.

Women can do it, we have no doubts about that. We don't believe that enough of them to make up 53 percent ever will. But there will always be the few, and for those few the top of the ladder may not be out of reach. Ferraro got within shooting distance, after all.

．　　■　　■

So where are political women in the late 1980s? Further than they were ten years ago and, we hope, not as far as they'll be ten years from now. It's not only women who hold that hope: one of the men we talked to who was optimistic was Mitch Daniels, then the political director at the White House. We talked with him in one of those large airy offices in the West Wing where powerful men lean back at their ease. Women have never been in the inner circles of the West Wing, not in this administration or any previous one, but even there the change is beginning: at the secondary level there are a few women's faces, a few women's voices heard at staff meetings.

"I think the changes in the place of women in political life, like so many changes in society, are really breathtaking if you step back a couple of feet, and are accelerating," Mitch told us. "One could say that it just can't come fast enough, and it can't, but the fact of it and the pace of it are both pretty evident. I think you see a very rapid and steady progression of women up the chain—in fact, I think the appetite, the public appetite and probably the political leadership's appetite, for women in top positions exceeds the supply right now. I'm convinced of that. Just this last [1984] election, motivated to some extent by the fact that the Republican party doesn't do as well with women as with men, and because the party was being criticized as being less sensitive to women's rights and so forth, we announced in advance that we were going all out to recruit as many women to run at the Senate level as we could, that we would provide the maximum possible assistance to any woman nominated, regardless what the polls said or how bleak the outlook might be. In a couple of cases, we provided the allowable money from the party ahead of the nomination, which became very controversial, for example, out in Nebraska. We nominated more women than the party ever had before—four of them. Regrettably, we didn't elect any of the challengers. But that demonstrates how strong the interest was." Nancy Kassebaum was reelected, of course.

There does seem to be a genuine push to find good women candidates, particularly for some high-visibility races. Part of the motivation is undoubtedly a cosmetic one, a cynical desire to find a gimmick that works, but to claim it's all window dressing is to underestimate ungratefully the efforts of the men who have tried to give women a fair shake.

If there are three stages to women's political development—the first being the hopeless, stubborn races where the woman is jeered at as a fool and as a shame to her sex, the second being the stage in which a very few women are accepted as anomalies in the system, but always as the exceptions to the normal rules, and the third being the nirvana in which a woman candidate expects, and gets, matter-of-fact acceptance as a candidate depending on her qualifications—we seem to be wallowing along somewhere between stage two and stage three. Is gender-neutrality ever a possibility? Probably not: sex appears to be too interesting a concept to the human organism. But perhaps we can look for the day when gender will be *a* fact about a candidate and not *the* fact.

We still have so few women stars, names that ordinary people can put faces to: Ferraro, Kirkpatrick, Schroeder. But there are thousands of less famous women taking an active part in government: eighteen thousand women in elective office alone. It's not enough, it should be more, but we can take some pride in the fact that there are eighteen thousand of them. Behind them are the host of women pols, moving skillfully behind the scenes, women who got bitten by the bug and remain excited by the drama and potential of the next election, even when they're licking their wounds from the last one. Somewhere out there, among those women and the younger ones who are just making their first tentative exploration into the promises and follies of working politics, is the next generation of stars, learning the system, mastering the rules, honing their skills.

Those women are going to make it. And someday, down the road, nobody is going to consider that remarkable at all.

Notes

Unless otherwise credited, all quotations are taken from personal interviews conducted by the authors.

Statistical information about women in political office, unless otherwise credited, is derived from the National Information Bank (NIB) on Women in Public Office, a service of the Center for the American Woman and Politics (CAWP), Eagleton Institute of Politics, Rutgers University.

The primary source for congressional information, unless otherwise noted, is Michael Barone and Grant Ujifusa, *The Almanac of American Politics 1986* (Washington, D.C.: National Journal, 1985).

1. Banners, Bunting, and All That

1. Jane Perlez, "Will Pat Schroeder Be the First Woman President?" *Vogue* (April 1986), p. 178.
2. Ibid.
3. *Los Angeles Times*, November 6, 1983, p. 16.
4. *New York Times*, November 9, 1972, p. A18.
5. Prince Michael of Greece, "I Am Fantastically Lucky," *Parade* (July 3, 1986), p. 7.

2. Hitting the Hurdles

1. Ruth B. Mandel, *In the Running: The New Woman Candidate* (Boston: Beacon Press, 1983), p. 34.
2. Susan Tolchin and Martin Tolchin, *Clout: Womanpower and Politics* (New York: Coward, McCann, and Geoghegan, 1974), p. 13.

216

3. Sandra Baxter and Marjorie Lansing, *Women and Politics: The Visible Majority*, rev. ed. (Ann Arbor: The University of Michigan Press, 1983), p. 17.

4. Tolchin and Tolchin, p. 14.

5. T. H. White, *The Making of the President 1972* (New York: Atheneum, 1973), p. 179.

6. Tolchin and Tolchin, p. 34.

7. White, p. 186.

8. Tolchin and Tolchin, p. 58.

9. Tolchin and Tolchin, p. 32.

10. Mitchell Locin, "A Woman's Place Is in the House," *Sunday: The Chicago Tribune Magazine* (April 13, 1986), p. 13.

11. Baxter and Lansing, p. 139.

12. Locin, p. 23.

13. *Newsweek*, May 21, 1984, p. 10.

14. Barbara M. Trafton, *Women Winning: How to Run for Office* (Boston: The Harvard Common Press, 1984), p. 52.

15. Susan J. Carroll, *Women as Candidates in American Politics* (Bloomington: Indiana University Press, 1985), p. 26.

16. *New York Times*, June 29, 1987, p. A12.

17. *New York Times*, March 2, 1987, p. A9.

18. Jeane J. Kirkpatrick, *Political Woman* (New York: Basic Books, Inc., 1974), p. 231.

19. Mandel, p. 82.

20. Barbara Williams, *Breakthrough: Women in Politics* (New York: Walker and Company, 1979), p. 110.

21. Kirkpatrick, p. 3.

3. The Campaign Trail

1. Margaret Carlson, "The Fight of the Decade," *Savvy* (January 1987), p. 45.

2. Ibid., p. 46.

3. "No More Petticoat Politics," *TIME* (September 22, 1986), p. 26.

4. Larry J. Sabato, *The Rise of Political Consultants* (New York: Basic Books, 1981), P. 31.

5. Barbara M. Trafton, *Women Winning: How to Run for Office* (Boston: The Harvard Common Press, 1984), p. 128.

6. Ruth B. Mandel, *In the Running: The New Woman Candidate* (Boston: Beacon Press, 1983), p. 63.

7. *New York Times*, March 15, 1987, p. A14.
8. John McLaughlin, "Women Pols," *National Review* (December 5, 1986), p. 24.
9. Mandel, p. 180.
10. Daryl Glenney, "C & E Interviews: Matt Reese," *Campaigns & Elections* (July–August 1987), p. 18.
11. *The Autobiography of Eleanor Roosevelt* (Boston: G. K. Hall & Company, 1984), p. 109.
12. Carlson, p. 75.

4. The Money Game

1. Bill Whelan, "Hill May Be Ready to Place a Lid on Campaign Spending," *Insight* (April 13, 1987), p. 18.
2. Ibid.
3. Edwin Diamond and Stephen Bates, *The Spot: The Rise of Political Advertising on Television* (Cambridge, Mass.: The MIT Press, 1984), p. 374.
4. Xandra Kayden and Eddie Mahe, Jr., *The Party Goes On* (New York: Basic Books, 1985), p. 193.
5. *New York Times*, March 22, 1987, p. E5.
6. Whelan, p. 19.
7. Michael J. Malbin, ed., *Money and Politics in the United States* (Washington, D.C.: American Enterprise Institute for Public Policy Research, 1984), p. 275, n. 84.
8. Whelan, p. 19.
9. Steven V. Roberts, "Politicking Goes High-Tech," *New York Times Magazine* (November 2, 1986), p. 39.
10. Ibid.
11. Barbara M. Trafton, *Women Winning: How to Run for Office* (Boston: The Harvard Common Press, 1984), p. 84.
12. Diamond and Bates, p. 6.
13. Howard Baker, Speech to the American Society of Newspaper Editors, San Francisco, April 10, 1987.
14. Whelan, p. 18.
15. Malbin, p. 262.
16. *New York Times*, November 14, 1986, p. A16.
17. *New York Times*, March 22, 1987, p. E5.
18. *New York Times*, November 7, 1986, p. A18.

19. Larry J. Sabato, *PAC Power* (New York: W. W. Norton, 1985), p. 7.
20. Whelan, p. 19.
21. Theodore J. Eismeier and Philip H. Pollock III, "Political Action Committees: Varieties of Organization and Strategy," in Malbin, p. 123.
22. *New York Times*, April 18, 1987, p. A7.
23. Ibid.
24. *Business Week*, October 27, 1986, p. 86.
25. John McLaughlin, "Women Pols," *National Review* (December 5, 1986), p. 24.
26. Mark Green with Michael Waldman, *Who Runs Congress?* (New York: Dell Publishing Company, 1984), p. 24.
27. Ruth B. Mandel, *In the Running: The New Woman Candidate* (Boston: Beacon Press, 1983), p. 182.
28. Mary H. J. Farrell, "The Political Power Gap," *Savvy* (June 1986), p. 57.
29. McLaughlin, p. 24.
30. *New York Times*, November 7, 1986, p. A18.
31. Trafton, p. 87.
32. Geraldine Ferraro with Linda Bird Francke, *Ferraro: My Story* (New York: Bantam Books, 1985), p. 195.
33. Xandra Kayden, *A Handbook for Women Entering Politics* (Cambridge, Mass.: Women Involved, Inc., 1973), p. 8.

5. Women among Men

1. Jeane J. Kirkpatrick, "Why I Think More Women Are Needed at the Pinnacle of World Politics," *Glamour* (September 1985), p. 178.
2. Estelle Ramey, as told to Vera Glaser, "Men vs. Women," *The Washingtonian* (February 1987), p. 87.
3. From ABC/*Washington Post* exit polling figures.
4. *New York Times*, November 7, 1986, p. A18.
5. Kathy A. Stanwick and Katherine E. Kleeman, "Women Make a Difference," in *Bringing More Women into Public Office* (New Brunswick, N.J.: Center for the American Woman and Politics, Rutgers University, 1983).
6. Milton Coleman, "Rep. Lynn Martin: A Woman's Face in the

GOP Crowd," *Washington Post National Weekly* (June 2, 1986), p. 14.
7. Mitchell Locin, "A Woman's Place Is in the House," *Chicago Tribune Magazine* (April 13, 1986), p. 14.
8. *New York Times*, April 20, 1987, p. A10.
9. Ibid.
10. *Washington Post*, October 15, 1978, p. 9.

6. Other Women
1. Alice Fleming, *The Senator from Maine* (New York: Thomas Y. Crowell Co., 1969), p. 70.
2. Fleming, p. 103.
3. *New York Times*, January 28, 1987. p. A31.
4. Geraldine A. Ferraro, with Linda Bird Francke, *Ferraro: My Story* (New York: Bantam Books, 1985), pp. 46–47.
5. Ibid., p. 48.
6. Mary H. J. Farrell, "The Political Power Gap," *Savvy* (June 1986), p. 55.
7. *New York Times*, July 17, 1977, p. A24.
8. Jeane J. Kirkpatrick, *Political Woman* (New York: Basic Books, Inc., 1974), p. 124.
9. Susan Tolchin and Martin Tolchin, *Clout: Womanpower and Politics* (New York: Coward, McCann, and Geoghegan, 1974), p. 261.
10. Ferraro, p. 215.
11. Quoted in Kathy A. Stanwick, "Political Women Tell What It Takes," in *Bringing More Women into Public Office* (New Brunswick, N.J.: Center for the American Woman and Politics, Eagleton Institute of Politics, Rutgers University, 1983), p. 9.
12. Ibid., p. 19.
13. Alice Kresse, "Lights, Camera, Activism," *Washington Post National Weekly* (November 3, 1986), p. 11.
14. Ibid.
15. Ibid., p. 12.
16. Quoted in *News and Notes about Women Public Officials*, Vol. 5, No. 1, "Women's Money in the 1986 Election: An interview with Ellen Malcolm," Center for the American Woman and Politics, Eagleton Institute of Politics, Rutgers University (December 1986), p. 4.
17. Ibid.

7. The Retrospective View

1. Jeane J. Kirkpatrick, "Why I Think More Women Are Needed at the Pinnacle of World Politics," *Glamour* (September 1985), p. 178.
2. Ibid.
3. Cindy Adams, "A Very Candid Conversation with Jeane J. Kirkpatrick," *Ladies' Home Journal* (May 1986), p. 177.
4. Ibid., p. 108.
5. Fred Barnes, "Queen Jeane," *The New Republic* (July 8, 1985), p. 11.
6. Kirkpatrick, p. 180.
7. Susan J. Carroll and Wendy S. Strimling, *Women's Routes to Elective Office* (New Brunswick, N.J.: Center for the American Woman and Politics, Eagleton Institute of Politics, Rutgers University, 1983), pp. 145–146, 169.
8. Barbara Jordan and Shelby Hearon, *Barbara Jordan: A Self-Portrait* (Garden City, N.Y.: Doubleday, 1979), p. 254.
9. Ibid., p. 255.
10. Malcolm Boyd, "Where Is Barbara Jordan Today?" *Parade* (February 16, 1986), p. 12.
11. Ibid., p. 13.
12. *Newsweek*, May 21, 1984, p. 10.
13. Lavinia Edmunds, "Women Who Won," *Ms.* (January 1987), p. 33.

8. Where Do We Get to from Here?

1. *New York Times*, June 29, 1987, p. A12.
2. *New York Times*, July 19, 1987, p. A22.
3. *New York Times*, July 22, 1987, p. A12.
4. From *Congressional Quarterly's* "Green Guide," 100th Congress pocket edition (Washington, D.C.: Congressional Quarterly, Inc., 1987).

Index

222